The Castle Lectures in Ethics, Politics, and Economics

CONSTITUTIONAL PROCESSES AND DEMOCRATIC COMMITMENT

Donald L. Horowitz

Yale UNIVERSITY PRESS
New Haven & London

Published with assistance from the Mary Cady Tew Memorial Fund.

Yale University Press books may be purchased in quantity for educational, business, or promotional use. For information, please e-mail sales.press@yale.edu (U.S. office) or sales@yaleup.co.uk (U.K. office).

Set in Janson type by Newgen North America, Austin, Texas.
Printed in the United States of America.

Library of Congress Control Number: 2020951772
ISBN 978-0-300-25436-5 (hardcover : alk. paper)

A catalogue record for this book is available from the British Library.

This paper meets the requirements of ANSI/NISO Z39.48-1992 (Permanence of Paper).

10 9 8 7 6 5 4 3 2 1

Parts of this book were given as the Castle Lectures in Yale's Program in Ethics, Politics, and Economics, delivered by Donald L. Horowitz in 2016.

The Castle Lectures were endowed by Mr. John K. Castle. They honor his ancestor the Reverend James Pierpont, one of Yale's original founders. Given by established public figures, Castle Lectures are intended to promote reflection on the moral foundations of society and government and to enhance understanding of ethical issues facing individuals in our complex modern society.

For Justin, Stephanie, and Jadyn

Contents

Preface

This book emerged out of a longstanding work in progress on constitutional processes and design for severely divided societies. As I wrestled over the years with what I initially thought were aspects of a single subject, I eventually came to believe that constitutional processes and institutional designs for severely divided societies were best treated separately. With respect to the former, the result is this study, which attempts to learn something about the goals that constitutional processes might serve and the experience that observers and participants have had with multiple constitutional processes.

Many students of constitutional design have argued that societies riven by ethnic or religious conflict need some special institutions to help mitigate their problems. Yet the constitutional processes by which such societies might adopt appropriate institutions are a neglected subject. There is, however, a literature on constitutional processes in general. True enough, deep disagreement in constitutional processes for severely divided societies will most likely fall along lines of the most prominent cleavages in the society and may have more negative and long-lasting effects than disagreements manifested in processes for societies not so divided. For this reason, constitutional processes for severely divided societies may also require somewhat more attention to criteria for securing agreement and to certain other features of the process than other societies might require.

Nevertheless, constitutional processes for any society aspiring to democracy, stability, and peaceful accommodation of contention have much in common. The conditions surrounding the inception of the process, the procedural choices available, the standards by which those choices might be evaluated, and the sources of process failure have a common vocabulary in which they are described and analyzed. In short, constitutional processes form a compact subject, separable from institutional design. Most, but not all, of the evidence adduced in this book is drawn from severely divided societies, and along the way I highlight some special process considerations that must apply to societies I shall define as severely divided. Even so, this is also a book about constitutional processes in general, processes intended to lead to democratic outcomes that have some staying power.

That staying power cannot be assumed. Much of the book concerns the problem of spanning the chasm between what is agreed and written down in constitution making and the reneging behavior that not infrequently follows. Some part of this gap—but by no means all of it—is likely to be related to the processes by which commitments are made, in particular who is involved and how the processes are conducted.

The plural *Processes* in the title of the book is deliberate. Considering the number of bodies that can be formed to take part in the making of constitutions, the qualifications of their members, the ways in which they can be convened, chosen, and organized, the tasks that can be assigned to each, the sequences in which they might do their work, and the methods by which their work product might be approved or disapproved, it is clear that no two processes can be or ought to be identical. That makes the evaluation of various process alternatives unusually difficult and contingent, for the evaluation of one feature of a process can easily be affected by a change in the total configuration of features. Underlying all such evaluations, as I hope to make clear, is a concern that certain critically important objectives be recognized and realized. These I shall make explicit as we go along, but this is not a cookbook for designing processes: it emphasizes certain criteria but contains no specific recipes. It merely advances a perspective on and a critique of constitutional processes, based upon certain objectives and methods for their probable attainment.

Portions of this book were presented in the Castle Lectures on Ethics, Politics, and Economics at Yale University in the fall of 2016. I am pleased to record my gratitude to the benefactor of the series, John K. Castle, and to Nicholas Sambanis, who, as director of the Yale Program on Ethics, Politics, and Economics, was kind enough to invite me to deliver the lectures. During my stay in New Haven, I benefited from the hospitality afforded me by faculty and students and by Kellianne Farnham and Beth Iams Wellman, who managed the logistics seamlessly.

A project spanning a number of years, as this one does, would be impossible without support from foundations and research centers. For supporting the larger project from which this book is drawn, I am grateful to the Harry Frank Guggenheim Foundation, the Carnegie Scholars Program of the Carnegie Corporation, the United States Institute of Peace, the Woodrow Wilson International Center for Scholars, and the National Endowment for Democracy. I also benefited from released time afforded by the Bost Research Professorship at Duke Law School. Each of these grantors provided me with the opportunity at earlier stages to conduct pieces of the necessary research and writing.

I would also like to thank institutions that invited me in recent years to work on parts of this project while in residence in Germany, Malaysia, and Singapore: the American Academy in Berlin, where I held the Siemens Prize Fellowship; the Academic Icon Program at the University of Malaya; the Political Science Department at the National University of Singapore; the College of Humanities, Arts, and Social Sciences at Nanyang Technological University (NTU); and the Centre for Asian Legal Studies (CALS) at the Faculty of Law of the National University of Singapore (NUS). At these institutions, I was warmly welcomed by, at UM, Khadijah Md. Khalid, Emile K. K. Yeo, Danny Wong, and the late and sorely missed Lee Poh Ping; at NUS Political Science, Terry Nardin and Jamie Davidson; at NTU, Joseph Chin Yong Liow; at NUS Law, Dan Puchniak, Kevin Y. L. Tan, Andrew Harding, Jaclyn L. C. Neo, and Dian A. H. Shah; and, at all, an array of stimulating colleagues and helpful staff.

I am indebted for helpful comments on the book to the two anonymous readers for the Press and for comments on much earlier drafts to Lise Morjé Howard, Christina Murray, members of the audience at the Castle Lectures, and participants at the George Washington University Comparative Politics Workshop, the McGill University Legal Theory Workshop, the Minerva Center for Human Rights at Tel Aviv University, and the Nanyang Technological University, where very early and partial versions of this book were presented. At a late stage CALS workshop sponsored by the Konrad Adenauer Stiftung, and organized by Dian A. H. Shah, I received helpful comments on several chapters from CALS colleagues mentioned above and from Chang Wen-Chen, Melissa Crouch, Mario Gomez, Budhi Karki, Eugénie Mérieau, Jacob Ricks, and Ronojoy Sen.

For advice, research leads, and comments on particular issues in the book, I am grateful to Rehan Abeyratne, Evan Abramsky, Daniel Branch, Michael Breen, Federica Carugati, Nic Cheeseman, Rohit De, Neil De Votta, Rohan Edrisinha, Yash Ghai, Jill Cottrell Ghai, Mario Gomez, Sharan Grewal, Gehan Gunatilleke, Madhav Khosla, R. William Liddle, Mara Malagodi, Ali Malik, Jehan Perera, Abrak Saati, Dian A. H. Shah, and Steven Wilkinson.

Late in the book's development, three people went far out of their way to help with sources on particular issues. Christina Murray saved me from several errors and led me to new sources on Kenya. Jehan Perera and Rohan Edrisinha repeatedly facilitated contacts with participants in the Sri Lankan process described in chapter 8.

Of course, despite all the help I have received, responsibility for the product is mine alone. This is much more than a pro forma absolution, since I know that there will inevitably be disagreements between these exceedingly well-informed colleagues and myself on some issues.

Research for the book would also have been impossible without the support of outstanding librarians—Melanie Dunshee, Jennifer Behrens, and Tina Moore at Duke, as well as Emily Vaughn and Sarah Braun at the National Endowment for Democracy—all of whom have put up with numerous requests for an array of materials over the years with utmost efficiency and good cheer. Abundant thanks are also due to Lauren Maxey, who played an invaluable role in preparation of the final manuscript for publication, and to Margaret Otzel for her sharp eye and fine judgment in editing the manuscript.

As usual, I express my gratitude to Judy Horowitz, whose contribution was to prod and read in equal measure and whose constitutional practice for our household insures domestic tranquility and generates abundant mutual affection.

One final note: In this book, it is sometimes helpful to touch on the substantive elements of institutional design that were in play, mainly in order to help illuminate some aspects of constitutional process, but this is not the occasion or the place for extended discussion of the merits of one design or another. A constitutional process with certain features can be attractive regardless of particular institutional preferences. A good constitutional process alone, however, is insufficient to assure interethnic accommodation in severely divided societies. For that, an appropriate suite of conciliatory institutions needs to be chosen. The book I mentioned at the outset, on institutional design for interethnic power sharing, is still very much in progress.

Donald L. Horowitz
May 2020

CHAPTER 1

The Goals of Constitutional Processes

In the thirty years between 1989 and 2019, by one authoritative count, 189 new, interim, or reinstated constitutions were adopted by 100 national governments.[1] This figure shows two somewhat contradictory tendencies. First, the sheer number of constitutions bespeaks a high level of demand for documents encoding fundamental legal and political principles. That same number, however, suggests considerable breakdown in the ability to satisfy that demand. It is striking that so many previously adopted constitutions had to be replaced and that, during these three decades, as many as thirty-three countries needed to adopt more than one constitution, if we count both newly adopted and reinstated constitutions. If we drop out interim constitutions and reinstated former constitutions, we are left with 155 new constitutions over this period. (And these statistics do not reflect the number of new constitutions drafted but ultimately

1. The source is the Constitute Project, www.constituteproject.org, and the terminal date of this count is May 21, 2019. In a few cases, such as Andorra or the Vatican, the adopting territories could best be described as principalities. I am indebted to Jesse Baugher of the project for the count. I have added Indonesia, 1999–2002, to the list; it had been omitted because the new constitution was created by thoroughgoing revision of the old one, without a formal name change for the almost entirely superseded document.

not adopted.) Obviously, the Third Wave of Democratization was accompanied by a new wave of constitution making, although many of the new constitutions fell short of democratic standards.

Because constitutions are usually intended to be permanent, they may provide for amendment but not for replacement. For that reason, there is typically no authoritative process in place to produce a new constitution, and the circumstances in which replacement is needed are so variable that there is certainly no single standard way to do the job.[2] There may even be no authoritative method or forum to choose the process by which a constitution will be created and adopted. The choice, in other words, characteristically takes place in an unstructured or only modestly regulated, often tumultuous environment and is heavily affected by the exigency of the situation.

In these conditions, it is hardly surprising that the numerous process possibilities and sequences would give rise to a variety of prescriptions for good or even ideal processes of constitutional creation. These prescriptions respond to a variety of criteria—some explicit, some implicit, most of them quite reasonable—that lead to different procedural destinations.

If the objective of constitutional design for severely divided societies—in which a few birth-based ethnic or religious groups compete for state power—is a set of institutions that will foster durable democracy and conflict reduction, then constitutional designers must think about processes that might be conducive to such choices. In severely divided societies[3] characterized by high degrees

2 .For the common practice of using democratically elected legislatures as constituent bodies to enact new constitutions, see Gabriel Negretto, "New Constitutions in Democratic Regimes," in Negretto, ed., *Redrafting Constitutions in Democratic Orders: Theoretical and Comparative Perspectives* (Cambridge: Cambridge University Press, 2020), pp. 1–30.

3. A more precise definition of a severely divided society is one in which: there is conflict among groups possessing consciousness of differences that are putatively birth-based (that is, ascriptive); these ethnic differences are highly salient in politics;

of political and ethnic polarization,[4] constitutional processes are especially important to produce agreed rules of political behavior and to prevent domination of one group by another. There is little authoritative wisdom and considerable disagreement about how to structure such processes, and there are many starting conditions that constrain process choices. Among the common constraints are an atmosphere of crisis in which drafters must work, the frequent conflation of constitutional processes with peace processes to end civil wars, and a sense among constituents that dealing with disliked opponents might be illegitimate or at least distasteful. I shall mention more constraints as we go along.

A good constitution is only one piece of a large set of conditions that might facilitate the emergence or retention of democracy and intergroup conciliation: it is not the instant coffee of either. Where institutions are weak and democratic habits are insufficiently formed, as they are in many countries, even a well-designed constitution cannot make good these deficiencies in the short term. Nevertheless, agreed institutions can help create the governmental bodies, public procedures, habits, and restraints that cause political actors to modify their behavior in the light of new constitutional norms.

A good constitutional process should be conducive to creating carefully designed political institutions and to enlarging the perhaps-narrow initial area of agreement about how the polity will and should be governed. Yet, as I have said, there is by no means complete agreement on what a good process is. To some degree,

---

a few main groups seek power at the center or seek to avoid the domination of others; and there is a history or current experience of intergroup antipathy or suspicion.

4. There is an extensive literature on the connection between polarized group relations and ethnic conflict. As Michael W. Doyle and Nicholas Sambanis point out, polarization increases the risk of civil war occurrence, whereas high levels of ethnic fractionalization do not. *Making War and Building Peace* (Princeton: Princeton University Press, 2006), p. 37.

disagreements reflect underspecified objectives of the process and, to some degree, reflect divergent views about the means to common objectives.

This book makes the case for processes that are broadly inclusive of groups in the society, through the mechanism of elections, and that involve a high degree of consensus resulting from deliberation. The case I make for this type of process and its relation to a democratic outcome is an argument, not a proof. Still, there is evidence for it that unfolds as the book moves along—evidence from prior studies of process and of successful processes that had these attributes and, by contrast, of poorly constructed or failed processes that would likely have benefited from them.

The argument acknowledges that providing for the inclusion of a wide range of diverse actors is often at odds with seeking consensus and can create a stalemate if inclusion carried to its outermost limits. I shall note later that the electoral means to create inclusion should not facilitate widening the spectrum of participants to the point where extremists can easily act as spoilers in the constitutional process. Similarly, the high degree of consensus envisioned here would not give any of the participants an absolute veto, a weapon that can be fatal to a process in which disagreements are to be ironed out.[5] Rather, it is a level of consensus that can be expected often (but not always) when there is an exchange of reasoned argument in an atmosphere unburdened by temptations to undue passion or bombast and unconstrained by unrealistic deadlines. The rules favoring consensus cannot be rules of complete unanimity, but they can set a high standard for agreement. And since consensus cannot always be achieved, there needs to be room for bargaining, as well as argument, so that compromise outcomes become possible when consensus is not, and for voting when neither consensus nor compromise is possible.

5. See Douglas W. Rae, "The Limits of Consensual Decision," *American Political Science Review*, Vol. 69, no. 4 (1975), pp. 1270–94.

By *consensus* I mean agreement on a course of action that is shared across lines of political opposition by actors in the constitutional process.[6] Constitutional consensus entails convergence on what is regarded as the best provision or the best set of arrangements to achieve agreed objectives. Typically, consensus is achieved by persuasion and therefore requires deliberation, an exchange of reasons and arguments in order to decide what the best decision might be.[7] In framing a constitution, an effort to find consensus entails multiple iterations as specific provisions are considered, as well as agreement on the completed project as a whole.

Consensus on every provision is very difficult to achieve. The actors may have come to the constitutional forum with divergent demands, some of which may even be in mutual contradiction. These demands may be difficult to satisfy by argumentation and may require negotiation that produces compromise,[8] a mode of decision that acknowledges that consensus would be preferable but on some matters may be impossible to achieve.

The method appropriate to compromise is bargaining and exchange, leading to resolution of an issue in dispute by mutual or unilateral concessions in order for one or both or all sides to achieve partial satisfaction on that issue or satisfaction on another issue in dispute. Consensus, on the other hand, involves agreement on a course of action, or on a set of institutions, that is distinct from compromise in its outcome, but perhaps not entirely in its method. Compromise involves the negotiated exchange of goods, in which

6. What I have in mind here bears some resemblance to what John Rawls refers to as an "overlapping consensus," a shared scheme of social cooperation and a shared belief in the justice of the basic structure adopted, a consensus that can grow more stable over time. Rawls, "The Idea of an Overlapping Consensus," *Oxford Journal of Legal Studies*, Vol. 7, no. 1 (1987), pp. 1–25.

7. This is the formulation of Ian O'Flynn and Maija Setälä, "Deliberative Judgment and Compromise," *Critical Review of International Social and Political Philosophy*, https://doi.org/10.1080/13698230.2020.1737475.

8. For the relations of consensus and compromise, see ibid.

each side may not or may actually receive all that it has been aiming to gain, provided the other side receives some or all of what it seeks in return. Either way, compromise is dependent on reciprocal concessions and sometimes on mutual restraint in making demands on the other side. Because consensus concerns widespread agreement on a plan conceived in the best interest of the whole, there will need to be an element of reciprocity, for agreement to that plan requires the forbearance of the actors in pursuing their initial claims.

The difference between consensus and compromise lies in the outcome as well as the method. Compromise entails an element of tit-for-tat exchange. Those who create consensus, on the other hand, may decide to adopt a set of principles adhered to by all sides that satisfies what seem at first to be divergent demands of the actors by transcending them or by agreeing on the legitimacy of the diverging demands and incorporating them in what could be called an overlapping or global solution that receives the assent of the actors on all sides. Whatever the precise components, consensus in a constitution embodies a way forward on a political life in common, a prescription of rules and structures agreed across political lines. Later in this chapter, we shall review an example of consensus, drawn from ancient Athens, that is very much in that spirit.

Consensus has another meaning, too. It can refer to the formal standard for approving decisions—usually by something approaching unanimity. Consensus may be achieved for the overall approval of a constitution, even if decisions on particular provisions are based on compromise or voting. If a standard of near-unanimous final decision is met, that is generally a strong indication that decisions of a large body do reflect a substantial measure of agreement on a common course of action, even if some parts of the agreement are based on compromise or voting. Consensus at the conclusion of a process in which some decisions have been produced by negotiation or balloting may, nevertheless, reflect a widespread belief of participants in the process that the overall plan is the best in the circumstances, given the variety of interests and preferences of the actors involved, despite disappointment on particular provisions.

I shall refer to both uses of the term *consensus* in what follows. For practical purposes, it will be clear in the cases to which I refer that when the standard of overwhelming approval at the conclusion of a process is met,[9] that is generally a sign that consensus, in the sense of overarching agreement on rules for a common political life, has played a major part, albeit not necessarily the only part, in reaching such a result.

The closer a constitution is to a consensus document throughout, rather than merely at the conclusion of the process, the more likely I believe it is to be conducive to durable democratic commitment on the part of the participants. Consensus decisions help to impart definiteness and clarity to agreements, which can be relied upon later, so as to thwart perverse recollections and interpretations leading to defection and violation of constitutional provisions.

By contrast, constitutions reflecting heavy doses of compromise at important points may be picked apart if distasteful concessions invite subsequent regret and the possibility of defection from what was agreed. Compromise means something is lost or not attained in return for something gained. And so, in later self-interested formulations, acknowledgment of concessions made may be minimized, whereas benefits to be received may be exaggerated. Action of this kind is likely to be taken as regret grows, by those who conceded something or by their successors in interest, well after the compromise has been agreed. Renunciation or opportunistic reinterpretation of a compromise may also occur if satisfaction declines, because value received has fallen short of anticipation. Not uncommonly, disappointment with the downstream results of compromise

9. Provided that all formally included participants have taken part in the final decision. We shall see an exception in the case of Nepal in 2015, in which a significant category of included participants dissented by boycotting the final decision.

for one side or another manifests itself with the passage of time. Similarly, constitutions enacted by repeated majority votes invite the possibility of lingering disappointment by those on the losing side in some or all of the votes or by their constituents. In constitutional processes, compromise is the fallback criterion for decision when consensus cannot be achieved, and voting is the fallback criterion for decision when neither consensus nor compromise can be achieved.

Of course, regret and repudiation are not inevitable results of compromise and head-count decisions. Compromisers may be content with partial gains, and those who lose in fair votes may derive satisfaction from the opportunity to have had their arguments heard, if the proceedings have been unhurried, fair, and deliberative. On the whole, however, consensus outcomes are more likely to invite a sense of collective accomplishment and a shared belief that a wise plan was conceived—and on that account less likely to be subject to defection.

What are we to make of a constitution agreed by near-unanimity at the conclusion of the proceedings if some of its parts were agreed through compromise or through voting? As it happens, three constitutions to be considered in this book were adopted by unanimous or nearly unanimous consent, but in one of these certain provisions were adopted by voting, and in another some important provisions involved unilateral or mutual concessions that produced compromises.

Indonesia's constitutional revision produced a consensus document by the most exacting standard to reach that judgment. All provisions were adopted only by actual consensus, except that one provision reflected a compromise achieved by the proponents' withdrawal of a much more extreme and unpopular demand in exchange for a more modest concession on the part of the large majority who objected to the demand. That one compromise can scarcely impair the consensual status of the overall result.

Tunisia's constitution was adopted by a nearly unanimous vote in favor, but that achievement entailed a number of significant compromises about specific provisions. Those difficult compromises were reached, in my view, because the actors agreed on the fundamentals of a democratic dispensation despite great differences among them on matters of religion. The final vote reflected that consensus.

India's constitutional process also ended with a nearly unanimous vote in favor. Along the way, however, an array of disparate starting positions on specific issues had to be resolved by votes on many of those issues. Some analysts have nevertheless considered the outcome to reflect a consensus, while others use slightly more modest and nuanced terminology to characterize it. Because I think the final vote on the whole document did reflect an acceptance of many initially disputed items, I am inclined to refer to the Indian constitution as consensual.

The line between consensus documents and those achieved by compromise or by voting on specific issues is not always easy to discern. On the side of consensus, proponents of a position may relent after a lost vote on the issue and join the general approbation of what has been achieved. The same may be true of those who gained less than they had hoped because they were obliged to make concessions along the way. When they do, they may cast a ballot in favor of the total ensemble, embracing many such issues. A process involving scrupulous inclusion and extended deliberation seems most likely to produce this level of acceptance.

All processes will require opportunities for compromise and standards for voting, generally supermajority standards, when specific proposals do not command universal assent. Both fallback methods of reaching agreement need to be in the repertoire of constitution makers, even if they aim at consensus.

Some provisions of many constitutions can be made under something approaching a Rawlsian veil of ignorance, since participants will not be able to forecast their precise impact on themselves but can agree on provisions that seem fair to everyone. Very often, however, participants, especially those who represent well-defined ethnic, social, or partisan groups, will have, or think they have, visibility of interests concerning some or even many of the provisions. For this situation, as I have maintained, consensus may still be achieved by taking account of everyone's interests in framing institutions that will serve them. But if consensus cannot be achieved, or if it can be but only on some matters and not on others, compromise becomes indispensable,[10] and even then dissent from compromises may be unavoidable, which means that provision must be made, as a fallback, for approval by some arbitrary numerical standard for the approval of a constitution.

Compromise is a term that can cover a variety of outcomes. It can involve exchanges that serve the interests of the various segments of the public that are represented by those who sit at the table, usually politicians, and it can also allow for bargains that political actors find workable for their future relations and for the interests of their constituents. The need for compromise, however, can open the way to bargains that serve only the interests of the politicians who agree to them, sometimes at the expense of other politicians or the public or segments of the public that are excluded from their benefits. A good process should embody ways to avert this particular prospect.

10. For a good example, see Tom Ginsburg, *Judicial Review in New Democracies: Constitutional Courts in Asian Cases* (Cambridge: Cambridge University Press, (2003), p. 165, recounting a dispute in Mongolia in which the governing party "demanded a presidential system, in keeping with its tradition of strongman leadership, while opposition forces, knowing they had few candidates with the seniority and name recognition to win that post in the short term, wanted a parliamentary system. If there was to be a president, the reformists preferred it to be an indirectly elected position." The dispute ended in compromise, with a directly elected president possessing a veto over legislation, but subject to an override by two-thirds of the legislature, *and* a prime minister, nominated by the majority coalition in the legislature, whose cabinet appointments would be subject to legislative approval.

And there is yet another mode of constitution making that is inimical to the interests of the public: the constitution that is made by and for the government of the day. Rohan Edrisinha has made a cogent case that each of the two post-independence constitutions adopted in Sri Lanka favored the partisan political agenda of those who were instrumental in creating them, because they had temporary control of the government at the time, and he argues for a new constitution that caters to the interest of the public rather than the interest of current power-holders alone.[11] Many constitutions fall into the category Edrisinha criticizes.

In order to prevent the creation of constitutions that embody rent-seeking compromises or constitutions that simply empower those currently in office, some writers and many advisors have thought that widespread participation of the public at all stages of constitution making, including the very early stages, would protect public interests. My own view is that the benefits of this prescription are overstated, and its costs can be significant. The public can and should be mobilized to enter into dialogue with the drafters, to question them, and to provide feedback, but widespread participation at every stage of the proceedings would be counterproductive. I shall in due course explain why I think that is so. The standards for a good process advanced here—principally, inclusion of elected representatives and consensus reached through deliberation, with negotiation and compromise where necessary—are more likely to achieve a constitution oriented toward the interests of the public. Of course, the public needs to be informed periodically about what the constitution makers are producing. In addition to these criteria, we shall see that it is prudent to take some precautions against private, last-minute deal-making that can alter in fundamental ways what has been agreed.

11. Edrisinha, "The Need for a New Constitution for Sri Lanka," January 16, 2016, http://srilankabrief.org.

Just as there is little agreement on optimal constitutional processes, so, too, is there little agreement on the institutional contours of the end product with respect to the goal of interethnic conflict reduction, where conflict of this kind is severe. As I mentioned in the preface, these differences of opinion will not be addressed in this volume, because an appropriate process ought to be open to a variety of answers reached by the participants. Two additional goals of constitutional process, however, bear on the probability that the institutions adopted will serve their intended purpose. These are the coherence of conflict-reducing measures and other provisions (so that institutions do not work against each other) and the clarity of important constitutional provisions (so as to minimize inadvertent or willful misinterpretation later). These goals, too, are sometimes in conflict with some of the process-related goals just enumerated—and sometimes with each other as well—and so tradeoffs become essential.

Commitment is an overarching, if often latent, goal of constitutional processes. If a process achieves its other objectives, those who produced the constitution may become committed to the agreement that underlies the provisions of the document. There is, however, no assurance that they will be firmly committed. The temptations to depart at a later time from what has been agreed are many, especially in a polity in which divisions run deep. To the maximum extent possible, therefore, constitutional processes should be structured to facilitate commitment and reduce defection. And by using the term *commitment* I mean to embrace commitment to the constitution and the democratic regime as a whole and to particular agreed provisions that form part of its essential structure.[12]

12. I am aware of the vagueness of the phrase "essential structure." By emphasizing commitment, I obviously do not mean to foreclose amendment by the process provided in the constitution.

Despite many valiant efforts, there is no definitive account of all the elements determining the investment of constitution makers and their successors in the results of a constitutional process. It is customary to describe constitutions as instruments by which the polity, through its representatives, binds itself to certain governing arrangements, rights, and divisions of official responsibilities that are usually considered superior to ordinary law and are relatively difficult to alter. Nevertheless, since ambitious or discontented individuals or groups might choose to renege on constitutional commitments if they can, the sources of strong commitments—and, for present purposes, their connection to the process by which a constitution is created—become critically important subjects.

By strong commitments, I mean undertakings that effectively protect democratic constitutional arrangements against change except by specified procedures intended to minimize the chance of significant defection. Commitments of this kind imply investment in the outcome, reinforced by indicia of credibility, but they also usually mean that, because of the expected commitment of others, an obligation will be difficult or costly to dishonor.[13]

In the literature on constitutional commitment, elites are said to agree to self-limiting behavior—that is, they agree to accept rules even in subsequent instances when breaking them might benefit them—because cooperating with others on pre-set responses avoids

13. John Ferejohn and Lawrence Sager, "Commitment and Constitutionalism," *Texas Law Review,* Vol. 81, no. 7 (2003), pp. 1929–63, at pp. 1938–40. Thomas C. Schelling, who pioneered the study of commitment, especially in international politics, argues that, to increase the credibility of a commitment, a demonstration of seriousness to counterparties, including a willingness to incur costs to keep the commitment, is most effective. In international relations, this includes displays of vulnerability in the event of challenge (American troops in West Berlin during the Cold War, for example, to demonstrate to an adversary the inevitability of war in case that sector of the city were invaded). See Schelling, *Strategies of Commitment and Other Essays* (Cambridge: Harvard University Press, 2006), pp. 1–24; Schelling, *Arms and Influence* (New Haven: Yale University Press, 1966), pp. 38–91.

the problem of reciprocal vulnerability. They remove future options in advance in order to prevent suffering a loss (paying a cost) later if there were no mutual restrictions on the use of such options.[14] So, for example, minority rights are agreed as a conscious exercise in restricting collective, democratic autonomy in order to prevent minority oppression subsequently.[15] Similarly, violence is ruled out as a means of securing political advantage, because the constitution specifies approved methods of change. Commitment of this kind entails an implicit exchange of promises that are embodied in a constitutional document.

Often, political actors are willing to coordinate on such solutions after experiencing the adverse effects of predation, either by an autocrat or by competing political groups.[16] Violence or mutually experienced injury and a desire to avoid repetition are frequently in the background. Without those conditions, it might be difficult to induce both sides (or all sides) to forego future options. In this respect, cooperation emerges just as it does in repeated games of prisoner's dilemma.[17] In reiterated prisoner's dilemma

14. See Robert E. Goodin, "Institutions and Their Design," in *The Theory of Institutional Design*, ed. Goodin (Cambridge: Cambridge University Press, 1996), pp. 1–53, at pp. 23–24. See also Michael Gilbert et al., "Constitutional Locks," Virginia Public Law and Legal Theory Research Paper no. 2019-50, arguing that prohibitions on constitutional amendments for a specified period after adoption of a constitution ("constitutional locks"), present in forty-four constitutions worldwide, serve to promote principled deliberation, protect minorities, and create increased space for negotiation, thereby facilitating credible commitment.

15. Cristina Foroni Consani, "Constitutional Precommitment and Collective Autonomy: Can They Be Reconciled?" *Revista de Estudos Constitucionalis Hermenêutica e Theoria do Direito*, Vol. 7, no. 3 (2015), pp. 235–42.

16. Barry R. Weingast, "The Political Foundations of Democracy and the Rule of Law," *American Political Science Review*, Vol. 91, no. 2 (1997), pp. 245–63; Stephen Holmes, "Precommitment and the Paradox of Democracy," in *Constitutionalism and Democracy*, ed. Jon Elster et al. (Cambridge: Cambridge University Press, 1988), pp. 195–240.

17. Robert Axelrod, *The Evolution of Cooperation*, 2d ed. (New York: Basic Books, 2006).

games, cooperation is preferable to defection, but in early games neither player can count on the other to cooperate, and so each defects, thereby suffering mutual disadvantage. Over time, however, players learn to act reciprocally when others initiate cooperative action, and the sooner cooperative behavior begins, the better the results.[18]

With the proliferation of issues, if there is not complete consensus, the range of favorable and unfavorable outcomes usually discourages later defection on the occasion of any one loss.[19] If reciprocal cooperation proves helpful to political actors, they accept some losses once the cooperative arrangements have been put into place. In addition, actors understand that an absence of stability will be costly and that it will be difficult or perhaps impossible to agree on alternative arrangements once one set of arrangements is functioning, even if it turns out to be imperfect in its distribution of outcomes. Particular outcomes create new constituencies, especially among the winners, who then reinforce the arrangements. So, eventually, a certain amount of inertia and habituation begins to set in, supplementing mutual interest, and this helps to strengthen the force of constitutional rules.[20] Because of this, it is often said that such constitutions are "self-enforcing," in the sense that it is expected that actors will abide by what has been agreed. What starts out as a deliberate decision of political leaders, a consensus in response to

18. Ibid., p. 117.

19. On this mechanism in political coalitions, see Sven Groennings, "Notes Toward Theories of Coalition Behavior in Multiparty Systems: Formation and Maintenance," in *The Study of Coalition Behavior*, ed. Groennings et al. (New York: Holt, 1970), pp. 445–65. See generally Daryl Levinson, "Parchment and Politics: The Positive Puzzle of Political Commitment," *Harvard Law Review*, Vol. 124, no. 3 (2011), pp. 657-746, at pp. 693-94, 715, 742, 744, which describes many of the mechanisms usually postulated to be operative in producing commitment.

20. For the "veneration which time bestows on every thing, and without which perhaps the wisest and freest governments would not possess the requisite stability," see James Madison, *The Federalist*, No. 49, in *The Federalist Papers*, ed. Ian Shapiro (New Haven: Yale University Press, 2009), p. 257.

sharp differences, becomes a set of habits about solving political problems.[21]

This rather neat story, with its teleology of self-enforcement, is usually developed in accounts of the origin and persistence of Western constitutional democracies, for which it is, on the whole, a fairly helpful explanation. Even there, however, some of these mechanisms may not function in any given case. Furthermore, the commitment explanation, useful though it is in general, leaves open questions about the high incidence of constitutional defection and breakdown, where those occur. There are, after all, reasons for the profusion of new constitutions that I mentioned earlier. Many of these came into existence because previous constitutional orders broke down when commitments did not hold. For that reason, it is worth thinking about how constitutional processes can contribute to higher levels of commitment.

There are, of course, inhibitions on defection following agreements. Reneging typically has highly negative reputational consequences[22]—as Thomas C. Schelling says, an actor's rejection of a previous commitment discredits others the actor may actually wish to keep in place[23]—and it tends to give rise to tit-for-tat revenge,[24] which can be painful. Similarly, constitutional courts and other institutions may punish and publicize violations, thereby "inhibiting transgression."[25] For these reasons, defection might not be a routine

21. In addition to writings on commitment, see, on this point, Dankwart Rustow, "Transitions to Democracy: Toward a Dynamic Model," *Comparative Politics,* Vol. 2, no. 3 (1970), pp. 337–63.

22. Schelling, *Strategies of Commitment and Other Essays,* pp. 10–11; Douglas M. Gibler, "The Costs of Reneging: Reputation and Alliance Formation," *Journal of Conflict Resolution,* Vol. 52, no. 3 (2008), pp. 426–54.

23. Schelling, *Arms and Influence,* p. 66.

24. Axelrod, *Evolution of Cooperation,* pp. 27–54 et passim; cf. William Bernhard and Tracy Sulkin, "Commitment and Consequences: Reneging on Pledges in the U.S. House," *Legislative Studies Quarterly,* Vol. 38, no. 4 (2013), pp. 461–87.

25. Zachary Elkins, Tom Ginsburg, and James Melton, *The Endurance of National Constitutions* (Cambridge: Cambridge University Press, 2009), p. 212.

response to disappointment with constitutional arrangements and their results. Nevertheless, it does occur with some frequency in polities with major divisions, such as those in severely divided societies, as some commitment theorists recognize.[26]

If there are large power imbalances, the institutionalization of constitutional norms may be thwarted before it is complete, when a powerful group suffers or anticipates a serious loss. In such circumstances, defection may occur even if the loss is completely consonant with constitutional provisions, for then the costs of defection, compared to the benefits of acquiescence, might seem to be well worth paying. This problem has been noticed with peace agreements. Special modes of "transformative peacekeeping" have been recommended to deal with it. These involve intense and extended involvement of third parties, who are willing to call out violations and raise the costs of noncooperation early on.[27] Outside of this setting, however—where states are sovereign and third-party intervention is usually absent or, worse, where third parties have malign interests in the conflict in a neighboring state—these methods are not usually available.[28] And defection, even by stronger parties, may produce developments that surprise the defectors, as weaker parties organize for armed rebellion, often receiving support from neighboring states.[29]

Even at later stages, commitments may erode as their perceived costs cumulate and/or their perceived benefits decline. Recall that,

26. See, e.g., Weingast, "Political Foundations of Democracy and the Rule of Law," p. 256.

27. Doyle and Sambanis, *Making War and Building Peace,* pp. 52–58. Many others have lamented the inadequate power and staying-power of peacekeepers. See, e.g., Jean Arnault, "Good Agreement, Bad Agreement? An Implementation Perspective," Princeton University, Center of International Studies, unpublished paper, n.d.

28. Compare, however, Bosnia since 1995 and Macedonia since 2001, where international interveners have been active.

29. See Donald L. Horowitz, "Irredentas and Secessions: Adjacent Phenomena, Neglected Connections," in *Irredentism and International Politics,* ed. Naomi Chazan (Boulder: Lynne Rienner, 1991), pp. 9–22.

in severely divided societies, a few groups are competing for state power, and some leaders of these groups have a preference for power that excludes others. For both sides, the stakes may be so large that reputational costs, tit-for-tat revenge, publicity about violations, or sanctions of similar severity cannot deter reneging in all circumstances. And revenge for defection may actually produce escalation of the conflict rather than renewed compliance.

Durability of constitutional commitments is therefore a significant challenge. Its most serious manifestations are visible with respect to future generations who, having failed to experience the founding background events, often including violence that earlier generations worked to avert, may underweight the risks of reneging. This is especially probable if there have been changes in conditions that they see as unfavorable to the group with which they are affiliated. If they have been chosen wisely, the institutions embodied in the constitution will presumably exert some deterrent effect. Obviously, arrangements that are seen to be just—that is, just under the circumstances, including the condition of interethnic contention, if present—and that embody conflict-mitigating mechanisms and institutions that support them may contribute to durability. Likewise, habits of compliance with the constitution may be fostered by the efficacy and steadfastness of compliance bodies, such as courts and electoral commissions, whose decisions can create an aura of inevitability to the enforcement of constitutional provisions. But durability is certainly affected by the perceived fairness of results, insofar as they are traceable to the content of constitutional arrangements, results that may change over time, favoring one side or another disproportionately. Of course, opportunities for altering the constitution as results change will affect durability. For example, amendment processes will be available to change the constitution, and judicial review may allow reinterpretation. These and other features of the constitutional design may operate to change the calculus of dissatisfied actors in favor of continued commitment.[30]

The question here, however, is not durability in general or the occasions for defection in general. Rather, the question is whether *constitutional process* has any part to play in facilitating constitutional commitments and, at least to some extent, extending the likely durability of those commitments in order to avoid the catastrophes often befalling those countries that experience reneging behavior that results in oppression, conflict, and warfare.

In what follows, I make an argument for special attention to securing widespread agreement of politicians to any new constitutional dispensation. It is true that some military regimes have the power to thwart democratic constitutional change, as they have in Myanmar (Burma), Thailand, and Egypt. But when we are considering civilian-created constitutions in most countries, especially where civilians have seized the initiative or already possess the power to create a new constitution—generally even when citizens have triggered the process by their massed presence in the streets—the fate of those constitutions turns much more on their acceptance by civilian politicians. And by politicians I mean to include even politicians from the former regime, whether autocratic or democratic, and insurgent political leaders in countries emerging from civil war. Dissatisfied politicians, particularly those representing ethnic groups in conflict with others, constitute a serious threat to new institutions. New democratic openings do not always block opportunities for illiberal forces to return to undemocratic practices.[31]

---

30. Elkins, Ginsburg, and Melton find, for example, that democratic constitutions have a longer average life by 30 percent than do authoritarian constitutions. They also find that, within limits, ease of amendment has a positive impact on durability. See Elkins, Ginsburg, and Melton, *Endurance of National Constitutions*, pp. 137, 140.

31. H. Kwasi Prempeh, "Africa's 'Constitutionalism Revival': False Start or New Dawn?" *International Journal of Constitutional Law*, Vol. 5, no. 3 (2007), pp. 469–

The armed forces are, by themselves, generally a much less potent threat to new, democratic constitutions than are ambitious or dissatisfied politicians,[32] who have been responsible for democratic degradation in dozens of countries, from Hungary to Sri Lanka and from Lebanon to Burundi.

The adherence of politicians to a new set of democratic institutions is, therefore, of great importance. Political elites are the central actors in democratization,[33] and the same can be said for their role in constitutionalization. Especially in ethnically divided polities, as the risk of military coups has declined with measures to prevent them,[34] interethnic accommodation may become more attractive, but it comes with the risk of defection.[35] As I have suggested, there may be several motives for politicians to play or not to play by constitu-

506; Andreas Schedler, "What Is Democratic Consolidation?" *Journal of Democracy*, Vol. 9, no. 2 (1998), pp. 91–107, at pp. 95–96.

32. The number of military coups and coup attempts is a small fraction of what they were in the coup-prone 1960s and 1970s. Civilian democratic, autocratic, and semi-autocratic regimes greatly outnumber military regimes. The number of successful coups worldwide traced the following trajectory: 61 in the decade of the 1960s, 56 in the 1970s, 36 in the 1980s, 21 in the 1990s, 10 in the 2000s, and just 6 from 2010 to 2017. Drew DeSilver, "Despite Apparent Coup in Zimbabwe, Armed Takeovers Have Become Less Common Worldwide," Fact Tank, Pew Research Center, November 17, 2017, www.pewresearch.org. For this change in Africa and a compelling explanation for it, see Philip Roessler, *Ethnic Politics and State Power in Africa: The Logic of the Coup–Civil War Trap* (Cambridge: Cambridge University Press, 2016), pp. 87, 307 et passim. See also Kristen A. Harkness, *When Soldiers Rebel: Ethnic Armies and Political Instability in Africa* (Cambridge: Cambridge University Press, 2018), pp. 217–22; Duncan McCargo, "Are Military Regimes Going Out of Style?" *The Institute Letter*, Institute for Advanced Study, Princeton, New Jersey, Spring 2006.

33. Samuel P. Huntington, *The Third Wave: Democratization in the Late Twentieth Century* (Norman: University of Oklahoma, 1991), pp. 107–8; Larry Diamond, "Introduction: Political Culture and Democracy," in *Political Culture and Democracy in Developing Countries*, ed. Diamond (Boulder, CO: Lynne Rienner, 1993), pp. 1–33, at p. 3; Rustow, "Transitions to Democracy," passim.

34. For techniques of coup-proofing, see Donald L. Horowitz, *Ethnic Groups in Conflict* (Berkeley: University of California Press, 2000), pp. 532–59.

35. For a more nuanced statement of the variables at work in certain situations, see Roessler, *Ethnic Politics and State Power in Africa*, pp. 273–74.

tionally prescribed rules, among them incentives and disincentives that accompany ephemeral changes in conditions. A critical but neglected one is their attachment to the new constitutional dispensation at the time of its creation.

That consideration is the principal reason for the importance of deliberation and, to the maximum extent possible, consensus or at least a mutually satisfying set of compromises. The adherence of participating politicians should enhance the durability of the outcome. Among other things, constitutions lay out certain boundaries, observance of which depends on restraint and, hopefully, self-restraint of political actors. In the world of severely divided societies, where credible commitment of politicians to institutions often falls short, partly because legal institutions may not be adequate to hold public actors to their obligations and may even abet them in violating obligations,[36] it is worthwhile to underscore the critical importance of widely distributed political consent at the outset. As I shall argue later, citizen participation may be helpful at various stages of the process, but much more important is the behavior of the elected representatives of the citizenry. Without their inclusion consensus cannot be complete.

In severely divided societies, early, solid commitment might just be able to help with a recurrent problem of path dependence. If initial commitment to a constitutional regime of ethnic equality is weak or easily dislodged, ethnically biased policies may be enacted. Once they take root and create constituencies dependent upon them, these policies can become difficult to reverse or to modify. Organized interests congeal around them, and even when they have proved costly in terms of economic efficiency, or the maintenance of interethnic peace, or even basic fairness, the political parties that patronize those interests become fearful of antagonizing them, lest

36. I am referring here to perverse judicial interpretation solicited or encouraged by politicians, a subject I return to later.

other parties are willing to champion them in the name of ethnic solidarity.

As Theodore J. Lowi argued a half century ago, policy makes politics, as much as politics makes policy.[37] By this he meant that politics "takes its shape from the functions the state performs."[38] In countries like Malaysia and Sri Lanka, there is abundant evidence for this proposition. In the former, a series of actions altered the constitution and practice agreed in 1957 (in Malaya, before the creation of Malaysia in 1963).[39] An elaborate regime of ethnic policies to favor Malays was put in place in the 1970s and 1980s, creating a large clientele of Malay business people and other beneficiaries of Malay preferences who became important members and constituents of what was until 2018 the main Malay party.[40] They have proved highly resistant to changes that several governments have contemplated in order to open market access to contractors and other competitors for the sake of efficiency and fairness to all ethnic groups. The same is true for rather harsh policies favoring Islam over other religions, despite guarantees of religious freedom in the constitution, as we shall see later. In Sri Lanka as well, policies and constitutional re-

37. Lowi, "Public Policy and Bureaucracy in the United States and France," in *Comparing Public Policies: New Concepts and Methods,* ed. Douglas E. Ashford (Beverly Hills: Sage, 1978), pp. 177–95, at p. 178; Lowi, "Four Systems of Policy, Politics and Choice," *Public Administration Review,* Vol. 32, no. 4 (1972), pp. 298–310, at p. 299. The idea goes back to E. E. Schattschneider, *Politics, Pressures, and the Tariff* (Hamden, CT: Archon, 1963).

38. Lowi, "Public Policy and Bureaucracy in the United States and France," p. 178.

39. Malaysia incorporated the Federation of Malaya with the Borneo states of Sabah and Sarawak, as well as Singapore, into a new federation called Malaysia. Singapore departed Malaysia two years later. The constitution of the new country was and is based on a heavily amended version of the original constitution of Malaya.

40. See Donald L. Horowitz, "Cause and Consequence in Public Policy Theory: Ethnic Policy and System Transformation in Malaysia," *Policy Sciences,* Vol. 22, nos. 3–4 (1989), pp. 249–88.

visions favoring Sinhalese Buddhists over various minorities have proved difficult to modify, as organizations benefited by the policies, including the Buddhist Sangha or priesthood, became powerful interest groups able repeatedly to thwart change,[41] again as we shall note at later points.

These policies in both countries were easy to adopt in the decades following independence, because commitment to initial constitutional protections for minorities was either thin or vulnerable to defection by second-generation politicians. Once these biased policies were implemented, path dependence did the rest of the work to thwart a return to norms of equality. When expectations become embedded and a class of beneficiaries and potential beneficiaries is established, anticipated reductions in tangible or symbolic benefits are experienced as a loss. The palpable benefits of these policies and the influence of their proponents on the electorate have made and still make them hard to modify.

Repeatedly, efforts were made in Malaysia to scale back what had become a regime of privileges for Malays, experienced by non-Malays as discrimination and even as attempts at their exclusion from the national community. Each time, proposals to modify the regime of preferences provoked reactions from beneficiaries and their representatives that thwarted the progress of such proposals at the outset. Even after a new multiethnic coalition government finally came to power on a reform agenda in 2018, plans to amend provisions for Malay preferences and also to reform the extremist Islamic administration at the central-government level were stymied

41. See generally Robert N. Kearney, *The Politics of Ceylon (Sri Lanka)* (Ithaca: Cornell University Press, 1973); Benjamin Schonthal, *Buddhism, Politics, and the Limits of Law in Sri Lanka* (Cambridge: Cambridge University Press, 2016). For some of the particulars, see Neil DeVotta, *Blowback: Linguistic Nationalism, Institutional Decay, and Ethnic Conflict in Sri Lanka* (Stanford: Stanford University Press, 2004), pp. 153–55.

by reactions that created fear of electoral reversal in the new government, with its vulnerable majority.[42]

Similarly, as we shall explore in some detail in chapter 8, repeated attempts to redress the discriminatory treatment of minorities in Sri Lanka have come to naught, each time effectively vetoed by threats of Sinhalese opposition parties to defeat the proponents of reform at the polls. As soon as these threats surfaced, they caused governing parties to back away from taking the electoral risk. Even after protracted ethnic warfare and a subsequent election in 2015 that brought constitutional reformers to power, a serious attempt to create a new constitution that might bring equal treatment to the Tamil and other minorities was frustrated by the reluctance of reform leaders to risk retribution by the opposition at the polls.

In each case, the commitment to equality, having been breached, created entrenched interests that made the costs of rectification appear to be insurmountable even after still-later generations came to understand the need for changing course. In both Malaysia and Sri Lanka, the initial constitutional arrangements were put in place by commissions created by the departing British colonial regime, albeit in close consultation with the ascendant leaders who would take over the newly independent governments. While elements in the new governments were committed to the constitution, that commitment was not necessarily widely shared. The initial constitutional process was not geared to produce wide or very deep commitment on the part of those who would take power and would soon share power with others who had not participated and become committed in the first instance. The constitution-framing task at independence

42. See Lily Zubaidah Rahim, "Resurgent Ethno-Religious Nationalists, Ambivalent Democrats, and the Challenge of Policy Reform in the 'New Malaysia,'" paper presented at the 2019 annual meeting of the American Political Science Association. In 2020, that government fell as a result of defections to a coalition that consisted heavily of members of the former opposition.

was conceived as making acceptable rules that would govern and, in some respects, limit government action. Commitment was more or less taken for granted.

Departures from those rules that affect identifiable groups create a long-term conundrum. The difficulty of reversing departures from initial constitutional principles over time, especially when the policies that depart from those principles take root and create strong constituencies that will fight to retain those policies, argues strongly for a greater emphasis in constitutional processes that produce firmer and more durable commitment. At times of democratic opening or reopening after periods of authoritarian rule, processes need to be geared carefully toward that end.

To be sure, no claim can be made that strong initial commitment alone is enough to assure the growth of a constitutionalism sufficient to fight off forces of ethnic dissensus and the quest for advantage in a contentious milieu. Among other things, good institutions, especially rule-of-law institutions, are also required in order to make defection more difficult and even implausible. That means that constitutional processes need to focus hard on the substance of institutional design or re-design. Many forces, including civil society organizations, no doubt also need to be brought to bear to persuade interested groups to abide by what has been agreed in order to stem the growth of recalcitrant political constituencies and interest groups dedicated to revisionist projects of radical ethnic inequality in a society that might otherwise enjoy tranquility and a measure of harmony, if not interethnic friendliness. Nevertheless, if we are speaking of constitutional process, then measures of securing maximal commitment through such a process is a very important place to start. The most secure foundations for commitment seem to me to be inclusion, deliberation, and consensus.

Inclusion of all major groups and political tendencies minimizes the number of possible players who, because they were not present, may not feel bound by what has been agreed and may have been overlooked in the apportionment of benefits and obligations.[43] "Groups must have an interest in the constitution to maintain it," argue Elkins, Ginsburg, and Melton in the conclusion to their careful study of constitutional endurance. "Inclusion in the making of constitutions can promote a unifying identity and invite participants to invest in the bargain . . . ."[44] Inclusion also prevents rent-seeking conspiracies hatched by those who are there at the expense of those who are not.

Deliberation involves reason and persuasion in the search for good answers to the questions confronting decision makers. Much of the writing on credible commitment concerns actors who wish to be believed and who genuinely intend to honor their commitments and to bind others to do so. Christine Bell contends that many constitutional processes begin with the rudiments of an elite deal.[45] (Some do, and many do not.) If such a deal is to grow into a constitutional settlement,[46] the participants—a more inclusive group—need time to rethink the deal, explore its implications, and flesh them out, trying to persuade each other about what arrangements might work well. A deal, after all, is not a design, although it may contain the kernel of one. At least the same deliberation time, and probably more, is needed in the absence of an antecedent deal. There is evidence that longer constitutions, those with more detail (within limits) last longer.[47] Longer constitutions are very likely to be the product of inclusive representation and extended deliberation.[48]

---

43. On inclusion and "self-enforcing" constitutions, see Elkins, Ginsburg, and Melton, *Endurance of National Constitutions*, pp. 78–81.

44. Ibid., p. 211.

45. Christine Bell, "Introduction: Bargaining on Constitutions—Political Settlements and Constitutional State-Building," *Global Constitutionalism*, Vol. 6, no. 1 (2017), pp. 13–32, at pp. 14, 20–21.

46. See ibid., p. 31.

47. Elkins, Ginsburg, and Melton, *Endurance of National Constitutions*, p. 210.

48. Ibid.

Some actors, however, may not be genuine, or their commitments may be equivocal, shaky, or contingent. By giving participants extended contact in the course of argumentation, deliberation helps, or should help, each to ascertain the genuineness of commitments of others. After all, as Schelling suggests, the presence of faking in many activities implies that humans have developed some capacity to detect it,[49] and a thorough review of psychological literature indicates that gullibility on matters of importance to the listeners is strictly limited.[50]

Repeated interaction in a structured setting, in which participants have an expectation of further interaction, is likely to give rise to a reciprocal understanding of "their colleagues' intentions, their trustworthiness, and the political constraints they are facing . . . ."[51] They learn which assertions are genuine and which are merely negotiating tactics, and they reject continued interaction with those who have deceived them previously.[52] This kind of interaction can provide useful knowledge for producing a constitutional dispensation that all sides can live with. In situations of adverse interest, repeat players are more likely than single-shot players to initiate cooperation.[53] Extended deliberation has a good chance of generating cooperation and discourse that is conducive to consensus. There is, then, a case for an unhurried constitutional process.

Moreover, deliberation should be conducive to commitment through shared experience, but the degree of commitment also

---

49. Schelling, *Strategies of Commitment and Other Essays,* p. 21.

50. Hugo Mercier, "How Gullible Are We? A Review of Evidence from Psychology and Social Science," *Review of General Psychology,* Vol. 21, no. 2 (2017), pp. 103–22.

51. Mark E. Warren and Jane Mansbridge, "Deliberative Negotiation," in *Political Negotiation: A Handbook,* ed. Mansbridge and Cathy Jo Martin (Washington, DC: Brookings Institution Press, 2016), pp. 141–96, at p. 172, quoting Amy Gutmann and Dennis Thompson, *The Spirit of Compromise* (Princeton: Princeton University Press, 2012), p. 170.

52. Warren and Mansbridge, "Deliberative Negotiation," p. 167.

53. Axelrod, *Evolution of Cooperation,* pp. 77 et passim.

depends on whether the proceedings leave disaffected dissenters recurrently on the losing side of majority or even supermajority votes. For that purpose, attempts to achieve consensus on particular items, whenever possible, can be helpful, particularly in societies where intergroup political divisions are pronounced.

Consensus decisions have a number of highly significant virtues. They guarantee that the inclusion of ethnic minorities will be meaningful, whereas otherwise their preferences could be neglected in favor of the will of the majority. They help to impart definitiveness and clarity to what has been decided that can be relied on later. Consensus requirements can also improve the quality of argumentation and deliberation. Careful studies of deliberation in Belgium and Colombia found that consensus standards for agreement elicited more reasoned and serious justifications than simple-majority standards did.[54] Equally important, widespread consensus reflects at least minimal satisfaction on the part of those who subscribe to it and so under most conditions renders subsequent defection much harder to justify. Consensus on a total constitutional package should create greater inhibition on defection than does separate agreement on pieces of the package. Those who seek to undo particular pieces of what was agreed to as a whole threaten to unravel the entire agreement, a possibility likely to be met with stern opposition. A consensus based on inclusive representation should be more difficult to undo than are other forms of agreement.

---

54. Didier Caluwaerts, *Confrontation and Communication: Deliberative Democracy in Divided Belgium* (Brussels: Peter Lang, 2012), pp. 136-37; Juan E. Ugarriza, "When Adversaries Talk: The Experimental Effect of Engagement Rules on Postconflict Deliberation," *Latin American Politics and Society*, Vol. 58, no. 3 (2016), pp. 77-98. Caluwaerts also found the higher standards produced more attentive consideration to others' arguments, and Ugarriza found consensus fostered more "common-good" arguments and fewer that were self-interested. Similar results have been obtained in studies of unanimous versus majoritarian rules of jury deliberation. See, e.g., Dennis J. Devine, "Jury Decision Making," *Psychology, Public Policy, and Law*, Vol. 7, no. 3 (1999), pp. 622-727, at p. 669.

Widespread consensus signals widespread commitment. Credible signals that inhere in consensus constitutions are important first steps in a longer process by which actors are likely to (but, in some cases, may not) find it in their interest to play by democratic rules.[55]

Participants in significant activities tend to take pride in the work of their own hands. The more that inclusion and consensus produce a successful conclusion to the process, the more pride there is likely to be, and the more commitment should result. This is speculative, of course, but it is not without foundation. In recent decades, psychologists have been studying the relation of motivation to emotions, finding that certain emotions motivate people toward certain goals. Experimental research has shown that an experience of success in a task is associated with high levels of pride, a finding that holds across multiple cultures. Individuals who experience pride in response to success in task fulfillment are more likely to persevere in subsequent similar tasks. Indeed, pride is an emotion more apt to be related to the pursuit of success in long-term goals than are most other emotions. It promotes continued achievement-oriented behavior, often in the same field of endeavor.[56] Needless to say, these studies do not demonstrate a link between pride in constitutional creation and democratic commitment, but the continuing

---

55. See Stathis N. Kalyvas, "Commitment Problems in Emerging Democracies," *Comparative Politics*, Vol. 32, no. 4 (2000), pp. 379–98, at p. 391. There is, of course, the earlier-mentioned problem of later generations who were not involved in the consensus and whose commitment cannot be taken for granted. If the constitution develops around itself an aura of success, especially if present conditions contrast favorably with conditions in the period preceding the constitutional adoption, defection may become more difficult for later generations.

56. See Alec T. Beall and Jessica L. Tracy, "Emotivational Psychology: How Distinct Emotions Facilitate Fundamental Motives," *Social and Personality Psychology Compass*, Vol. 11, no. 2 (February 2017), pp. 1–17, https://doi.org/10.1111/spc3.12303; Jessica L. Tracy and Richard W. Robins, "Emerging Insights into the Nature and Function of Pride," *Current Directions in Psychological Sciences*, Vol. 16, no. 3 (2007), pp. 147–50; Daniel Hart and M. Kyle Matsuba, "The Development of Pride in Moral Life," in *The Self-Conscious Emotions: Theory and Research*, ed. Jessica L. Tracy, Richard W. Robins, and June Price Tangey (New York: Guilford Press, 2007), pp. 114–33. See also the literature on "the IKEA effect."

motivational effects of pride after successful task completion suggest that it can motivate this kind of commitment.[57]

As I have said, consensus requires deliberation, and it therefore requires time to achieve it, so to opt for a goal of consensus is also to minimize decisions taken in haste. Especially important, at least for severely divided societies, consensus on the fundamental rules of politics connotes at least a modicum of respect for the other side, a development that can scarcely be overvalued in such a society, where mutual respect may generally be absent. That is another good reason for attempting to cultivate consensus in a deliberative process that is inclusive and thus not limited to a small and perhaps unrepresentative body of constitution makers.[58]

There is yet another reason for aiming at consensus. If a constitution is to be privileged as the supreme law of the land, a principal justification for that superior status is the higher standard for adoption: the vast majority of people legitimately involved in producing it gave its contents serious consideration and agreed with the outcome.[59] This reason, of course, squares with the argument for commitment by political actors, but it also provides an argument for compliance on the part of those who were not so involved.

Durable constitutional consensus is not a new idea. In the late fifth century B.C.E., Athenian oligarchs and democrats, reflecting on

57. To test this proposition, consider arguments likely to be made to potential defectors after a successful, inclusive process involving extensive deliberation and ending in consensus. To a threat of reneging on an issue previously settled, other participants will probably respond that they had been over that ground thoroughly before, and it had all been thrashed out. After a great deal of hard work and against many obstacles, defection risks undoing the accomplishment of consensus. These are serious reproofs that would reflect pride in what had been achieved compared to the status quo ante and commitment deriving from success in producing it.

58. In chapter 6, we shall encounter a constitutional agreement made by a small group of leaders across ethnic lines that was undone by the defection years later by more radical politicians who had not been included.

59. I was prompted in this direction by a question about the justification for "supreme law" status posed by Chang Wen-Chen in Hong Kong on July 5, 2011.

a decade of violence, gradually agreed on legislative institutions and procedures, as well as measures to protect property, personal freedom and dignity, and a set of rules about making rules—in short, a suite of arrangements amounting to a constitution. As described by Federica Carugati in an intriguing book,[60] the Athenians concentrated a good bit of attention on enforcement, including methods of challenging the validity of new laws.[61] The previous regime had been characterized by frequently imposed decrees and legislation that, by unsettling legal obligations, adversely affected the interests of the oligarchs. The emphasis on personal rights, on the other hand, was to assuage the grievances of the democratic majority against the arbitrary actions of oligarchs. The interests of both sides had been vulnerable.

The eighty-one-year duration of this constitution was due to the consensus that had been achieved. That consensus bound both oligarchs and democrats and was observed even by the latter, although they had won the preceding civil war. Consensus was based on an understanding of the failures of the previous regime, including its legal instability and the insecurity of property, and on a turn to legality inspired by Athens' early lawgivers, most notably Solon (ca. 630–560 B.C.E.).[62] After a long period of conflict, it was understood across lines of contention that a regime based on legality, correcting the lawlessness of the democrats and providing rights against the oligarchs, would be preferable for both sides.

I have simplified the argument of the Carugati book in an effort to illustrate some of the relationships between consensus and commitment. It might be said, of course, that underlying the Athenian consensus was a sense of reciprocal concession bordering on, if not actually consisting of, compromise. I concede that the line between

60. Carugati, *Crafting a Constitution: Law, Democracy, and Growth in Ancient Athens* (Princeton: Princeton University Press, 2019).

61. Ibid., pp. 69–71.

62. See esp. ibid., pp. 40–74.

the two is sometimes imperfect, for in an environment of diverging interests the idea of exchange cannot wholly be excluded. But, in my view, what makes this story principally a matter of consensus, in the face of the mutual recognition of differing if not always opposing interests, was agreement on the overall features of a desirable, legally binding regime, buttressed by its legitimation in a well-understood past. Legality was its overarching theme, a theme broad enough to provide confidence that the grievances felt by the population would not recur or, if they did, would be redressed. Almost everywhere in constitution-making forums there are divergent interests, and if resolution of those are enough to stamp the resulting agreement as a compromise, then the concept of consensus becomes useless in constitutional processes. The mere existence of an undercurrent of reciprocity is not enough to warrant the label *compromise,* provided there is overarching agreement on the new dispensation as a desirable way to engage in political life together and, therefore, worthy of commitments intended to be durable. This agreement on the new legal dispensation seems to me the best explanation for the durability of the Athenian regime.

Of course, consensus is more likely if there is a veil of ignorance concerning the interests of constitution makers. But in Athens, where interests were visible, the consensus on legality as a course that would serve both sides was the mode of constitution making.

It is encouraging that in fraught conflict situations negotiators do not always push demands to extremes. They may not opt for the best deal but settle for one that is good enough.[63] Winners have been known to accept self-limitation, sometimes when it is costly to themselves, or take risks in the national interest that jeopardize their

63. On "good enough," as opposed to interest maximization, see Michael Slote, "Moderation and Satisficing," in *Varieties of Practical Reasoning,* ed. Elijah Millgram (Cambridge: MIT Press, 2001), pp. 221–35.

own prospects.[64] There are, nevertheless, reasons to think compromise less desirable than consensus, as I have contended, inasmuch as many people compromise only reluctantly, and the durability of compromise outcomes depends, in considerable measure, on satisfaction with what the bargains produce for the respective sides years later. From both of these standpoints, regret and reneging, consensus is indeed more desirable.

Yet, in the long run, compromise is not in all respects a distant second-best. In the ordinary politics that follows the adoption of a constitution, the ability to compromise is an essential skill, and for leaders of groups in severely divided societies with divergent interests and preferences it is especially critical. In formerly authoritarian countries, constitutional processes can provide on-the-job training in compromise by forcing the players to engage with the claims of political opponents and to develop a familiarity with the interests and preferences of other actors that may have been long suppressed. In the very best case, negotiating and arriving at a compromise can be "one way by which people can come to see that there are points of view other than their own, and it is just such contexts that an attitude of toleration is likely to be developed."[65] A constitutional process should be judged not merely by the agreement it produces but also by the legacy it leaves in the human capital of

64. Consider the examples of Civic Forum in negotiations upon the demise of communism in Czechoslovakia, when it conceded an electoral system unfavorable to itself, and of B. J. Habibie after he assumed the presidency of Indonesia upon the resignation of Suharto, when he risked alienating prospective supporters for his own election by offering East Timor a referendum on independence—which did in fact kill his chances. See, respectively, Jon Elster, Claus Offe, and Ulrich Preuss, *Institutional Design in Post-Communist Societies: Rebuilding the Ship at Sea* (Cambridge: Cambridge University Press, 1998), p. 114; R. William Liddle, "Habibie's Transforming Politics," *Indonesia's Presidents: Constraints, Resources, and Choices*, in manuscript, chap. 2.

65. Albert Weale, *Democracy*, 1st ed. (Basingstoke, U.K.: Macmillan, 1999), p. 183.

those who participate in it. This is a neglected but very important proposition.

Even short of the best case, however, the probable relationship of some of these attributes of a constitutional process to genuine, credible commitment seems rather clear, as is their likely functionality for operating a polity after adoption of a constitution. Of course, even with clear criteria of this kind, an optimal process is elusive, perhaps impossible to devise in practice. Sometimes the attributes deemed desirable are in contention with one another, and process tradeoffs are required.[66] Nevertheless, conceptions of a desirable process can be helpful as a standard of judgment against which to measure actual processes.

It would be too grand to claim that these attributes add up to a full-blown theory of constitutional processes and the development of commitment. Rather, they comprise a series of highly plausible propositions about the elements of a constitutional process that are conducive to the commitment of politicians to the constitution that emerges from their efforts. As I mentioned earlier, these propositions are supported by evidence from some constitutional processes that were conducted in accordance with the enumerated attributes and from the failings of some that were not. In the existing state of knowledge, it is impossible to prove that any set of attributes of a constitutional process *necessarily* conduces to democratic commitment. There are just too many intervening variables, including antecedent conditions and idiosyncratic twists and turns in such processes, for a definitive level of proof. It is possible, however, to show that processes lacking the attributes on which I focus usually have adverse effects that often impair prospects for democratic commitment.

Obviously, then, I make no claim that these attributes inevitably lead to commitment or that there are no other routes to secur-

66. See chapters 5 and 6, below.

ing commitment. What I think is clear is that when widely shared, high levels of commitment to a democratic dispensation are present at the outset of a new constitutional regime, they facilitate peaceful political contestation in an agreed framework. My argument is that certain characteristics of constitutional processes seem more likely to generate those results than are processes lacking those characteristics.

Admittedly, the objectives I have laid out embody high standards that cannot always be met. Yet they are worth aspiring to because of the high rates of reneging and constitutional failure and the resulting lack of democratic durability of many constitutions. Given the absence of careful reflection on process issues accompanying the inception of many constitutional revisions, there is reason to think that attempts to achieve these objectives, if they were considered seriously at the outset, can be successful in more cases than might be imagined at first glance.

Like many others who write about these matters, I have so far spoken about the durability of constitutions and the durability of commitments as if the two were identical. But many constitutions can endure, in the sense of survive, even if the obligations undertaken at the inception become thoroughly debased over time, because of recurrent reneging that falls short of behavior that might bring the whole edifice down. We shall encounter examples of this behavior as we go along. Genuine commitment imparts integrity to a constitution—resistance to debasement—as well as durability of the document.

Most of what will be argued here might well apply to societies that are not severely divided in the sense in which I have used that term at the outset of this chapter.[67] The text that follows certainly is situated in and draws heavily on findings, discussions, and debates about processes that are not necessarily inspired by concern for the

67. See note 3, above.

future of divided societies. Nevertheless, the conflicts in such societies—among them Bosnia, Cyprus, Iraq, Lebanon, Macedonia, Malaysia, Nigeria, Somalia, Sri Lanka, and many others—prompted the inquiry that led to this volume. The problems of apt constitutional processes are important wherever constitutions are to be made, but they are more critical in severely divided societies than they are elsewhere. As we shall see, they are made difficult by the episodic nature of constitution making and the starting conditions typical of the enterprise.

CHAPTER 2

Knowledge, History, and Visibility

Certain elements in the constitution-making environment inhibit the planning and execution of sound processes. Inexperience among constitution drafters can limit their choice of processes and of apt institutions to consider for adoption to those that are familiar or that seem successful elsewhere. Severe time limits can prevent adequate deliberation, and external advisors often focus processes on goals that produce little proven payoff but incur heavy costs in lost deliberation time.[1] The presence of significant constraints and tradeoffs make choosing a suitable process and running it effectively a daunting task. Here I want to emphasize constraints involving knowledge, history, and the visibility of interests.

More often than not, constitution making is an exceptional event.[2] There is a great deal of experience in the world about the making of new constitutions (or the extensive amendment of old ones) but also a formidable problem of lost knowledge. Most people who make constitutions have never done so before and will never

---

1. On "participatory" constitution making, see chapter 7, below.

2. For more detail on matters discussed in the next several paragraphs, see my McDonald Lecture at the University of Alberta Centre for Constitutional Studies, published as Donald L. Horowitz, "Constitution-Making: A Process Filled with Constraint," *Review of Constitutional Studies*, Vol. 12, no. 1 (2006), pp. 1–17.

do so again. After the fact, their experience will generally not be recorded or utilized, and so their successors will have to start over from scratch. In many constitutional processes, there is a need for greater expertise than constitution makers are likely to possess.

Of course, in recent decades, constitution making has become an international and comparative exercise in ways that it was not previously. There is accessible literature on how to do the job, there are foreign advisors and organizations proffering advice—sometimes unwanted advice[3]—there are conferences on constitution making, and there are many ways to learn something from the experience of other states. There are strong trends in constitutional adoption, such as constitutional courts[4] and certain electoral systems,[5] although these adoptions are often implemented in very different ways from country to country. There are also advocates of certain modalities of constitution making that pass as universal prescriptions, some of which will be discussed at a later point.

Yet the impact of these changed conditions is not entirely benign. Conferences on constitution making are frequently attended by people who have made constitutions but rarely by those who will be called upon to do so in the future. Some constitution makers use international involvement as window dressing to demonstrate the democratic character of the process of constitutional choice, but the decisions are the same as would have been made without that involvement.

---

3. It is worth recalling the story told to me by the chair of an African constitutional commission. As soon as he was appointed, he was approached by an American consulting firm that offered to run the entire constitutional process for him, assuring him that there would be no cost involved, as a grant could be secured to cover all costs incurred. The offer was declined. Negotiation consultants made a similar offer at the outset of the South African constitutional process.

4. See Tom Ginsburg, "The Global Spread of Constitutional Review," in *Oxford Handbook of Law and Politics*, ed. Gregory Caldeira et al. (Oxford: Oxford University Press, 2008), pp. 81–98.

5. See Andrew Reynolds et al., *Electoral System Design: The New International IDEA Handbook* (Stockholm: International IDEA, 2005).

Foreign experts are often numerous, and their work can be intensive. Sometimes their advice is modest, and even then it is frequently rejected,[6] for reasons sound or unsound. In some cases, international involvement produces unpromising leads that need to be chased down.[7] Constitution makers are often ambivalent about international advice, and they are sometimes suspicious of the motives underlying the advice of local experts. They tend to be skeptical of unfamiliar foreign models. That skepticism leads them to choose from a much less than complete menu of possible institutions and constitutional processes.

Even when foreign experts bring good, useful comparative knowledge, constitutional planners and drafters may ignore it, fail to recognize its significance, or misconstrue it. There is a particularly large gulf in communication between first-time constitution makers and academic experts who might contribute useful information on similar experiments elsewhere.

Much advice is concerned with having participants reach agreement. If "getting to yes" is the objective, the content of the agreement may matter less than its achievement, although there may be many different agreements to which the participants could assent, some more and some less apt for their particular predicament. The

6. Wiktor Osiatynski, "Paradoxes of Constitutional Borrowing," *International Journal of Constitutional Law,* Vol. 1, no. 2 (2003), pp. 244–68.

7. Afghanistan's constitution makers had this experience in 2003 in connection with the assertion of certain constitutional advisors about the advantages of a very broad scope of judicial review for a constitutional court that was (it was thought) to be headed by a strong—and strong-willed—Islamist. It took a good deal of time and effort to head off some of the more doctrinaire and ethnocentrically American proposals. (I was involved in a minor way in the effort.) The provisions that replaced the proposal for a constitutional court were, however, incomplete and confusing. A supreme court was accorded some, but apparently not all, powers of constitutional interpretation, while a separate commission was accorded other, ill-specified powers pertaining to the constitution. On the confusion, see Tom Ginsburg and Aziz Huq, "What Can Constitutions Do? The Afghan Case," *Journal of Democracy,* Vol. 25, no. 1 (2014), pp. 116–30, at pp. 124–26.

emphasis on reaching agreement, which happens to suit the interests of outsiders (and perhaps some insiders, too) to finish a job, may produce a bias against adequate deliberation time and conceivably produce agreements that embody mutually inconsistent provisions.

Constitution makers generally do not gain an encyclopedic knowledge of the advice on offer, and what is on offer may not be a fair sample of what is available. Not every organization offering constitutional advice is on the scene in every process. Furthermore, a certain amount of advice on process that is tendered can be characterized as standard operating procedures recommended for environments that are anything but standardized. As we shall observe when we return to expert advice in chapter 7, uniformity of prescriptions can make decision makers hesitant to depart from them, despite the acute diversity of situations from country to country.

Inapt advice can be given, and inapt provisions can be adopted, because we are all, to some degree, prisoners of our own interests,[8] culture, and parochial experience. To decide what comparative models might prove pertinent requires a considerable degree of abstraction and ability to compare the situation of the proposed source country to that of the proposed recipient country in which the constitution maker is working. It will require a sophisticated assessment of both countries for the constitution maker to decide whether the comparison is relevant. Very often, experience that comes from unfamiliar source countries will be rejected or received skeptically,[9] be-

8. On the obvious role of interest of the borrowers in whether and what to borrow, see Lee Epstein and Jack Knight, "Constitutional Borrowing and Nonborrowing," *International Journal of Constitutional Law,* Vol. 1, no. 2 (2003), pp. 196–223.

9. Christina Murray, "Constitutional Design in Africa: Is Mix and Match OK?" *Ethnopolitics,* Vol. 15, no. 5 (2016), pp. 528–32, at p. 529. When it was suggested to Indonesian constitution makers by a local NGO that they adopt the Nigerian presidential electoral system, they were reluctant to do so, and some wondered whether Nigeria had ethnic or religious problems as serious as Indonesia's. I am drawing on my field notes from a meeting in Jakarta with about fourteen members of the main committee to revise the Indonesian constitution, held on May 11, 2000, and also from interviews in Jakarta on August 1, 2000. Because of lack of familiarity with

cause constitution makers, like some of the experts advising them, know much more about their own country than about any others.

Constitution makers may be biased in favor of certain foreign models, such as the former colonial power, in whose educational institutions they may have studied.[10] Anglophone countries in Asia, Africa, and the Caribbean generally express an affinity for British institutions (save for the many imperial presidencies in Africa), including plurality elections. Francophone countries tend to prefer French institutions, such as presidential or semi-presidential systems and two-round elections. In process terms, colonial affinity often leads former British colonies to turn to elite constitutional commissions for constitutional change and former French colonies to choose an updated version of estates-general.[11]

Post-colonial preferences can and do change, but powerful networks, habits, and pressures can retard the changes. There is not yet completely free trade in constitutional innovation. In some seriously divided countries with aspirations to democracy, there is an attraction to countries such as Switzerland that have a high reputation for conciliatory politics or simply to what are regarded as the most successful democracies.[12] Decision makers in this situation might do better to

---

Nigeria or its elections, it took a long time for the Indonesian body to decide, but in 2002 the Indonesians adopted a version of the Nigerian system after that same Indonesian NGO conducted a protracted campaign for it. Unfortunately, as often happens, the adopters tweaked the borrowed provisions, and when combined with other features of Indonesian electoral arrangements, they proved to be less effective in achieving their intended purpose than they might have been.

10. Cf. Alan Watson, *Legal Transplants* (Edinburgh: Scottish Academic Press, 1974); Watson, *Society and Legal Change* (Edinburgh: Scottish Academic Press, 1977), emphasizing idiosyncratic overseas educational backgrounds of those who are instrumental in borrowing legal norms.

11. For observations on constitutional transfer, see Günter Frankenberg, "Constitutional Transfer: the IKEA Theory Revisited," *International Journal of Constitutional Law*, Vol. 8, no. 3 (2010), pp. 563–79.

12. The literature on policy diffusion is abundant. For alternative models, see Kurt Weyland, "Theories of Policy Diffusion: Lessons from Latin American Pension Reform," *World Politics*, Vol. 57, no. 2 (2005), pp. 262–95.

examine the experience of countries that had encountered problems like their own, in order to ferret out the causes of any improvements.[13]

That is what happened in a number of countries following the publication of the *Federalist Papers* in the United States. The papers were widely translated and discussed in Latin America and Western Europe. The Venezuelan constitution of 1811, Mexico's of 1824, the Central American Federation constitution of 1825, and Argentina's a year later were all influenced by the United States document of 1787. Federalism, presidentialism, and judicial review were adopted early on in Latin America, because constitutional theorists in Latin American countries saw in certain features of the original possible answers to problems that perplexed them. These were not cases of foreign constitutional missionaries bringing provisions from elsewhere but of local experts reading and studying innovations and their applicability for themselves—and not merely in Latin America but in Switzerland and in Germany as well.[14] For a variety of reasons, there is much less critical evaluation and careful importation in the twenty-first century.

If there has been a failed constitutional process in their country's history, constitution makers may begin with a strong inclination to create a process that is the polar opposite of the one that failed, even if the failure has an explanation that might render it irrelevant to current concerns. Two historically conditioned memories that shaped the constitutional reform process in Indonesia from

---

13. For a fuller discussion of such biases, see Donald L. Horowitz, "Constitutional Design: Proposals versus Processes," in *The Architecture of Democracy*, ed. Andrew Reynolds (Oxford: Oxford University Press, 2002), pp. 15–36, at pp. 31–32. On learning from "constitutions that have been successful in the most trying environments, not just the most favourable," see Nic Cheeseman, "Accommodation Works Better for Reducing Conflict," *Ethnopolitics*, Vol. 15, no. 5 (2016), pp. 538–45, at p. 542.

14. On the role of Alberdi and Sarmiento in Argentina and of Troxler and of von Mohl in Switzerland and Germany, respectively, see Donald L. Horowitz, "The Federalist Abroad in the World," in *The Federalist Papers*, ed. Ian Shapiro (New Haven: Yale University Press, 2009), pp. 502–32, at pp. 504–6.

1999 to 2002 can make this clear. These affected profoundly the way the reformers went about their business.

The first derived from the extensive violence that had accompanied previous regime changes and had begun to afflict the country again in the late 1990s. A large political party, led by Megawati Sukarnoputri, daughter of the deceased dictator Sukarno, had within it a significant faction that was strongly attached to Sukarno's constitution, which was still in force when his successor, Suharto, fell from power in 1998. This faction was opposed to major changes in the constitution. Important figures in the military, which was prominent in the regime to be transformed, were also opposed to wholesale change. To have appointed or elected a body dedicated to creating immediately an entirely new constitution would have invited a great deal of opposition, some of it violent and perhaps decisive. Gradual amendment over several years, leading to a substantially new constitution, based on a slowly growing consensus, was the safer course. That course was chosen. By its conclusion, military opposition was ineffectual, and most in Megawati's party were carried along on a wave of starting afresh.

The second memory related to a previous, aborted effort at constitutional change. Between 1956 and 1959, a deadlock had gripped the constituent assembly that was attempting to agree on a new constitution. That deadlock allowed Sukarno to terminate Indonesia's brief period of parliamentary democracy and create what he called "Guided Democracy," which was no democracy at all. Recollection of the deadlock was on the minds of constitutional reformers after Suharto's downfall, and it led to a legislative process, rather than the creation of a separate constituent assembly that might produce another deadlock.[15] That memory also induced legislators not to take votes—

15. To be perfectly accurate, it was not the legislature as such but the legislature as augmented by some appointed members that had the power under the preexisting constitution to amend the document and that conducted the constitutional renovation by that method. I refer to that body elsewhere in the book as either a legislature

for voting had exposed the deadlock in the earlier assembly—but to decide each issue by consensus (with an insignificant exception) as consensus developed among all the party factions in the legislature. Amendments to the constitution were put out only as and when they were agreed and were withheld if no consensus had gathered around them. The end result was a new constitution in the clothes of the old.[16]

The Indonesian process had its costs, to be sure, but there was no cost in legitimacy. The public has repeatedly told survey researchers that it is unhappy with its political parties but very happy with its democracy, despite some slippage in democratic practice since the constitutional reform.

Every country has its own historically based institutional imprints and memories, many of them relevant to constitution making. Many of those drive process choices by making some options appear attractive and others unattractive or even impossible. In Indonesia, these took the form of aversive memories, courses to avoid. Elsewhere, the delayed impact of earlier events, the embeddedness of standard operating procedures, long-established political affinities or grievances, recollections of previous crises, and myriad other phenomena lodged in history will rule in some courses of action—and the modes of organizing them—and rule out others.

Libya is a highly regionalized country with strong geographic loyalties. During the Arab Spring, when elections were held for the General National Congress, the western part of the country was allocated more seats than the east, on the basis of purported population ratios. This allocation caused great discontent and some violence in the east. At a later point, when a sixty-member body was being created to devise a new constitution, it was composed of twenty members from each of the three major regions, regardless of

---

or supralegislature, but its composition was, for practical purposes, very similar to that of the legislature proper.

16. On these processes, see Donald L. Horowitz, *Constitutional Change and Democracy in Indonesia* (Cambridge: Cambridge University Press, 2013), pp. 21–29.

population, just as was done the last time a constitution was drafted, in 1951. Indonesia avoided a previous model deemed unsuccessful; Libya emulated a previous model deemed successful.[17]

Most processes do not start completely fresh. Attractive and aversive memories are often present, as they were in East European processes after 1989, in Afghanistan's use of a traditional Loya Jirga process in 2003–04, and in the influential recollections of Myanmar's (Burma's) minorities in 2017 and after as they planned for their constitutional negotiations with the central government by reference to the gains they were promised at the Panglong Conference of 1947. These memories, of course, do not necessarily make the preferences that follow from them effective in producing a satisfying constitutional result.

Beneath these illustrations lies a deep impediment to the entirely free choice of process that resides in all particular histories. In an important book about how history shapes and constrains public choice, Paul Pierson argues for skepticism of what he calls "actor-centered functionalism."[18] By this he means accounts of how individual and collective actors opted for one, rather than another, institution or policy based solely on a calculus of anticipated benefits at a given moment of decision. Instead, he proposes a causal focus on development over time—that is, the ways in which long historical processes "condition the circumstances confronting" those who make political choices.[19] The freedom to choose is affected by a variety of events, interests, and habits that have their origins in previous critical episodes or in the slower, path-dependent evolution in a particular country.

---

17. Obviously, I cite the Libyan example not for its outstanding success in constitution making, which it did not produce, but for the decision to resort to a familiar past practice that limited violence over the immediate issue of how to constitute such a body.

18. Pierson, *Politics in Time: History, Institutions, and Social Analysis* (Princeton: Princeton University Press, 2004), p. 104.

19. Ibid., p. 133.

Not all countries will have had historical experiences that inhibit free choice of constitutional processes. Even for those that have had them, those experiences do not imply that constitutional processes are straightforwardly historically determined or that actors who must decide what processes to use are preprogrammed in a specific direction. But for those countries, it does mean that general criteria for successful processes may have greater likelihood of adoption than do the most detailed recommendations for how to go about constitutional renovation. Even on specifics, of course, decision makers can be persuaded, but it helps to know the historical slate on which they are writing.

Constitutions are forward-looking documents, but they are made by people who are deeply affected by their views of their own history and its constraints. The history to which constitutional drafters refer includes not only the long historical processes to which Pierson refers but also events that have brought about the transitional moment in which the constitutional renovators are working. What they decide to do and what they produce are very likely to be tailored to redress the deficiencies that have been most recently apparent. Foreigners may be ubiquitous, but local history is the unseen framer at the table.

In any collective decision, the visibility of the interests of the people at the table can be an obstacle to agreement. There may well be a tendency to exaggerate the existence of a Rawlsian veil of ignorance in constitution-making proceedings.[20] Political parties or individual politicians may have a sense of the institutions that, if adopted, will favor them and disfavor their opponents. Politicians can be proven wrong about what choice of institutions will benefit them, as they sometimes were in Eastern Europe after the demise of

20. Cf. Adrian Vermeule, "Veil of Ignorance Rules in Constitutional Law," *Yale Law Journal*, Vol. 111, no. 2 (2001), pp. 399–433, at p. 400.

communist regimes,[21] but, right or wrong, the decisions they take will be affected by what they see as being in their interest, when they think they have this foresight.

Nevertheless, drafters sometimes do have the luxury of creating a constitution behind a veil of ignorance. There was a veil of ignorance in Nigeria in 1978, when a constituent assembly sought to produce a constitution that could provide security against further ethnic conflict, the identity of whose victims the assembly could not foresee. As they saw it, any group might be vulnerable in the future. Operating behind the veil, they sought to install what they saw as ethnically neutral protections against that possibility.[22] Similarly, Indonesian constitutional designers seeking to leave behind the autocratic rule of Suharto had held elections in 1999. In those elections, no party had come close to winning a majority of seats. It was difficult to forecast who would be advantaged and who disadvantaged by any particular configuration of institutions, and so the designers set about trying to find a configuration everyone could live with. With one revealing exception: proponents of a presidential system in Indonesia actually favored direct election of the president for the first

21. For examples, see Elster, Offe, and Preuss, *Institutional Design in Post-Communist Societies,* pp. 79, 114–16; Gideon Rahat, "The Study of the Politics of Electoral Reform in the 1990s," *Comparative Politics,* Vol. 36, no. 4 (2004), pp. 461–79, at pp. 469–70.

22. These took the form of territorial distribution requirements for presidential elections—of the sort later adopted in Kenya and Indonesia—so that presidents would have widely distributed support, and what were called "federal character" requirements for the composition of various government bodies, so that no group could monopolize positions. 1979 Constitution of the Federal Republic of Nigeria, as amended, arts. 126, 14(3), respectively. These requirements were carried over into the 1999 constitution, which superseded the 1979 one. 1999 Constitution of the Federal Republic of Nigeria, as amended, arts. 133–34, 14(3), respectively. The requirements have functioned only most imperfectly to achieve their intended purposes, but they do illustrate veil-of-ignorance adoptions. (I was present during the 1978 deliberations and consulted with an elected group of delegates on the presidential electoral formula, which had been proposed by a different group.)

time even though the party most reluctant to endorse the proposal had the candidate most likely to win that office in a direct popular election.[23] In other processes we shall examine, political parties had very clear ideas early on about what institutions they preferred, and in still others they only began to assess their relative strengths and weaknesses once a commission's electoral reform proposals had been elaborated in its report.[24]

A veil of ignorance is, then, highly variable and undoubtedly much less common than is at least some visibility of interests, even at the beginning of a constitutional process. Visibility typically grows as the process rolls on and concrete proposals are made. The more limited the visibility, the greater the deliberation. The greater the visibility, the more prevalent is negotiation as the mode of decision. Moreover, the presumed visibility of interests may make negotiations difficult, enlarge the sphere of bargaining, narrow choices to those that politicians think will favor them or the group they represent, and risk incoherence of at least some provisions of the resulting constitution—although complete coherence is not assured no matter what the mode of decision. If they do not have this degree of visibility at the outset of the process, participants are more likely to acquire it once they see a more or less finished draft, at which point they can imagine more clearly how its various provisions will probably affect them, bearing in mind that they could be wrong in their forecasts. As we shall observe, this progression in visibility makes it very important that the process of final review of drafts be deliberate, highly inclusive, and at least relatively open, lest undue logrolling and rent seeking take over the process.

In severely divided societies, there are two more general versions of the problem of conflicting group interests that can appear

23. See Horowitz, *Constitutional Change and Democracy in Indonesia*, pp. 108–22.

24. I am referring here to Kenya 2009–10 and Fiji 1997, respectively. Both are discussed in chapter 6, below.

even at the outset of proceedings. The first is that politicians who benefit from hostile sentiment toward other groups and the concrete results of that sentiment in the political system are not likely to transform the conflict-prone environment that supports their political careers. The second is the asymmetry of group preferences. Majorities want unimpeded majority rule, whereas minorities want guarantees against majority rule. This form of group political interest is a major impediment to constitutional planning. As a result, severely divided societies, which may be most in need of institutions to reduce conflict, may have the greatest difficulty adopting them.

The sum of these constraints is, again, to choose from a more limited menu than is available for institutional choice. On the whole, this is probably unfortunate, but perhaps not uniformly so, because it can render whatever is chosen, whether in process or institutions, more likely to resonate with local norms and experiences.

The choice of constitutional process is subject to similar limitations. In the abstract, a particular set of constitutional processes might serve a given state very well if it were free to choose them, but the circumstances in which it finds itself may limit its ability to make the best choices. This is especially true of severely divided societies, in which a few ethnic or religious groups compete for state power. There the tradeoffs among choices of process can be unusually difficult, because they are often working in the presence or aftermath of insurgent violence, but tradeoffs are important everywhere.

It does not help that a task that is not performed with any degree of regularity and that, therefore, may have no set organizational or procedural protocols must be accomplished under the pressure of deadlines. Even if there are no formal deadlines, influential outsiders, with their own time constraints, may urge the participants simply to "get to yes," any yes to which the participants can sign on—based on the specious assumption that the main objective is agreement and that whatever they agree to, even in great haste, will prove adequate for their problems. And, of course, agreement will allow the outsiders, if they are not based in-country, to proceed to other business elsewhere.

Merely to ask the most basic questions about whether to draft a new constitution or to amend an existing one (and, if so, how extensively), whether to entrust drafting to a newly created body or an existing body, whether initial drafting should be done by a commission of experts, how to select members of the drafting body or bodies, how the body will go about its work and whom it will consult, whether its proceedings will be open or closed, what its rules of decision will be, whether its draft will need to be approved by another body or bodies or by the public—to contemplate these questions is to sense the possibilities for numerous permutations of constitutional processes.

Underlying these possibilities are fundamental choices, some based on reasoning about the objectives and tradeoffs involved, some on the country-specific historical experience shaping the leaders' view of the situation, some on the state of the knowledge of those who must choose, some on ideas or advice about how to proceed, and some based simply on preexisting conditions. By that last phrase, I mean what I referred to just now: the unique circumstances in which the state finds itself by dint of recent events. These recent events may include a civil war, the overthrow of an authoritarian regime, or an exceptionally surprising election result—any one which may require a prompt and decisive response in the form of institutional rejuvenation. The choice of processes takes place within a world of constraint.

Note that constitutional process may not be the most important determinant of constitutional outcomes—whether the exercise produces a democracy, whether conflicting groups accommodate each other, or whether the constitutional dispensation is seen as the legitimate source of rules by which politics is to be conducted. Studies of various process configurations show—with two very important exceptions, to be discussed later—no clear relation between process and outcome,[25] but this is likely to be because there are so many permutations of processes: by one count, nine; by another, eighteen. Undoubtedly, too, a wide range of contextual variables can intervene. Controlling for these would be exceptionally difficult. On these grounds, the creators of a large database recommend "an important role for the careful work of case study literature to try to untangle the causal relationships."[26] Nevertheless, process is virtually certain to have *some* effect—in some cases a determinative one, either for better or for worse—for we know from other fields that process and outcome are causally tied together, and we shall see their connections in this field in particular cases once some of the work of disaggregation is done.

Yet it is not always easy to specify these connections. After all, good processes may result from good relations among contesting parties before they embark on a process, or they may result from pre-process discussions or agreements, or they may result from clear thinking based on previous experience, including past process failures. And bad processes may result from the exigencies of bad starting conditions or unclear thinking about previous experience. Sometimes, then, it requires a deep dive into country data to explain results. Fortunately, a good deal of diving has already been done, and we shall do more.

None of the limitations on free choice of process makes serious thinking about more and less preferable processes futile. Choice is always constrained. The limitations actually make it more important for constitutional renovators to use their limited freedom wisely and concentrate on trying to import into their process those attributes that are likely to matter most.

---

25. Tom Ginsburg, Zachary Elkins, and Justin Blount, "Does the Process of Constitution-Making Matter?" *Annual Review of Law and Political Science,* Vol. 5, no. 5 (2009), pp. 201–23; Jennifer Widner, "Constitution Writing in Post-Conflict Settings," *William and* Mary *Law Review,* Vol. 49, no. 4 (2008), pp. 1513–41.

26. Ginsburg, Elkins, and Blount, "Does the Process of Constitution-Making Matter?" p. 218.

CHAPTER 3

Starting Conditions

One starting condition is very common, if not quite universal: a sense of crisis, a time when wars or insurgencies have occurred, or when existing arrangements have been shown to be illegitimate, as in Eastern Europe after 1989, or ineffective and illegitimate, as in Indonesia after 1998. New constitutions are not usually made when things are going very well. But things may have gone wrong in a variety of ways that can limit or channel possibilities about how to proceed.[1]

If, for example, a constitution is meant to end a civil war, then it will likely be negotiated in the same setting as a peace agreement. Public participation will usually be negligible. There will probably be no newly elected decision-making body. Even if there is formal separation of the peace process from the constitutional process, bargaining between defined sides, often accompanied by international mediation, will be the mode of decision. Representation will almost surely be less than fully inclusive of all segments of the society, as it was in Liberia in 2003 and in the Dayton Accords for Bosnia in 1995.

1. See Bruce Ackerman, "Three Paths to Constitutionalism—and the Crisis of the European Union," *British Journal of Political Science*, Vol. 45, no. 4 (2015), pp. 705–14.

It is generally undesirable to draft a constitution as part of a peace process. Participation is too narrow, both because armed groups may not be representative of opposition civilian constituents and because, if there are several armed groups, not all of them will necessarily come to the table. Furthermore, creation of durable institutions will have lower priority than will adoption of measures to end the violence.[2] An agreement is negotiated that may involve—or purport to put in place—fundamental changes in institutions and personnel, with the exclusive consent of the people at the table, whose claim to represent citizens may be dubious.[3] There is also the danger that armed groups will end up with a disproportionate share of power under the resulting dispensation, thereby producing a demonstration effect by which others are encouraged to shoot their way into power.[4] Even then, those armed groups that are at the table tend to be more interested in provisions conducive to exclusive benefits attained through rent seeking than to conflict reduction and democracy. They may be more focused on looting the treasury than on building institutions.

In spite of these high costs, some constitutional processes have been used to end insurgencies or other episodes of serious violence. The processes are too often a form of "fire-engine diplomacy."[5] They are generally ad hoc and hurried, they do not involve deliberation, and they fail to canvass all relevant options for a new constitutional dispensation. In some cases, they produce constitutions or

2. See Hallie Ludsin, "Peacemaking and Constitution-Drafting: A Dysfunctional Marriage," *University of Pennsylvania Journal of International Law*, Vol. 33, no. 1 (2011), pp. 239–311.

3. Andreas Mehler, "Not Always in the People's Interest: Power-Sharing Arrangements in African Peace Agreements," University of Manchester, Brooks World Poverty Institute Working Paper Series, January 2008.

4. Dennis Tull and Andreas Mehler, "The Hidden Costs of Power-Sharing: Reproducing Insurgent Violence in Africa," *African Affairs*, Vol. 104, no. 416 (2005), pp. 375–98.

5. Andreas Mehler, "Peace and Power Sharing in Africa: A Not So Obvious Relationship," *African Affairs*, Vol. 108, no. 432 (2009), pp. 453–73, at p. 455.

constitutional amendments, but in many they merely create what purport to be binding peace agreements between the sides, sometimes with the objective of incorporating the agreement into a hastily devised constitution. Usually, these are compilations of provisions spatchcocked together to meet the market-clearing price for an end to hostilities. Unsurprisingly, many such agreements fail to endure, and those that do endure are disproportionately supported by powerful international interveners,[6] such as the European Union and the United States in Bosnia and Macedonia.

Myanmar's (Burma's) protracted peace process has gone on for more than a decade, and very soon the subject matter began to overlap topics related to a constitutional dispensation. Rebel groups were not prepared to put down arms unless they knew what kind of regime they might be joining. Not only does such an overlap risk the exclusion of noncombatants; it also risks constitutional outcomes dictated by the positions of forces on the ground. For this reason, it would be preferable to settle on an interim agreement: a ceasefire with minimal arrangements for governing and, if necessary, a skeletal interim constitution that allows time for trust to build while a process is being devised to do the job properly.[7] A durable ceasefire and an interim constitution can kill the need for haste, give civilian politicians and their constituents a chance to be involved, and

6. Barbara F. Walter, "Conflict Relapse and the Sustainability of Post-Conflict Peace," World Bank Development Report, no. 2011, September 13, 2010; Donald Rothchild, "Reassuring Weaker Parties after Civil Wars: The Benefits and Costs of Executive Power Sharing in Africa," *Ethnopolitics*, Vol. 4, no. 3 (2005), pp. 247–67. In a manuscript-in-progress, I deal with a large subset of such agreements and find that only a minority of those intended to be permanent proved durable, and many of those were shaky, stalemated, or heavily weighted toward dominant groups.

7. Charmaine Rodrigues, "Letting Off Steam: Interim Constitutions as a Safety Valve to the Pressure-Cooker of Transitions in Conflict-Affected States?" *Global Constitutionalism*, Vol. 6, no. 1 (2017), pp. 33–62; Kimana Zulueta-Fülscher, "Interim Constitutions: Peacekeeping and Democracy Building Tools," IDEA Policy Paper, Stockholm, October 2015.

organize elections for whatever forum is chosen to do the deliberative work of constitution making. Of course, an interim constitution, even with adequate time for full inclusion, deliberation, and consensus, may "shape and constrain" the constitution that follows it in ways that are far from ideal.[8] There is no foolproof way to prevent this, but it is best to keep the interim document as narrowly tailored to its limited purpose as possible. And if an old constitution, unsatisfactory though it may be in general, is sufficiently serviceable to work on an interim basis, reliance on it might just be preferable.

Violence and distrust can poison constitutional processes. The presence of either can make constitution making premature. Premature processes can either fail to produce an agreement satisfactory to all sides, as we shall see in the case of Yemen, or produce a constitution that fails to include essential provisions, as in the case of Somalia. Bad timing is one of several ways to produce a failed constitution. It becomes important to judge whether the time is right for constitution making, as many conspicuous failures involve bad timing. Premature constitutional processes can do worse than fail. The results can be so disappointing as to escalate conflict and perhaps discourage future efforts at accommodation.

In international negotiation, there is much discussion of the advantages of prenegotiation or talks about talks. For constitution making, there needs to be more discussion about ripeness, methods of separating discussions about violence and provisions for ending it from the constitutional process, and ways to agree to disagree temporarily, rather than forcing agreement before a genuine process can begin.

The process before the formal process can be an important prelude to success in producing a democratic, conflict-regulating constitution. South Africa's interim constitution paved the way for a rather

8. Bell, "Introduction: Bargaining on Constitutions," p. 24.

different, majoritarian constitution,[9] but the point extends far beyond interim documents. The more prior understanding there is, the more likely it is that the contending parties will choose an inclusive, consensual process. Members of Tunisia's opposition, secular as well as Islamic, had years of meetings beginning in 2003, while it was in exile during the dictatorship of Zine al-Abidine Ben Ali. It built trust and political solidarity that facilitated constitutional agreement years later, in the face of further problems that appeared during the constitutional process.[10] Egyptian opposition groups did not have such meetings under the regime of Hosni Mubarak, and they entertained very different ideas about appropriate institutions after Mubarak fell from power. The unsatisfactory results are well known. Kenya's failed constitutional process in 2005 had produced multiple drafts that had been carefully considered and provided "a strong foundation" for yet another effort at constitutional agreement, one that produced agreement.[11] Leaders of four of the five major ethnic groups campaigned for approval of the new draft. Christina Murray attributes their agreement in 2010 to "a long incubation period,"[12] although we shall see later that the legislative review of what had been accomplished in earlier phases was indeed rushed and less than satisfactory.

9. Hassen Ebrahim, *The Soul of a Nation: Constitution-making in South Africa* (Oxford: Oxford University Press, 1999).

10. Al Stepan, "Toward a 'Democracy with Democrats' in Tunisia: Mutual Accommodation between Islamic and Secular Activists," paper presented at a Columbia University conference on Tunisia, March 27–28, 2015; Monica Marks, "Tunisia's Unwritten Story: The Complicated Lessons of a Peaceful Transition," paper presented at Columbia University, ibid.; Marks, "Purists vs. Pluralists: Cross-Ideological Coalition Building in Tunisia," paper presented at Columbia University, ibid. As we shall see, those who stayed behind in Tunisia had much less opportunity for extended discussion with each other. At least partly for this reason, some matters were left imperfectly resolved at the conclusion of the process.

11. Christina Murray, "Kenya, 2008–2010: Constitution Making in the Shadow of the GNU," unpublished paper, n.p., n.d., p. 17.

12. Ibid., p. 18.

Of course, pre-process communication does not always yield agreement.[13] Sometimes pre-process meetings of known antagonists can harden differences, as they did in Sri Lanka before the drafting of the 1972 constitution. That document solidified the preeminent position of Buddhism and the Sinhalese language in the state and alienated the Tamils, who walked out of the constituent assembly.[14] Indonesia had few fruitful meetings of opposition leaders before it embarked on its constitutional process following the resignation of Suharto in 1998, but it used an effective substitute: an incremental, multiyear process to produce a constitution agreed by consensus.[15] The consultations conducive to consensus can take place before a formal process begins or during the process, if it is not rushed.

Very often, however, good relations do not exist among participants, and even clear thinking about previous experience is in short supply. A common source of such problems is an embedded sense of antagonistic interest between groups. The starting positions of antagonistic groups about a future dispensation are often very far apart. To take one of many examples, in Myanmar (Burma), the majority Bamar (Burmans) and the many minorities who have been fighting a civil war for decades have had widely different views about one of the key issues in their conflict: the configuration of a future federal state. The minorities, some of whom have been fighting the central government for more than a half century, have expressed a desire for the highest degree of autonomy for the federal units in

13. Cf. James Putzel and Jonathan DiJohn, "Meeting the Challenges of Crisis States," Crisis States Research Centre Report, London School of Economics, 2012; Asli Bâli and Hanna Lerner, "Constitutional Design without Constitutional Moments: Lessons from Religiously Divided Societies," *Cornell International Law Journal*, Vol. 49, no. 2 (2016), pp. 227–308, at pp. 297–98.

14. Hanna Lerner, "Constituent Assemblies in Divided Societies," paper presented at the conference on Perspectives on Constituent Assemblies, University of Oslo, April 2016, pp. 7–9.

15. Horowitz, *Constitutional Change and Democracy in Indonesia.*

which they reside. The differences between the sides have extended to the most basic matter of representation of ethnic groups and nationalities in central government bodies, a subject on which they have also entertained polar positions.[16] In situations of this kind, where armed violence continues periodically, such issues tend to be negotiated in formal sessions in which the sides present their views and then return to their home bases.

Ethnic antagonism is sometimes accompanied by the desire of one group to deny national belonging and occasionally even formal citizenship to members of another. In Myanmar, hostile relations between Bamar (Burmans) and certain other Buddhist groups, on one side, and Muslim Rohingya, on the other, are just an extreme example of a fairly widespread phenomenon. A sense of indigenousness on the part of one group and of the alienage or lesser status imputed to another produces very unfavorable conditions for constitution making or long-term acceptance of conciliatory constitutional arrangements after they have been adopted. Over the many decades following Sri Lankan independence, some among the Sinhalese majority have developed the sense that the Sri Lankan Tamils (who migrated from what became India, on average, about a millennium ago) are actually recent immigrants, rather than indigenes, and have reduced their willingness to accommodate Tamil claims accordingly. There are many other cases where such views have been held from time out of mind. But even short of these conditions, empathy across group lines is not a typical starting condition.

These conditions raise the question of when to start a serious constitutional process. Premature efforts to create a constitution escalated violence in Yemen in 2015, when distrustful Houthi rebels apprehended that the division of north Yemen into four federal

16. For the differences among the three major collective actors, see Nyi Nyi Kyaw, "Democracy First, Federalism Next? The Constitutional Reform Process in Myanmar," Institute of Southeast Asian Studies (ISEAS), Singapore, Perspective Series, no. 93 (November 8, 2019).

units in a new constitutional arrangement would dilute their power, whereupon they accelerated their rebellion. The premature character of the Yemeni proceedings was also attested by the incomplete representation of the south, which was experiencing a secessionist movement of Hiraaks, many of whom failed to attend—another case of incomplete inclusion.[17]

Similarly, Somalia's wartime experience left it with a constitutional draft that was far from finished, because it was far from agreed. The Somali process began at a time when the violent Islamic Courts movement and the Transitional Federal Government were in a standoff, and it concluded at a time when the violent al-Shabaab movement controlled significant parts of the country's territory. Under the circumstances, constitution making could scarcely be done democratically. The first draft was completed by a committee selected by clan leaders in proportion to the number of clans, with a committee of Somali experts to advise the drafters. Deemed unsatisfactory by the UN Political Office for Somalia, that draft was peremptorily cast aside. Over the objections of the initial committee and its experts, a new committee was appointed under international auspices, with its membership kept secret. A National Constituent Assembly was also appointed to approve the new draft, without really considering it. Pressured by international bodies, it did so by 96 percent in 2012.[18] This sham approval was designed to get some blueprint down on paper.

17. The Yemeni process is discussed more fully later in this chapter and in chapter 5.

18. This is a greatly abbreviated account of a complex sequence of events. See Afyare Abdi Elmi, "Revisiting the UN-Controlled Constitution-Making Process for Somalia," e-international relations, September 12, 2012, www.e-ir.info/2012/revisiting-the-un-controlled-constitution-making-process; Abdihakim Ainte, "Somalia: The Legitimacy of the Provisional Constitution," *Accord*, no. 25 (2014), pp. 60–64; Kirsti Samuels, "An Opportunity for Peacebuilding Dialog? Somalia's Constitution-Making Process," *Accord*, no. 21 (2010), pp. 81–82. "Clans" in Somalia are the functional equivalent of large ethnic groups elsewhere.

The new document provided for a semi-presidential system and for federalism, but no elections could be conducted, and the first legislature was entirely appointed. Federalism was essential if secessionist Somaliland (the former British portion of Somalia) and autonomous Puntland (in the northeast of the country) were to be brought back into a unified Somalia, but there was no agreement in the constitutional process on elections or on the number, boundaries, or powers of the constituent federal units. The articles of the constitution on all these subjects state that they will be determined at a later date by the upper house of the legislature,[19] but completion of this task was delayed for years.

Ironically enough, there was no need for Somalia to engage in this premature constitutional exercise. The 1961 democratic constitution, drafted with Italian assistance, was available for use until conditions for revision were ripe. It was not federal, but neither is a federal constitution without federal units, boundaries, or powers. Old constitutions, however imperfect, may have their uses if the time is not right for renovation. As we have already seen and shall soon see again in the case of Yemen, there is value in pre-constitutional discussions among antagonists, even if violence precludes a constitutional consummation. Somalia might have benefited from such discussions, even without moving to actual drafting.

If there is no ongoing civil war but still great discontent with the way the existing constitutional structure has worked and therefore a felt need for major departures, an expert commission may be created in order to produce at least a first draft, which may then be sent to a representative body, either a sitting legislature or a specially elected constituent assembly, for reworking the text. There may be a searching examination of history and an openness to borrowing structures from other countries that seem to have avoided the problem that gave rise to constitutional reexamination. Many countries have fol-

19. 2012 Provisional Constitution of the Federal Republic of Somalia, arts. 47–53.

lowed such a course. Post–civil war Nigeria did so in 1978, as did Kenya in 2005 and 2010. At the time of decolonization, many former British colonies had also utilized an expert commission draft, with a variety of approval processes, some more adequate than others, prior to the transfer of power to the newly independent government.

If there is a sitting autocrat to overcome, a self-appointed opposition body may be constituted, as several were (a few with some success) in Francophone West Africa in the 1990s.[20] It may conduct public proceedings and welcome wide participation in order to overpower the authorities it opposes. If it achieves consensus, with or without expert assistance, it may succeed in making at least the initial constitutional decisions.[21] Needless to say, many such bodies, even if appointed by authoritarian regimes themselves, do not succeed in creating and implementing the democratic constitutions that were contemplated. If, however, the authorities signal willingness to negotiate, as they did in Eastern Europe during the same period, the opposition and the authorities may negotiate not just a transition to democracy but some of the constitutional parameters of the new regime.[22] In such circumstances, there may be a great deal of pre-commitment. Despite its failings, the National Dialogue in Yemen in 2013 created a subcommittee on "the Southern Question" that committed the government to a federal constitution, guaranteed 50 percent representation for the South in all government branches and in the military, and opened the possibility of special veto rights for the South,[23] provisions likely to be revived in later

20. John L. Heilbrunn, "Social Origins of National Conferences in Benin and Togo," *Journal of Modern African Studies*, Vol. 31, no. 2 (1993), pp. 277–99.

21. Jonathan Wheatley, "Constitution-Making in West Africa: Keeping the President in Check," in *Patterns of Constitutional Design*, ed. Jonathan Wheatley and Fernando Mendez (Burlington, VT: Ashgate, 2013), pp. 69–86.

22. See Elster, Offe, and Preuss, *Institutional Design in Post-Communist Societies*.

23. Outcome of the Subcommittee of the Southern Working Groups [of the National Dialogue]: Agreement on a Just Solution to the Southern Question, unpublished paper, Sana'a, Yemen, December 23, 2013.

processes. In cases such as this, when a new regime comes into existence later, some of its constitutional choices—even beyond procedural choices—may already have been made, at least tentatively, in the swirl of events.

Inherited circumstances constitute deep constraints on process choice. Suppose a discredited autocrat has been deposed after mass demonstrations, but the instruments of force are still in place, and no one in the government or in a fragmented opposition is in a position to exert legitimate authority, either to govern or to create a constitution to replace the authoritarian constitution. In that case, there will need to be an assurance of free elections for a new legislature, which might then draft a new constitution. In such a situation, which resembles that of Indonesia after the fall of Suharto in 1998, the forum for constitution making may not be entirely foreordained, but the election, having legitimated a new government, might also impart to it just enough authority to produce the new constitution. Indonesia benefited from having a history of pseudo-democratic elections, which could be converted into democratic elections, in which political parties, both those that had participated in the authoritarian regime's elections and those that could be created rapidly on a foundation of preexisting religious organizations, could participate. South Africa had similar advantages, and newly elected bodies in both countries could, with unhurried deliberation, proceed to craft new constitutions that enjoyed a considerable measure of legitimacy. Iraq, on the other hand, had no such history and was accorded insufficient time to do the job.[24]

These examples are not exhaustive. Many initial conditions affect the availability of process choices, but unevenly. The initial conditions in Indonesia merely made probable a certain choice

24. On the utility of authoritarian elections in facilitating the later emergence of electoral democracy, see Staffan Lindberg, ed., *Democratization by Elections* (Baltimore: Johns Hopkins University Press, 2009); Lindberg, *Democracy and Elections in Africa* (Baltimore: Johns Hopkins University Press, 2008).

of constitutional forum, and the free and fair elections that were conducted also mitigated the sense of crisis so as to allow drafting without a firm deadline. That is as far as they went. Other conditions that were not produced by the events surrounding the fall of Suharto—more deeply embedded conditions, in fact—determined the mode of proceeding, the decision about whether to amend or redraft from scratch, the rules of decision (by voting or consensus), the open or closed nature of the proceedings, and the need for approval beyond the drafting body. By contrast, ending a civil war by producing a new constitution in addition to a peace agreement more or less dictates the mode of proceeding (entirely by negotiation) and the participants (usually limited to leaders of the combatants), while a public movement to supplant an unpopular autocracy may involve a much wider range of participants, but this is variable. In Ghana, there was discussion of a draft prepared by a nine-member committee of experts,[25] and in Benin the National Conference appointed a temporary legislature, which then drafted a constitution.[26]

The initial events following the fall of dictators during the Arab Spring of 2011 show that there are still choices to be made about constitutional process, despite a general similarity of those events. Consider first the careful process developed in Tunisia, which can then be contrasted with events in Egypt and Libya.

In Tunisia, where the regime truly was overthrown, there were serious doubts among the many strong secularists and the politicians who represented them about the possible influence and intentions of a strong Islamist party, Ennahda. A 155-member commission was formed to discuss choices to be made before elections could be held. That body recommended elections to a hybrid legislature-constituent assembly. The assembly was elected on the basis of list-system

25. Wheatley, "Constitutional Design in West Africa."

26. Chris Allen, "Reconstructing an Authoritarian State: 'Democratic Reversal' in Benin," *Review of African Political Economy*, no. 54 (1992), pp. 1–34.

proportional representation in order to obviate the possibility that Ennahda might secure a strong majority of seats on a plurality of votes, dominate the assembly, and alienate smaller secular parties. In the event, Ennahda won the largest fraction of seats, 41 percent. A rule of the assembly explicitly provided that committee chairs "shall seek to encourage agreement in the committee's work through the discussion of differing points of view, proposals and opinions." The rule continued: "Where consensus cannot be achieved, the facts shall be recorded in the committee's report and an opportunity provided for the Assembly to decide the matter in plenary sitting."[27]

After serious disputes had emerged in the assembly, its president managed to convince each party to speak with only "one voice" in contested decisions that were referred to a Consensus Committee. This was a major step in the effective inclusion of small parties. The Consensus Committee was aided by ideas advanced by an outside group, which was engaged in conciliation. It was also agreed to take no votes in the Consensus Committee, but to utilize instead a sense-of-the-meeting standard for decisions whenever more than two-thirds of the committee appeared to agree. After a seriously deliberative process, the assembly produced what Al Stepan called "an inclusive, consensual and democratic constitution."[28] The final vote was 200 yes, 12 no, and 4 abstentions.

Tunisia was fortunate that its authoritarian military and police were heartily detested by the population, and the regime had therefore been unequivocally overthrown in 2011. In Egypt, where

27. Tunisian National Constituent Assembly, Rules of Procedure, unpublished paper, December 16, 2011, rule 57. For reflections on the process, see Duncan Pickard, "The Current Status of Constitution Making in Tunisia," Carnegie Endowment for International Peace, Washington, DC, April 19, 2012.

28. Stepan, "Toward a 'Democracy with Democrats' in Tunisia." Stepan details the many conciliatory interventions that facilitated the ability of secularists to work with Ennahda.

Hosni Mubarak was displaced but his government and his relatively popular military remained in place, legislative elections were held first, and a subset of legislators was appointed to draft a constitution, which was later supplanted. No firm understanding on process was reached between the Muslim Brotherhood and secular politicians, in stark contrast to Tunisia, and neither deliberation nor consensus was sought. In Libya, following Muammar Gaddafi's overthrow and assassination, legislative elections were conducted. The new legislature chose experts to do the drafting. But then there was a reversal—a decision that a constituent assembly needed to be elected, now, as we have already seen, apportioned by region rather than by overall national population. Interregional disputes were never really resolved. In each case,[29] there was some latitude to choose varying sequences and, at various points, different drafting bodies. The overthrow of an autocracy provides more latitude to choose a process and a sequence than does an ongoing conflict, but only in Tunisia was the latitude utilized in a deliberative way. In Egypt and Libya, early decisions were often taken hastily and then reversed.

Time constraints are frequently severe. There may be a deadline set for a constitutional commission or assembly to issue its report. In general, deadlines constrict options. They limit consideration of anything unfamiliar, and they limit time for argumentation and debate, thus channeling decisions toward proposals with historical or cultural resonance or with support among external advisors who can certify the international respectability of the choices made. And they often provide for decisions by majority or supermajority vote, leaving losers dissatisfied. Both the prevalence of deadlines and the

29. See Ann M. Lesch, "Troubled Political Transitions: Tunisia, Egypt and Libya," *Middle East Policy*, Vol. 21, no. 1 (2014), pp. 62–74, at p. 73, attributing Egypt's authoritarian outcome to the rush to elect a new government and the inordinate haste to promulgate a divisive constitution.

crisis atmosphere in which constitutions are frequently made inhibit deliberation and the generation of consent.

So does the fact that staff is usually assembled for the task in a rushed fashion. Lines of authority may not be clear, and the ability of outside experts to connect with staff may be more difficult than it might otherwise be. The infrastructure that supports the constitution makers can suffer from the same circumstantial disabilities as the constitution makers themselves do.

And then there are the specific circumstances in which constitution makers find themselves, with many variations: whether there is a sitting regime or whether it has been overthrown; whether there is a unified or divided opposition; whether there is already a workable, if defective, constitution in force; if so, whether that constitution has any remaining legitimacy and, therefore, utility in getting the process started; whether elections are needed and can be held before a constitutional process begins; and so on. These variations more or less guarantee that constitutional processes come in a variety of shapes and sequences. The one constant is likely to be a sense of crisis.

Even in urgent circumstances, however, many process choices may still be open: to use or not to use the old constitution while creating the new; to elect or appoint drafters, or do both; to have an elected constituent assembly, with or without an expert drafting commission, or to allow the legislature to do the job; to hold elections before drafting or reverse the sequence; and what mechanism to use for final approval. Of course, how these choices are made is usually determined in each case by country-specific or (sometimes) internationally contagious conditions and preferences, some of which are quite limiting. But, before we get lost in the welter of possibilities for process decisions, it is best to step back in order to consider what specific aims a constitutional process might be set up to achieve, on the assumption that there is at least some freedom to choose. In many cases, that freedom may contract, sometimes severely, under the weight of particular histories and current circumstances.

With so many diverse starting conditions, it is not possible to specify anything resembling detailed, uniform process prescriptions. What is more useful is to keep our eyes on the truly important ends and means that it is worth struggling to put at the center of any process decision.

CHAPTER 4

The Forum and the Method

Constitutions are documents crafted for the future by people concerned not to repeat an unsatisfactory past, burdened by their own present interests and those of their constituents, and often deprived of adequate information about the likely effects of their actions on the prospects for their respective countries.[1] There is no shortage of recommendations about what they should enact but little real wisdom about how they should be organized and go about their job.

Jon Elster has thought incisively about this subject. His approach is subtle but minimalist. Elster begins by acknowledging deficiencies of knowledge, both normative and empirical, about the benign or malign effects of institutions. This leads him to eschew affirmative attempts to produce good outcomes or choose good decision makers.[2] Instead, he is merely willing to advocate measures to prevent "mischief,"[3] by which he means the risk that emotion, bias,

1. Similar points have been well made by Kim Lane Scheppele, "A Constitution Between Past and Future," *William and Mary Law Review*, Vol. 49, no. 4 (2008), pp. 1377–1407.

2. Jon Elster, "Excessive Ambitions (II)," *Capitalism and Society*, Vol. 8, no. 1, article 1 (2013), pp. 1–34.

3. Jon Elster, *Securities Against Misrule: Juries, Assemblies, Elections* (New York: Cambridge University Press, 2013), pp. 1–8.

or prejudice might rule the decision process. Of the three general qualities likely to pervade decision processes—reason, passion, and interest—Elster aims to minimize passion, interest, and its manifestation, bargaining and logrolling, while maximizing reason, particularly that aspect of reason that conduces to public-regarding outcomes.

Now, of course, maximizing the prevalence of reason and argument is not a merely negative goal but a commendable, positive one. Yet this seems to me a mere quibble, for in my view the collective ignorance, normative and empirical, that drives Elster's admirable abstemiousness, while considerable, is not complete. Merely because we do not know everything—and we are certainly very far from knowing everything—does not mean that we know nothing about what he calls "positive institutional design." Preventing harm, while studiously avoiding potential benefits, may deprive an institutional design of a benefit that is indeed verifiable. In other cases, suspending judgment about benefits allows reversion to preexisting default positions that, had judgment been exercised, might have been deemed less desirable than available alternatives. Many institutional decisions are just not matters that should be left to indifference. We may not know what is best, but on some matters we may know what is better and worse.[4] Beyond that, constitution makers and those who choose them cannot abstain because of ignorance; they are obliged to make such determinations.

Elster's carefully reasoned treatment of the issues of constitutional process contains numerous useful insights and can open the door to even more. Not that these will produce any single ideal constitution or perfect constitutional process. We have already seen that starting conditions are far too varied for a single specification of process. There is a sharp limit to what can be prescribed. More fruitful

4. See my commentary on "Excessive Ambitions (II)," which I call "Excessive Skepticism," *Capitalism and Society*, Vol. 8, no. 1, article 4 (2013), pp. 1–8.

is attention to some major goals and general methods of achieving them. Even so, it is possible to pursue questions of constitutional process by beginning with some of Elster's major points. These concern secrecy of the proceedings, the crisis atmosphere common to many constitutional processes, and the size of the deliberating body.

If the constitutional forum, such as a constituent assembly, requires secrecy in deliberations, says Elster, that will be conducive to more naked, self-interested bargaining than might occur in a public forum, because publicity induces argument from general principles and makes horse trading more difficult. But, Elster adds, secrecy also prevents participants from being too firmly committed to positions that they articulate early in the process, and so in that way it renders them more open to argument.[5]

Experience confirms these insights. In Kenya in 2000–2004, according to Jill Cottrell and Yash Ghai, the latter of whom chaired the Kenya constitutional commission of that time, open proceedings "may have made it harder to achieve consensus," because newspapers habitually reported "heated and polemical debates, which encouraged delegates to take extreme positions. By contrast, leaders on both sides of the ethnic divide in Fiji," where Ghai served as legal counsel to certain political parties in the 1990s, "considered that concessions and compromises would be easier if they could be negotiated in secrecy," and that is how they operated when they reviewed a commission draft that had been submitted to a select committee in parliament.[6]

---

5. Elster, *Securities Against Misrule*, p. 230; Elster, "Arguing and Bargaining in Two Constituent Assemblies," *University of Pennsylvania Journal of Constitutional Law*, Vol. 2, no. 2 (2000), pp. 345–421, at pp. 410, 413.

6. Jill Cottrell and Yash Ghai, "Seeking Democratization, Accountability, and Social Justice: The Constitution Building Process in Kenya (2000–2004)," *Democratization*, Vol. 14, no. 1 (2007), pp. 1–25, at p. 25 n.36. Unfortunately, as we shall see later, secrecy at a very late stage of constitution making in Fiji, coupled with limited participation of members of parliament, facilitated negotiation of an arbitrary deal by only two members of the committee that inadvertently changed some of most

South Africa had a similar experience. In the early so-called CODESA (Convention for a Democratic South Africa) proceedings, which were largely public, the pronouncements of delegates exposed the wide gulf between their understandings, thereby contributing to tension rather than consensus. After CODESA failed, a new forum, the Multiparty Negotiating Process, was created. It was "smaller, more efficient, and further from the public's pressurising eye."[7] Similarly, when Nepal's deliberations were held in open sessions, members took party positions and engaged in "'plebiscitary rhetoric' to affect public perception of the debate," whereas in closed sessions they "negotiated as Nepali citizens, not as party members."[8] Secrecy in deliberations, in order to facilitate argumentation, persuasion, and testing ideas without prior commitment to them—and also some serious bargaining—can be most valuable to the proceedings.[9] Spain's legislature used secret—and inclusive—nighttime meetings, to which nonmembers of the legislature were sometimes invited, to work on the difficult problems of Spain's regions and their relation to the center.[10] The inclusive feature is important, because the presence

---

important ethnically conciliatory provisions of the proposed constitutional design—and with decidedly negative effects. There is a major difference between, on one side, secrecy in a commission formulating proposals for public scrutiny or a large deliberative forum that does the same and, on the other, secrecy in a much smaller group that functions at a later stage and has the ability to undo major features of what has been agreed without according them serious scrutiny.

7. Erik Doxtader, *With Faith in the Works of Words: The Beginnings of Reconciliation in South Africa, 1985–1995* (East Lansing: Michigan State University Press, 1998), p. 182.

8. Amanda Snellinger, "The Production of Possibility Through an Impossible Ideal: Consensus as a Political Value in Nepal's Constituent Assembly," *Constellations*, Vol. 22, no. 2 (2015), pp. 233–45, at p. 238.

9. "By now, the empirical evidence on the deliberative benefits of closed-door interactions seems incontrovertible." Mark Warren and Jane Mansbridge, "Deliberative Negotiation," in *Political Negotiation*, ed. Mansbridge and Cathy Jo Martin (Washington, DC: Brookings Institution, 2015), pp. 145–95, at p. 177.

10. Andrea Bonime-Blanc, *Spain's Transition to Democracy: The Politics of Constitution Making* (Boulder, CO: Westview Press, 1987), pp. 59, 64.

of members from all parties discourages the pursuit of rent seeking, as does the periodic disclosure and explanation of decisions reached in secret deliberations.[11]

Secrecy in the balloting at a constitutional assembly is equally ambiguous in its effects. Ballot secrecy makes logrolling very difficult, because it renders the credibility of promises unverifiable, and for Elster putting impediments in the path of logrolling is a positive result. Yet ballot secrecy also makes accountability for decisions impossible.[12]

Crisis, as Elster trenchantly suggests, cuts both ways: it gives rise to passion, in the form of fear, but it can simultaneously conquer self-interest,[13] and it can also spur enthusiasm for creating new constitutions.[14] Crisis also gives rise to urgency, which will probably result in "suboptimal investment in information,"[15] but the time pressure it creates tends to equalize bargaining power, which is a benefit.[16] Crisis may, and frequently does, greatly attenuate the time necessary for adequate deliberation, and so it may impair both consensus and the coherence of the resulting product. On balance, steps that can end the crisis and reduce the time pressure are worth pursuing. As they do this, skillful political actors can turn crisis into opportunity for innovation.[17]

Any large group, such as an assembly, may produce incoherent compromises, leading to institutions that do not fit together or work

11. Warren and Mansbridge, "Deliberative Negotiation," pp. 178–85.

12. Elster, *Securities Against Misrule*, p. 232.

13. Ibid., pp. 203–4.

14. Jon Elster, "The Political Psychology of Constitution Making," in *Constituent Assemblies*, ed. Elster, Roberto Gargarella, Vatsal Naresh, and Bjørn Erik Rasch (Cambridge: Cambridge University Press, 2018), pp. 207–45, at p. 230.

15. Ibid., p. 205.

16. Elster, "Arguing and Bargaining in Two Constituent Assemblies," pp. 360, 400.

17. See John Kingdon, *Agendas, Alternatives, and Public Policies*, 2d ed. (London: Longman, 2003).

well together.[18] Relatively large bodies generally prevent manipulation of an assembly, but they may require delegation of some of the assembly's work to committees in order to benefit from the expertise that may be sacrificed in a large assembly.[19] Large bodies make it less likely that the resulting constitutional draft will be a coherent product. In severely divided societies, where there are conflicting prescriptions for institutional design, it is easy to find compromise provisions that may work against each other and be inadequate to mitigate severe conflict, as I shall illustrate later. But even though a coherent product is difficult to achieve, Elster's optimal design of a constituent assembly does not consider the combination of an expert commission with a representative assembly to review the draft, a combination that I shall note can sometimes have its own advantages and problems.

Beneath these insights, validated by close examination of actual assemblies, lie a few assumptions that are laid out explicitly. As reason is preferable to interest for Elster, so arguing is preferable to bargaining and logrolling over constitutional terms. As I have already noted, arguing and persuasion are certainly preferable, because they can lead to consensus, but negotiation and compromise need to take over where persuasion and consensus end. Delegate self-interest and conflict of interest are likely to be manifested in such assemblies, and considerable attention needs to be devoted to subduing them or channeling them in constructive directions.[20] A preference for reasoned deliberation reduces the probability that delegates will arrive with fixed positions that remain stubbornly unaltered throughout the proceedings and heightens the likelihood that the results are not

18. Elster, *Securities Against Misrule,* p. 193.

19. Ibid., pp. 219–22.

20. This is also the theme of Elster, "Forces and Mechanisms in the Constitution-Making Process," *Duke Law Journal,* Vol. 45, no. 2 (1995), pp. 364–95.

merely different from initial preferences but actually better—and, equally important, believed by the participants to be better.[21]

Yet there are no formulaic answers to these problems. The size and composition of an assembly, the rules of publicity and secrecy, and human tendencies to passion, interest, and reason all interact. Secrecy can undoubtedly be helpful in facilitating deliberation, but at late stages, when small groups are negotiating in closed proceedings to get the best deal, secrecy may be conducive to importing incoherence into the product or facilitating rent-seeking arrangements that advantage some actors at the expense of others, as we shall see. Decisions about constitutional process, as Elster rightly says, involve multiple tradeoffs among desirable ends.[22]

If that is so, then it is worthwhile examining some additional goals that might be added to the mix. The utility of this strategy can be demonstrated by an illustration of goals not considered by Elster. In an early article, he makes a strong case for precluding members of a constitutional assembly from serving subsequently in a legislature, for fear that members of the assembly might create provisions that could benefit them later as members of the legislature.[23] For similar reasons, Elster prefers that specially assembled bodies, rather than legislatures, produce constitutions. He suggests that the elimination of legislators from such assemblies also replaces bargaining with argumentation, "since there will be nothing to bargain about."[24] But surely delegates to constituent assemblies, often members of political parties, also represent various interests in the polity, and bargaining cannot really be banished from the proceedings.

21. See Horowitz, *Constitutional Change and Democracy in Indonesia*, p. 159.

22. Elster, *Securities Against Misrule*, p. 232.

23. Elster, "Forces and Mechanisms in the Constitution-Making Process." This view is reaffirmed in Elster, "Ways of Constitution-Making," in *Democracy's Victory and Crisis*, ed. Alex Hadenius (Cambridge: Cambridge University Press, 1997), pp. 123–42, at p. 137.

24. Elster, *Securities Against Misrule*, p. 235.

In this account, the evils of conflict of interest and rent seeking loom large. But has a tradeoff been missed here, in the quest to suppress vice but not to pursue virtue?

If a legislature deliberates long and hard over a protracted period and finally achieves consensus on a new constitution, there may well be three benign and important side effects of its labors. First, legislators may find the agreed institutional structure to be workable, in ways that they might not find parts of a constitution designed entirely by others to be. Put simply, they have decided they can live with what they created. Second, as I stated in chapter 1, they may entertain feelings of commitment to the product of their labors. Having taken credit for the accomplishment, they may be discouraged from violating or overthrowing the constitution later. Constitutions are notoriously short lived.[25] Anything that deters the overthrow of a democratic constitution and promotes the efforts of politicians to work within its confines must be accounted a benefit. Third, a point particularly important for divided societies, in which legislators come from and represent different groups, often with divergent objectives and cultural dispositions: when a legislature works over a considerable period to achieve consensus on a constitution, its members may, in the process, come to understand each other's fears, aspirations, and habits of thought. That was certainly a very important side benefit of the lengthy legislative processes of constitutional revision in Indonesia and Tunisia.[26] In a severely divided society, mutual understanding among politicians of different groups that are

25. The median constitution adopted between 1789 and 2005 endured a mere nineteen years; democratic constitutions lasted twenty-one years. Elkins, Ginsberg, and Melton, *Endurance of National Constituions*, pp. 129, 137.

26. Horowitz, *Constitutional Change and Democracy in Indonesia*, pp. 76, 264; R. William Liddle and Saiful Mujani, "The Islamic Challenge to Democratic Consolidation in Indonesia," unpublished paper, Ohio State University, 2002, p. 30; Tereza Jermanová, "From Mistrust to Understanding: Inclusive Constitution-Making, Design and Agreement in Tunisia," *Political Research Quarterly*, 2020, doi 10.1177/1065912920967106, at p. 10.

in conflict is a rare but supremely important virtue that can translate into habits of cooperation. In this and other ways, legislative constitutional deliberation can strengthen legislative capacity, whereas capacity achieved by specially assembled drafting bodies can be lost when they are dissolved, especially if their members are disqualified from later service in the legislature.

These observations lead me to conclude that legislatures should not always be foreclosed from making constitutions. Research thus far does not support the suspicion that constitutions crafted by legislatures provide unusually generous power to the legislative branch or crimped power to the executive.[27] Two studies find that constitution-designing legislators do not create stronger legislatures than constituent assemblies do. According to one, the latter actually give legislatures more power.[28] Another study finds no differences between constitutional revisions done by legislatures and those done by constituent assemblies.[29] In Indonesia, the legislators who drafted the constitution created a new, directly elected presidency and abjured many powers formerly possessed by the legislature. An

27. See Elkins, Ginsburg, and Melton, *Endurance of National Constitutions*, pp. 17–18; Ginsburg, Elkins, and Blount, "Does the Process of Constitution-Making Matter?" p. 213. Elster, "Political Psychology of Constitution Making," p. 227, disputes these findings based on concerns about the sample. Gabriel L. Negretto reaches conclusions similar to those of Elkins et al. Negretto, "Constituent Assemblies in Democratic Regimes: The Problem of a Legally Limited Convention," in *Constituent Assemblies*, ed. Elster et al., pp. 31–56, at pp. 39–41, But on the limited question of legislative involvement in parliamentary government formation, see also Cristina Bucur et al., "Constitution Making and Legislative Involvement in Government Formation," in ibid., pp. 186–206, at pp. 200–201.

28. Zachary Elkins and Tom Ginsburg, "Can We Trust Legislators to Write Constitutions?" paper presented at the conference on The Gap Between Parchment and Practice: Ambivalent Effects of Constitutions in Developing Countries, American University, Washington, DC, May 28–29, 2013.

29. Ana Torney and Nina Massüger Sànchez Sandoval, "Constituent Assemblies in Swiss Cantons," in *Patterns of Constitutional Design*, ed. Jonathan Wheatley and Fernando Mendez (Burlington, VT: Ashgate, 2013), pp. 119–44.

additional advantage for legislatures: they usually have permanent staff, rather than a need to gather staff from scratch.[30]

If legislators are not to be disqualified from constitution making, that possibility bears on the sequencing of elections. It is sometimes thought that new constitutions should precede elections, rather than vice versa.[31] Given the dubious legitimacy of many sitting legislatures in transitional states, the tendency of such a sequence will be to reduce the occasions for legislatures to draft constitutions and so will limit the choice of forum. In any case, constituent assemblies should generally also be elected, to assure their representativeness.

None of this means, of course, that legislatures always can or should be the forums in which constitutions are made. There is, of course, the possibility that a body with two important tasks will neglect one or the other or will be distracted by its multiple responsibilities,[32] but this problem can be greatly mitigated by allowing ample time for a legislature to produce the constitution, where that is deemed desirable. What is paramount is that the deliberative constitution-making body be elected.

The legislative process for creating the Polish constitution of 1997 began with an array of interparty conflicts that threatened to undermine the constitutional project. As Wiktor Osiatynski describes it: "The mingling of the Constitution with ordinary politics was the

30. Cf. Arun K. Thiruvengadam, *The Constitution of India: A Contextual Analysis* (Oxford: Hart, 2017), p. 32.

31. That was, for example, the view of Paul Bremer, the United States representative in Iraq after the invasion of 2003. See Larry Diamond, *Squandered Victory: The American Occupation and the Bungled Effort to Bring Democracy to Iraq* (New York: Henry Holt, 2006), p. 47. There is a literature on the dangers of premature elections. See, e.g., Jack Snyder, *From Voting to Violence* (New York: Norton, 2000). Those dangers, however, are not universal. Often elections should come first, lest the status of the constitution and whatever else is done in the name of the polity is contested in undemocratic ways, because of their illegitimacy.

32. Jon Elster et al., "Introduction," in *Constituent Assemblies*, Elster et al., pp. 1–12, at p. 9.

cardinal reason for its repeated delays in Parliament. Because the drafting process took place in the lion's den of daily politics, the very legitimacy of the framers was repeatedly called into question. This also had a significant impact on the final content of the document. More often than not, compromises were struck by adding into the draft constitution everything that everyone wanted. As a result, the 1997 Constitution teems with declarations and promises."[33]

Osiatynski goes on to say that promises are not enforceable under the Polish constitution, so their inclusion amounted to mere surplusage. He also explains that the reason for the conflation of legislative politics and constitutional politics was the need for newly formed parties to mobilize a clientele by the only means they had at hand: they had to "invent quarrels to attract supporters."[34] The new parties used the proceedings to build their support. This practice suggests that any drafting body (constituent assembly or legislature) with elected members and their inevitable party affiliations would have had the same problem, provided the parties' support was not already established and substantial. Had the parties' bases been more established, the process would have been consumed with fewer distractions.

Completion of the Polish constitution was delayed—a delay enabled by the prior passage of an interim "Little Constitution" in 1992. In the end, however, Osiatynski's judgment is that the constitution that emerged from the lengthy process did what it needed to do with respect to the distribution of power, the control of its abuse, the rights of citizens and their protection, and numerous other matters. Others writing in the same symposium had a more reserved view of the many compromises in the process, but none saw the product as anything other than a democratic dispensation in a society

33. Osiatynski, "A Brief History of the Constitution," *East European Constitutional Review,* Vol. 6, nos. 2–3 (1997), pp. 66–76, at p. 66. The article is part of a symposium on the Polish constitution.

34. Ibid., p. 70.

with some fairly prominent socioeconomic and secular-religious divisions.[35]

As we have seen, the circumstances in which forum decisions are made are highly variable. In Indonesia, the successor to Suharto, the unpopular vice president B. J. Habibie, was able quickly to convince his opponents that he was committed to holding free elections for the legislature. As they began the task of constitutional renovation, the newly elected legislators had available a deeply flawed but, in its specification of amendment procedures, still-serviceable constitution whose legislative powers had been traduced by Suharto. That constitution, its democratic features revived, could be used for a lengthy, extensive reform process that eventually produced an essentially new constitution masquerading as an amended version of the original.[36] Of course, it is possible that legislative constitutional innovation will be preempted by the nature of the occasion that prompts the constitutional revision or by other conditions that impair the legislature's legitimacy. Nevertheless, the possibility that legislative representation is likely to be inclusive and that legislators may be able to reach high levels of constitutional consensus should not be neglected.

The failure of Nepal's democratically elected legislature, sitting as a constituent assembly, to produce any constitution after years of deliberation, beginning in 2008, provides a useful counterpoint to Indonesia's (and Poland's) success, but not because the Nepalese legislature, sitting as a constituent assembly, attempted to write in rules that would favor the legislature later. There was also no dispute at the outset over where Nepal was to end up. Under amendments to the Interim Constitution, enacted in 2007, after a peace agreement

35. See Ewa Letowska, "A Constitution of Possibilities," ibid., pp. 76–81; Leszek Lech Garlicki, "The Presidency in the New Polish Constitution," ibid., pp. 81–89; Pawel Spiewak, "The Battle for a Constitution," ibid., pp. 89–96. (Interestingly, Spiewak foresaw some rule-of-law problems that eventually did come to pass.)

36. See Horowitz, *Constitutional Change and Democracy in Indonesia*.

that had ended an insurrection begun by Maoists, there was a commitment to create a democratic federal system that recognized the desire of indigenous ethnic groups, those living in deprived regions, and other minorities, especially the numerous people of the Madhesh (along the long boundary with India), to enjoy a significant measure of territorial autonomy.[37] Many reasons have been asserted for the failure of the first Constituent Assembly (2008–12) to reach that goal, but among them a few stand out.[38]

The first is that, for years, government formation and reformation took precedence over constitutional work. In the initial phase, 2008–12, no party had a majority in the legislature, but the largest party, the Communist Party of Nepal (Maoist), tried repeatedly to capture executive authority, and others tried, sometimes successfully, to wrest it away. By contrast, Indonesia, which had a multiparty legislature with no party in the majority, had a fixed-term presidency, and this sort of struggle over control of the executive, which might otherwise have occurred, was preempted by that fact.[39]

---

37. Rohan Edrisinha, "Debating Federalism in Sri Lanka and Nepal," in *Unstable Constitutionalism: Law and Politics in South Asia,* ed. Mark Tushnet and Madhav Khosla (Cambridge: Cambridge University Press, 2015), pp. 291–319. I am grateful to Rohan Edrisinha for a discussion of the process in Nepal, where he spent four years as a constitutional advisor for UNDP. The interpretation, however, is mine.

38. The literature on the Nepalese constitutional process is considerable. See, e.g., Saurab Chaudhary and N. P. Chaudhary, eds., *Constitutional Evolution in Nepal* (New Delhi: Pentagon Press, 2012); Hari P. Bhattarai and Jhalak Subedi, eds., *Democratic Constitution Making: Experiences from Nepal, Kenya, South Africa, and Sri Lanka* (Kathmandu: Nepal South Asia Centre, 2007); Mahendra Lawoti, "Shifting Tides in South Asia," *Journal of Democracy,* Vol. 25, no. 2 (2014), pp. 131–45; Sumit Bisarya, "Forces and Mechanisms in Plurinational Constitution-Building in South Asia," in *Annual Review of Constitution-Building in South Asia,* ed. Bisarya et al. (Strömsberg, Sweden: International IDEA, 2016), pp. 51–65; André Lecours, "The Politics of Diversity Treatment in Contemporary Nepal: From Difference Elimination to Difference Management," *Nationalism and Ethnic Politics,* Vol. 20, no. 4 (2014), pp. 373–92.

39. In Indonesia, a crisis along the way produced impeachment and removal of a sitting president, but this was not tied to struggles within the drafting body

Because of the widespread distrust of the rather obviously undemocratic ambitions of the Nepali Maoists during this period, even serious bargaining could not have been expected. And yet, in this, the first of two Constituent Assemblies, leaders undertook to engage seriously with each other. Nevertheless, progress was slow. There was much debate on whether federal units should be based on ethnic and caste identity or on administrative and economic viability. A preference for the first would produce more federal units; choosing the second would produce fewer. As time wore on, the CA was obliged to seek extensions of time from the Supreme Court, which it received on several occasions. The last request, however, was denied, and the first CA was therefore dissolved before it could reach consensus.

The second problem encountered in Nepal was a very heavy load of fundamental caste and ethnic problems—as well as enormous differences in ethnic preferences relating to the form of government, federalism, electoral system, affirmative action, language, religion, and more. Parties took positions on these issues that, in the beginning, could scarcely be reconciled, a problem made more difficult by the assembly's resistance to appointing an expert drafting committee. There was a high level of apparent visibility of group and party interests, which usually makes agreement more difficult. Previously dominant high-caste groups favored fewer federal units, facilitating continuation of the control they had exercised nationally, while low-caste and regional minority groups favored more units

about who would be the chief executive. Among other reasons, there was a firm rule that the sitting vice president would succeed a president no longer eligible to serve. After the president was removed, the vice president simply succeeded him in office without any objection, even though the successor was female, a fact that rankled some Islamist legislators. Adherence to the rules as written was a useful exercise, emblematic of the seriousness with which members approached the job of laying down new rules.

that would cater to local particularisms. In the face of great division, the most important conclusion to draw is that deliberation takes time and is inconsistent with rigid deadlines.

The Nepal experience does not discredit legislative constitution making. It does, however, suggest that a legislature's success in such a job will be greatly facilitated if, in a parliamentary system, the composition of the executive is firmly established early in the legislature's term, so it is not always at issue to tear at interparty relations and distract attention from constitution making.

The two largest parties in Nepal tended to represent castes and ethnic groups that had been traditionally dominant. The Maoists, on the other hand, were identified with the cause of excluded minorities and low-caste groups. They argued for a federalism that would accommodate the aspirations of those groups by placing them in favorable positions in multiple states. A map published by a Maoist-controlled committee in 2011 contained as many as fourteen federal units, with disadvantaged groups very strongly represented in several of them, but no single group constituting a majority in any of them. The influence of minorities and low-caste groups would have been assured by the considerable measure of geographic separation from high-caste groups in the Maoists' map, but dominant groups favored federal units based on economic and administrative capacity rather than ethnic or caste affinity. A High-Level Restructuring Committee could not agree on the number of units. The majority favored eleven; a dissenting report, reflecting the reluctance of dominant groups to concede much to minorities, proposed only six units.[40] When the end came years later, the dissenters would prevail.

40. There was real agreement that Nepal should be a federal republic but no consensus on its design. See Krishna Khanal, "Federalism Discourse in Nepal: An Appraisal," in *South Asia: Nation Building and Federalism,* ed. Lok Raj Baral and Krishna Hachhetu (Delhi: Vij Books, 2014), pp. 134–56; Budi Karki and Rohan Edrisinha, eds., *The Federalism Debate in Nepal* (Kathmandu: UNDP Nepal, 2014).

The first Constituent Assembly proceedings dragged on for nearly two more years. During this time, the three main parties agreed on a map with eleven states, with boundaries drawn largely along ethnic and caste lines. One large minority group, however, the Madhesi, who live in the Terai area along the long southern border with India and are often disparaged as "Indians," objected to the map because it excluded some Madhesi from the two proposed Madhesi states, even though the proposed boundaries had also excluded dominant high-caste groups from Madhesi territory—a favorable development from the Madhesi point of view. Still, the dissent of the Madhesi killed Maoist support for a dispensation that would have met most of their demands. After four years, the Constituent Assembly had not produced a constitution, despite very considerable efforts to reach agreement as the final deadline approached.

In fact, it would take until 2016 and a newly authorized Constituent Assembly after the failure of the first in 2012 to produce a draft that commanded the assent—but, by no means, universal assent—of the body.[41] Even then, the same caste and ethnic problems deeply affected its reception.

This brings us to the third major process problem in Nepal: a crucial failure of consensus and an unfortunate victory for untrammeled majority rule in a constitutional process for a divided society. The second Assembly was elected in 2013. This time the Communist Party of Nepal (Maoist Centre) came in a distant third, with only 80 seats out of 601, eliminating the fear of the two largest parties, which together held one seat short of a majority in the new assembly, that the Maoists could engineer an undemocratic dispensation. Still, dissensus was strong in the chamber and in the country, especially

41. See Michael G. Breen, *The Road to Federalism in Nepal, Myanmar, and Sri Lanka* (London: Routledge, 2018). I am indebted to Michael Breen for several exchanges on Nepal, but the conclusions expressed here are entirely my own.

among Madhesi, represented by their own ethnic parties as well as by the Maoists. Had deliberations continued, consensus might have been reached. Unfortunately, the severe earthquake of April 2015 upended deliberation by creating public pressure to settle on a constitution. The two largest parties were determined to use their majority to comply with that pressure. Greatly weakened, the Maoists were forced to give way on the main elements of their formula or, in a more cynical view, proved that they were only weakly committed to the Madhesi cause, for they failed to follow through on a threat to take to the streets if the constitution passed with less than a genuine consensus.

Despite the absence of consensus, the constitution was approved, with the Maoists actually voting in favor and small Madhesi parties boycotting. In the 2015 draft, there were only six states, not a surprising number considering the reluctant federalism of dominant caste and ethnic groups. Following protests, a seventh state was created to satisfy a dominant caste group, but Madhesi demands to redraw the map in order to reverse the dilution of their power in one state and incorporate Madhesi populations outside the boundaries of the two states in which they were concentrated fell on deaf ears.[42] Comparable complaints by the Tharu, a disadvantaged ethnic minority also living in the Terai and unhappy about being combined in a federal unit with dominant, high-caste hill populations, were also ignored.

The Maoists also lost on the characteristics of the federal system. The larger parties favored not only fewer states but also a more centralized federal system that would be parliamentary in form, with a first-past-the-post-electoral system. On all of these and related matters, the Maoists had different views, and on only one was

42. There were amendments in 2016 to increase the proportional share of legislative seats and to enhance the fraction elected from the Terai, as demanded by Madhesi, but the boundaries of the federal units that concerned them and the Tharu were untouched. See 2015 Constitution of Nepal, as amended, arts. 42, 84, 286.

there serious compromise.[43] A hybrid electoral system was created, with first-past-the-post and list-system proportional seats, the latter of which the Maoists wanted in order to facilitate the representation of small groups.

The lengthy Nepalese constitutional process produced a constitution identified with the large parties and with long-dominant caste and ethnic groups. Demonstrations in the Terai, many of them quite violent, followed its adoption; at least fifty people were killed. For years afterwards, dissatisfaction festered among Madhesi and Tharu, together comprising at least 30 percent of Nepal's population,[44] very nearly the same population size as that of the dominant caste and ethnic plurality.

Opinions of the outcome vary, but one thing is clear. In the early stages of the second CA, there were efforts to find consensus, as there had been in the first CA. In the final stages, the process was the antithesis of an inclusive, consensus-driven product. Even compromise was only minimally in evidence, and when it was offered Madhesi dismissed it as "unilateral," rather than the product of a serious dialogue.[45] In later years, some Madhesi began to discuss secession.

In practical terms, the inclusion of minorities in Nepal was, at best, incomplete. A majority, representing portions of the polity, imposed its will, with little deliberation.[46] Unpopular minorities were, in the end, not heard. The contrast with Indonesia's legislative

43. The extent of the Maoists' loss can be gauged by other provisions as well. All unspecified, residual powers reside in the central government. An interstate council, created to settle disputes between the central government and the states, is composed of three central government representatives and only one state member. In these and other ways, a strongly centralized federation was created.

44. In spite of the apportionment of ethnic populations, Madhesi parties did manage to win a majority in one province in the election of 2017.

45. *Himalayan Times* (Kathmandu), January 26, 2016.

46. For a similar critique, see Mara Malagodi, "The Rejection of Constitutional Incrementalism in Nepal's Federalisation," *Federal Law Review*, Vol. 46, no. 4 (2018), pp. 521–40.

process of consensual constitutional reconstruction could hardly be sharper.

Constitutions are all over the map when it comes to the method of their creation. In Cyprus, the 1960 constitution was largely dictated by Britain and followed the demands of the Turkish minority. To the chagrin of the Greek majority, Britain's highest priority at the time was good relations with the Turks. Of course, when the Turkish-Cypriot vice president subsequently overplayed his hand and exercised his veto too liberally, the Greek president of Cyprus dissolved the partnership—and the constitution—in 1963. Efforts since that time to put the divided country back together have been a mix of persuasion and negotiation, but when the Turks agreed to a new constitution, the Greeks did not—and vice versa—so time inconsistency has kept the two sides apart for half a century. Malaysia's independence constitution, by contrast, was a collaborative venture between the British-appointed but multinational commission and the multiethnic coalition about to take power from Britain: it involved both deliberation by the commission and negotiation inside the coalition. Sri Lanka's independence constitution was produced by a British commission, which, for the most part, rejected minority demands. Its two post-independence constitutions were drafted by the governing parties of the day. Bosnia, like Cyprus, was a victim of diktat, but by the Americans, who acceded to the demands of Serbs and Croats in order to stop the warfare in 1995. Bosniaks had to agree, or there would be an end to American military aid, and the war might resume, to the disadvantage of the Bosniaks. Since that time, no amount of argumentation has convinced the Serb and Croat minorities to modify the rather sclerotic form of government practiced—or, rather, not practiced—in Bosnia. Kenya's 2010 and Fiji's 1997 constitution were the product of an experts' report and a commission report, respectively, modified at the last stages before adoption by negotiated deals in parliamentary committees. Northern Ireland's Good Friday constitution was very much the product of a deliberative-persuasive, but not fully inclusive, process. The process was pushed ahead by international pressure and was facilitated by the nonparticipation or desultory participation of those with extreme agendas but concluded with institutions that moderates from both sides were convinced were in their interest. These examples suggest the range of possibilities, which is very wide.

Although consensus is a major goal of a good process, most processes will need some balance between arguing and bargaining, and in some cases voting. Given the prevalence of ethnically based parties or ethnic organizations in severely divided societies, most members of a constituent assembly or a constitution-drafting legislature in such societies arrive at the forum principally as representatives of one segmental group or another. Their legitimacy to conduct constitutional business derives (at least for most of them) from their representative status. For the groups they represent, constitutional satisfaction, the belief that the new constitution reflects an accommodation that they regard as acceptable, is based on a sense that their group self-interest is being served rather than thwarted. This depends in part on a sense that concessions to their ethnic opponents are reasonable given their opponents' position in the society.[47] If there is too little negotiation, some ethnic interests may be neglected, for bargaining and exchange may be the only way to satisfy them. Reasoned argument does not always convince antagonists with deeply held beliefs about the justice of their cause, and this point does not apply only to ethnically divided societies.

These criteria give negotiation and reciprocity significant utility in a constitutional process, although they do not foreclose a preference for provisions based on reason and intended to benefit all regardless of future position or, as a participant in the South African

47. By "position in the society," I mean whether a group's opponents are perceived as indigenes or immigrants (or, worse, settlers or exploiters), traditional enemies, allies of a foreign power, crafty competitors, and so on.

process put it, provisions based on "the ability of negotiators to consider the merits of particular proposals independent of the group or 'personalities' that advanced them."[48] When, however, consensus is beyond reach, negotiation needs to be available.[49]

Moreover, severely divided societies require repeated, post-constitution legislative bargaining over conflicting ethnic interests. Often this must occur in the face of ethnocentric strictures on the part of extremists against conceding anything—or anything further—to ethnic opponents. Compromise is very hard to achieve in severely divided societies. Antipathy and the perception of hostility on the other side make compromise difficult, just as it does in international relations between antagonists.[50] In the background to the negotiation of each issue is its severability from the overriding question of domination; concessions are harder when the two are seen to be linked.[51]

Nevertheless, compromise may be possible even among participants whose respective constituents have recently been mutually hostile. As mentioned earlier, the 1957 Constitution of Malaya (later Malaysia) was crafted by a commission created by the departing British colonial regime. On a number of important contested issues, it was largely the product of compromise between representatives of Malays, then 49 percent of the population, and Malayan Chinese, then 38 percent. (Indians comprised 11 percent.) At the time, Chi-

48. Doxtader, *With Faith in the Works of Words*, p. 180. The phrase in quotation marks, described by Doxtader as "Rawlsian," is, except for "personalities," a paraphrase by Doxtader, rather than a direct quotation.

49. Yet, as Jamal Benomar aptly cautions, a constitution that is purely the product of compromise puts at risk the creation of strong democratic (and, he might have added, conflict-reducing) institutions. Jamal Benomar, "Constitution-Making and Peace Building: Lessons Learned from the Constitution-Making Processes of Post-Conflict Countries," United Nations Development Program, New York, August 2003, p. 6.

50. Robert Jervis, *Perception and Misperception in International Politics*, 1st ed. (Princeton: Princeton University Press, 1976), pp. 104–6.

51. Cf. ibid.

nese and Indians, who mainly arrived during British rule, were often considered unwanted guests. During World War II, a Malayan Chinese insurrection against Japanese occupiers was supplied by forcible expropriation of foodstuffs from Malay villagers. After the war, Malays took revenge in widespread episodes of deadly violence against Chinese, and eventually local Chinese communists organized a guerrilla insurrection that had barely been brought under control when constitutional negotiations began.

What drove Malay, Chinese, and Indian parties together in a coalition were, in the first instance, electoral needs, for there were other parties organized outside the nascent multiethnic coalition. An obvious hope for a durable peace among groups with the capacity to injure each other was another motivation, reinforced by British reluctance to leave Malaya without a stable government. Not long before the constitutional negotiations, influential Malay voices were calling for no negotiations with the Chinese, but in the end a powerful sense of reciprocal interest, coupled with determined leadership, drove the constitutional bargain.[52]

Even when leaders of contending ethnic or religious (or caste) groups agree on future arrangements or on policies, the incidence of outright reneging on commitments or stalemate about fulfilling them is high,[53] and we shall soon see examples of this in later years in Malaysia. To the extent that bargaining in the constitutional process accustoms the participants to the need for bargaining and compromise thereafter, especially if the constitutional process is regarded as having been successful in producing a mix of consensual solutions and acceptable compromises, the process must be accounted

52. The formation and development of the Malaysian interethnic coalition are described in Horowitz, *Ethnic Groups in Conflict*, pp. 397–404.

53. In my book manuscript-in-progress on the problems of interethnic power sharing, I assess the shortfall in durable compromise in severely divided societies. For a very early taste, see Donald L. Horowitz, "Ethnic Power Sharing: Three Big Problems," *Journal of Democracy*, Vol. 25, no. 2 (April 2014), pp. 5–20.

a success. Each stage in a good constitutional process can serve as a learning experience for the next stage.

The idea of the educational functions of constitution making has been explored by Madhav Khosla with respect to the Indian constitution.[54] In his view, the work of the Constituent Assembly, which sat for three years and also served as a provisional legislature, was "conceived as a pedagogical tool,"[55] against a background of pessimism about India's democratic prospects. The assembly, states Khosla, was an exercise in political education to build a civic culture across various lines of division, to defeat antidemocratic sentiments in the polity, and to produce democratic citizens.

Little attention in the general literature on constitution making has been devoted to the potential educative functions for the constitution makers themselves. A constitutional process has the capacity to show the participants not merely that they can agree and what they can agree on but also *how* they can agree. In many cases, this goal may not be achieved, but constitution makers have the possibility to become specialists in both consensus building and compromise, if the process goes well.

To be sure, bargaining in a constitutional process for a severely divided society must take place within limits, for such a society ideally needs a coherent set of institutions to mitigate conflict, rather than an incoherent mix.[56] Still, gains achieved through bargaining should produce commitment by participants to the constitutional product. Just as constitutional process as experiential learning is too

54. Khosla, *India's Founding Moment: The Constitution of a Most Surprising Democracy* (Cambridge: Harvard University Press, 2020), pp. 1–26.

55. Ibid., p. 22.

56. For skepticism regarding the likely delivery of a truly coherent set of institutions, see Donald L. Horowitz, "Constitutional Design: An Oxymoron?" in *Designing Democratic Institutions*, NOMOS XLII, ed. Ian Shapiro and Stephen Macedo (New York: New York University Press, 2000), pp. 253–84.

little emphasized, so is its potential for creating habits of credible commitment.

Put more broadly, there is potential for a good process to produce not only a good constitution but also to promote good political practice thereafter. In some cases, of course, these benefits will be merely aspirational, as opportunistic reneging proves irresistible, especially to later generations. Yet a good process may leave a substantial residue of respect for the institutions that have been created and for the methods that created them. In this sense, constitution making may not be so much an exercise in pre-commitment, as it is sometimes portrayed, as it is in post-commitment, in the sense of attachment to collective accomplishment.

CHAPTER 5

Inclusion and Consensus

There is an important tradeoff between inclusion and consensus. By inclusion I do not mean direct participation by individual citizens. (We shall deal more with public participation separately in chapter 7.) Social groups, including ethnic groups, may be included if their legitimate representatives have been chosen fairly, typically by free and fair election, and are present and heard at the proceedings. But inclusion and consensus are often at odds. The more players there are, the greater the potential obstacles to high levels of agreement.

The omission of any significant group from a constitutional forum can be fatal to the result. The ill-starred and poorly drafted Iraqi Constitution of 2005 had this defect.[1] The legislature from which the constitutional body was chosen had been elected by list-system proportional representation, with the whole country as a single constituency. The ostensible reason for a single nationwide constituency was that there had been no census in Iraq that could apportion population, and therefore seats, reliably among provinces. (Miraculously, by the time of the next election, it was discovered that ration cards is-

1. See Jonathan Morrow, "Iraq's Constitutional Process II: An Opportunity Lost," United States Institute of Peace Special Report no. 155, Washington, DC, November 2005; "Unmaking Iraq: A Constitutional Process Gone Awry," International Crisis Group, Middle East Briefing no. 19, Brussels, September 26, 2005.

sued by the Saddam Hussein regime could be used as a proxy for the population of each province!) The decision to hold the first elections in a single, undifferentiated constituency proved to be disastrous. A Sunni boycott of those elections meant that Sunnis were dramatically underrepresented in the legislature. Had the representatives been apportioned by province, Sunnis would have been elected proportionately, even if the boycott had prevailed and few had voted. This is because several provinces had strong Sunni majorities.

The absence of Sunnis from the constitution-drafting body allowed the Kurds and Shia who dominated that body to draft a federal constitution that served their interests but was at odds with Sunni views of Iraq as a unitary state with an Arab identity. The Kurds wanted a loose federation, with liberal power of the provinces to amalgamate in order to form multi-province regions; a single Kurdistan was their aim. The largest Shia party could be convinced that amalgamation of provinces into regions was also in its interest, because that party did not control oil-rich Basra.[2] As the largest party in the south, however, it would be able to control an amalgamated southern region, which would then include Basra. Intra-Shia party competition and the desire of one party to exclude others facilitated the creation of the Kurdish-Shia duopoly in the constitutional process. And that duopoly was founded upon blatant rent seeking on the Shia side. As party politics evolved, Shia leaders later became less enthusiastic about regional amalgamation and more enthusiastic about Shia-majority rule in the whole country, but that constitutional provision survived.

Because of the boycott, Sunnis were not really involved in this bargaining. Although the United States persuaded the constitutional committee to coopt some Sunni members, they did not participate

2. The largest party in the south was the Supreme Council for the Islamic Revolution in Iraq or SCIRI, as it was then called. In Basra, however, a smaller rival, Fadhila, and others were more powerful.

in an important way in crafting the constitution. The Kurds and Shia then met privately, and Sunnis subsequently turned against the constitution.[3] Most Sunnis voted against approval in a referendum, but they were not quite numerous enough in critical provinces to defeat the new constitution. It is worth underscoring here the importance of a single early decision—in this case involving the design of elections—that shaped not only the constitution and its neglect of Sunni interests but the violence and disintegration that followed.

Of course, there is no guarantee that, had Sunnis been included from the beginning, agreement could have been reached. Kurdish desires for regional autonomy were very far removed from Sunni preferences for a unitary Iraq. In divided societies such as Iraq, maximal inclusion—and here I have neglected even to mention the interests of other minorities, such as Assyrians, Chaldeans, Yazidis, and Turkmens, several of which suffered grievously later—is likely to make consensus difficult to achieve. There is a great temptation in many processes to ignore the interests of third or fourth groups,[4] especially if the two largest groups comprise a significant majority of the population, but this can be a fatal mistake, as the Iraq experience shows. The exclusionary aspects of the constitutional process have been linked to the development of authoritarianism in Iraq.[5] In Iraq, there was a failure of inclusion, which led to failures of deliberation, consensus, and compromise, a veritable cornucopia of failure.

The omission of a significant group from a constitutional process, allowing majority domination of the proceedings or the collusion of two or more included groups, at the expense of others, is

3. On the Sunni exclusion, see Andrew Arato, *Constitution Making under Occupation* (New York: Columbia University Press, 2009), pp. 211–33.

4. Cf. Nenad Stojanović, "Political Marginalization of 'Others' in Consociational Regimes," *Zeitschrift für Vergleichende Politikwissenschaft*, Vol. 12, no. 2 (2018), pp. 341–64.

5. Toby Dodge, The Politics of Iraq: The Exclusive Elite Bargain and the Rise of a New Authoritarianism," *Adelphi Series*, Vol. 52, nos. 434–35 (2012), pp. 147–80.

one problem. Another is the ability of minorities to obstruct the proceedings or make demands that majorities can ill afford to meet. Carefully designed decision rules cannot, by themselves, solve these problems, but badly designed rules can facilitate majority domination or minority obstruction. It is necessary to spell out standards for consensus decisions.

Many constituent assemblies have rules of decision that allow adoption of provisions or of the whole document on the basis of a majority or a two-thirds vote of delegates, but a genuine constitutional consensus, especially in a severely divided society, may require approval by an even higher standard, sometimes, perhaps, closer to—*but not equivalent to*—unanimity.[6] Two reasons underlie this assertion: (1) fear of majority domination; and (2) the related need to prevent disaffected minorities and politicians representing them from later turning against the constitution.

Where the assembly is divided into delegations or factions, consensus might entail unanimity or near-unanimity of various ethnic or party delegations or factions, even if they themselves opt for less-than-unanimous supermajority decisions *within* those delegations or factions, as they should, lest agreement be impossible to reach.

The Yemeni dialogue process of 2013, which preceded the formal constitutional process by a year, was structured in a way to maximize this kind of consensus.[7] The conference of 565 delegates was composed of eleven "constituencies" selected to produce

---

6. For a defense of unanimity standards in foundational decisions, see James M. Buchanan and Gordon Tullock, *The Calculus of Consent: Logical Foundations of Constitutional Democracy* (Ann Arbor: University of Michigan Press, 1962), pp. 73–77. For persuasive critiques, see Ian Shapiro, *The State of Democratic Theory* (Princeton: Princeton University Press, 2003), pp. 18–19; Rae, "Limits of Consensual Decision." My rationale for a high standard of consensus is, however, quite different from the one animating Buchanan and Tullock's argument for actual unanimity.

7. See the excellent description by Christina Murray, "Yemen's National Dialogue Process," manuscript version of a paper published in *Anayasa Hukuku Dergisi* (*Constitutional Law Review*) (Turkey), Vol. 2, no. 4 (2013), pp. 167–202.

representativeness in the absence of elections.[8] The conference was then divided into nine working groups, each focused on a different set of issues. Every proposal had to attain 90 percent approval in a working group before it could be considered by the whole conference. Any proposal falling short of that standard would be sent to a "consensus committee," whose function was to mediate disagreements. If the mediation efforts failed to produce 90 percent agreement in the committee in which the proposal originated, the proposal could then move forward with only 75 percent agreement in the committee. The same standards and procedure, including, if necessary, the mediation process, applied for decisions in the conference as a whole.

These standards would make it difficult to ignore the views of small groups, and indeed the standards were supplemented in the conference as a whole by an additional protection. That protection provided that if every member of any two of the eleven constituencies, each of the two comprising at least 5 percent of the total number of delegates, objected to a proposal, it would not be adopted. Complex though these rules were, they were designed to prevent both majority domination and obstruction of the proceedings by insignificant minorities.

Although Yemen later descended into full-scale civil war, the dialogue process was not the source of the failure.[9] The conference

8. For the purpose of explicating the rules of decision adopted in Yemen, I ignore the absence of elections in choosing representatives. The inability to elect representatives, ordinarily an indispensable feature of any constitutional process, is a tell-tale sign of the premature character of the proceedings. Nevertheless, the rules of decision were well crafted and worthy of study.

9. For perspectives on the outcome of the dialogue process and its relation to the warfare in the country, see Arab Center for Research and Policy Studies, "Outcomes of Yemen's National Dialogue Conference: A Step Toward Conflict Resolution and State Building?" Doha, ACRPS Policy Analysis Unit, February 2014; Charles Schmitz, "Yemen's National Dialogue," Middle East Institute, Washington, DC, March 10, 2014; Thomas Hueglin, "The Case of Yemen: Failed State or Failed Federal Concept?" unpublished paper, n.d.

produced a large number of recommendations for the later constitutional process. The most important subject on which it was impossible to reach agreement in the conference was the number of units into which a federal Yemen was to be divided. As we have seen, this issue affected the ambitions of two groups: southern separatists, who were inadequately represented, and Houthi rebels in the north. Both rejected a recommendation, produced after the dialogue process and later incorporated in the draft constitution, for six federal regions.

No dialogue or constitutional process could have resolved this contentious issue in the face of Houthi arms. Indeed, no constitutional process should have been convened in the face of ongoing violence by both the Houthis and Al-Qaeda in the Arabian Peninsula. It is clear in retrospect that a peace process should have been pursued before details of state structure were to be considered. The decision rules of the dialogue process were very well crafted, however, even though the process suffered from inadequate inclusion of all contenders, and the subsequent constitutional proceedings were premature.

As I have suggested, neglect of minority interests is only one risk. As Robert H. Mnookin has pointed out,[10] multiparty negotiations provide participants with incentives to prevent agreement. They may do this in order to increase their share in the outcome or in order to revert to the status quo ante when a proposed agreement benefits most, but not all, of the participants and when they are among those who have lost out. If there are several players, coalitions may form to share the benefits of an agreement among themselves while excluding others from benefits or even leaving them worse off than they were. These are seeds of dissensus.

---

10. Mnookin, "Strategic Barriers to Dispute Resolution: A Comparison of Bilateral and Multilateral Negotiations," *Journal of Institutional and Theoretical Economics*, Vol. 59, no. 1 (2003), pp. 199–220.

These possibilities for collusion and destabilizing reactions to it constitute important reasons for aiming at something closer to consensus in the sense of a supervening agreement, rather than a series of bargains, and in the sense of something closer to unanimity. Yet, if consensus close to unanimity is the aim, that very aim empowers spoilers, who may demand an unfair share or threaten to scuttle the negotiation by refusing to agree or engaging in violence to prevent agreement or to secure better terms for themselves.[11]

One solution to this problem is for those who would be greatly benefited by an agreement to make side payments to those who are insufficiently benefited or benefited not at all by the agreement. There may occasionally be opportunities to assuage the claims of potential constitutional spoilers in this way—for example, by according territorially concentrated groups asymmetric federalism or regional autonomy—but very often the claims of ethnic antagonists in a constitutional process cannot be satisfied by such measures. Moreover, side payments may offend prevailing notions of group entitlement, even when the prospective success of an agreement attractive to most participants will be jeopardized by failure to agree to such measures. Alternatively, they may produce agreement based on the side payment rather than on durable commitment.

For these reasons, bargaining failure becomes more likely as the number of groups participating in constitutional processes grows. The criterion of inclusion increases that number, and the criterion of something close to unanimity heightens the likelihood of failure.

In the South African constitutional negotiations of the 1990s, the concept of "sufficient consensus" across group and party lines was introduced. The objective was to achieve "the widest possible

11. On incentives for violence during negotiations, see Timothy D. Sisk, "Political Violence and Peace Accords," in *Violence and Reconstruction*, ed. John Darby (Notre Dame: University of Notre Dame Press, 2006), pp. 121–42.

consensus," and a variety of procedural devices—increased discussion time, reference of controverted issues to technical committees, adjournments, private consultations, and the like—was developed to try to break incipient deadlocks.[12] In the end, however, the chair was empowered to decide whether sufficient consensus existed on any issue. On one motion, the vote was fifteen delegations to eight, whereupon, to the dismay of the smaller parties on the losing end, the chair decided that the consensus was sufficient. In fact, what sufficient consensus came to mean in South Africa was agreement between the largest black party, the African National Congress, and the largest white party, the National Party. Third parties, both black and white, dissented from this practical meaning of the term.

The Northern Ireland negotiations of 1997–98 reached a similar result by a different route. In Belfast, sufficient consensus was said to consist of agreement supported by parties representing a majority of Catholics, a majority of Protestants, and a majority of all parties present as well as the governments of the United Kingdom and the Irish Republic. The departure of two Protestant parties from the negotiations simplified achievement of consensus by this standard. Moreover, a Catholic party, Sinn Féin, while present, scarcely participated in the proceedings. In practice, this meant that anything that could be agreed by the largest Protestant party, the Ulster Unionists, and the largest Catholic party, the Social Democratic and Labor Party, was deemed sufficient.[13]

Whatever the stated meaning of sufficient consensus, then, its operational meaning came down to anything that secured the

---

12. On some techniques used in South Africa to break deadlocks, see Nicholas Haysom and Sujit Choudhry, "Mechanisms for Resolving Divisive Issues in Constitutional Negotiation," Constitution-making in Focus, Interpeace Issue Paper, Geneva, 2010.

13. On the Northern Ireland process, see Donald L. Horowitz, "Explaining the Northern Ireland Agreement: Sources of an Unlikely Constitutional Consensus," *British Journal of Political Science*, Vol. 32, no. 2 (2002), pp. 193–220.

concurrence of the largest political party on each side of the main cleavage line. Essentially, multilateral negotiations were reduced to bilateral negotiations. For bipolar conflicts, this reduction may have some utility, but where each group is represented by more than one party, it may lay the foundation for opposition to the agreement, perhaps by parties on both sides. Fortunately for the fate of the Northern Ireland Agreement, opponents later found themselves forced to board a departing train,[14] namely the institutions established under the agreement, perhaps because they did not happen to be the opponents with the greatest capacity to oppose the agreement with violence. Opposition did, however, manifest itself in the subsequent referendum results and in the inter-party and intra-party dissent that made it difficult for the Ulster Unionist Party First Minister, David Trimble, to negotiate concessions across group lines once self-government took hold after the referendum.

Despite the great praise that has often been heaped on the South Africa–Northern Ireland versions of the sufficient consensus formulation, those versions have two major hazards. First, by emphasizing the adequacy of agreement between the two major players, they risk transforming multipolar conflicts into less tractable bipolar conflicts once other players sense that they had better line up behind one of the two major players if they are to have any influence down the road. Second, a sense that consensus is sufficient if it is shared between the two major players can hardly be applied in cases in which three or four sides cannot readily be reduced to two, even where the third and fourth groups are much smaller than the big two. What counts is whether the third or fourth groups are able to translate their dissent into action that spoils (or delegitimizes) the constitutional agreement or spoils the peace later, as Sunnis did in Iraq,

14. Cf. Stephen John Stedman, "Spoiler Problems in Peace Processes," in *International Conflict Resolution after the Cold War*, ed. Paul C. Stern and Daniel Druckman (Washington, DC: National Academy Press, 2000), pp. 178–224, at pp. 212–13.

or whether the inability to forge consensus in a multiparty process aborts the effort altogether, as it did in 2012 in Nepal, or renders the future of the constitutional bargain shaky, as it did in Nepal in 2015–16.

At a minimum, a constitutional consensus should attempt to include those with a capacity for violent obstruction,[15] but, given the fragility of many severely divided societies, any consensus should, if possible, be greater than that. It should attempt to embrace all major segments of all significant groups or else risk later destabilization of the agreement.[16] Repeated neglect of third, fourth, or fifth groups often has later costs if those smaller minorities have access to arms or develop inclinations toward separatism, or even if their persistent disaffection roils legislative comity. In short, the multiplicity of players makes an agreement hard to achieve, but it may well enhance the durability of a constitutional agreement once achieved. Although there is no perfect answer to this problem, the careful balance of something like the Yemeni standards looks more reasonable than the South Africa–Northern Ireland versions of sufficient consensus, which, as they focused only on minimizing obstruction of the proceedings, gave free rein to the two largest parties in each case. Interestingly enough, the two major parties that played the smallest role in the Northern Ireland process have each subsequently gained more seats than the two that negotiated the agreement, and these two have contributed most to the periodic, extended stalemates on fulfilling the stated objectives of the Good Friday Agreement that resulted from the process.

---

15. John Darby, *The Effects of Violence on Peace Processes* (Washington, DC: USIP Press, 2001), p. 52.

16. As I have noted earlier, there are many third, fourth, and fifth groups in severely divided societies whose interests are frequently ignored in constitutional proceedings. Consider Sunnis, Turkmens, and other groups mentioned previously in Iraq; Indians, Sabahans, and Sarawakians of various ethnic origins in Malaysia; Muslims in Sri Lanka; and the array of small but collectively significant minorities in Macedonia.

Division in the drafting body that corresponds to ethnic divisions quite obviously signifies a failure to gain the assent of representatives of a significant ethnic group, leaving it with a grievance. On the other hand, a sharp division within one or more ethnic group(s) opens the possibility of a later claim by the dissenters that those group members who assented signed on to a constitution that disserves the group. The dissenters could become spoilers. In a severely divided society, either type of disagreement about the constitution can be destabilizing. No doubt the disagreement that coincides with ethnic divisions is more serious, but both types are important. The South African and Northern Ireland processes acknowledged one but neglected the other. If institutional arrangements agreed in a constitutional process command the strong assent of most of the factions or parties of all of the groups included in the process, that is preferable to agreements that command the assent of any two of the largest participants while others dissent or are simply deemed irrelevant to resolution of the issue, which can precipitate a walkout by the dissenters and, of course, a lack of commitment or spoiler action later.

The strong assent of most parties or factions of all groups is, of course, a guarantee of consensus that crosses group lines. This standard has some clear benefits. For one thing, attention to the views of all groups should help preserve multipolarity where it exists, especially if reinforced by the creation of institutions that foster multipolarity. (In conflict-prone societies, multipolarity is far preferable to bipolarity.[17]) For another, after adoption of a constitution, sooner or later there will be those who object to interethnic compromise on some important issue or issues. When that occurs, the continued attachment to the constitutional arrangements by substantial segments

17. See Horowitz, *Ethnic Groups in Conflict*, pp. 36–41, 612, 632–38. This conclusion is supported by numerous subsequent studies finding a strong link between bipolar opposition and ethnic conflict. See, e.g., José G. Montalvo and Marta Reynal-Querol, "Ethnic Diversity and Economic Development," *Journal of Development Economics*, Vol. 76, no. 2 (2005), pp. 293–323.

of the objecting group may help avoid root-and-branch opposition of whole ethnic groups to each other. Tempting though it is, it is a serious mistake to focus merely on securing agreement. Maximizing the chance of the durability of the agreement is at least equally important.

The benefits of favoring both stringent inclusion and a high degree of consensus in constitutional processes can be formidable. If consensus is limited to the major players and the extremes have lost conspicuously in the constitutional process, the extremes may become more disaffected and dangerous when post-constitutional politics resumes. Consensus building works against this outcome. Moreover, the constitution-drafting body can be a school for arguing and bargaining, for crafting and understanding institutions and their logic, and for compromise. As I have said, these can become skills transferable to the political process the new constitution authorizes. The need for these skills argues for a highly representative body and the patience to seek broad agreement, in particular a degree of agreement that crosscuts groups and political parties, even if those groups or parties are, to some degree, internally divided in their constitutional preferences.

There is, however, an important downstream danger of rules requiring very high levels of consensus. It becomes possible that the institutional rules of the constitutional process may inadvertently spill over and become the constitutional rules adopted for the ordinary functioning of the polity that is created or re-created by the constitution, even though the aims of the two sets of rules are very different. Insisting on a very high degree of consensus might, then, end up biasing the drafting assembly in favor of a particular constitutional product, a regime that allows small groups to prevent action by the executive or the legislature. This can happen because extremists may well be able to foresee that they will habitually find themselves in opposition. If they have this degree of visibility, they may use the requirement of high levels of consensus to insist on a constitution that guarantees them a place in any subsequently formed government and even a veto over policy decisions, regardless of their agenda and their views and intentions concerning other ethnic groups. Although high levels of constitutional consensus are desirable, they should not be conflated with perfect unanimity, especially when those at the extreme points of the political spectrum use the desire for consensus to hold constitution makers hostage to a plan that requires creation of a regime that impairs the ability of government to get important work done.[18]

This is perhaps a small point in favor of constitution drafting by legislatures, rather than by specially elected constituent assemblies. Legislators will immediately understand that while consensus is important for producing a constitution, a very high degree of consensus for ordinary legislation is a prescription for frequent deadlock, and they are therefore unlikely to go in that direction.[19] (Others, of course, may see that danger as well, but legislators are bound to see it.) Beyond that, unanimity requirements in a legislative body are time-consuming; they implicitly privilege the status quo, and they can lead to economically dysfunctional pork-barrel politics.[20]

The rules of the constitutional process should not bias in *any* direction the configuration of democratic institutions to be adopted through that process.[21] That possibility is an important reason to keep any consensus requirements from allowing the capture of the

---

18. Note the caution of Andrew Arato regarding unanimity rules that might allow small veto groups to load up a draft with dysfunctional provisions and make agreement impossible. *Post-Sovereign Constitution Making* (Oxford: Oxford University Press, 2016), p. 103.

19. A point made explicitly by a member of the Indian constituent assembly-cum-legislature. See Granville Austin, *The Indian Constitution: Cornerstone of a Nation* (New Delhi: Oxford University Press, 1966), p. 317.

20. See the trenchant discussion in Weale, *Democracy*, 1st ed., pp. 127–28. Weale cites European Union agricultural policy as the quintessential example of pork-barrel politics under unanimity rules.

21. I am not agnostic about constitutional designs, but a dedication to deliberation cannot be squared with processes that import bias into the outcome of deliberation.

process by such veto players. Consensus requirements, if set too high, can thwart the process of deliberation about the institutions that should emerge from the process.

Given adequate deliberation time, a high level of consensus in a constitution-making forum is not always as difficult to achieve as it may seem. As I pointed out earlier, Tunisia was able to achieve this, despite numerous starting differences, major problems along the way, and a few dangerous issues left unresolved at the end, which we shall examine. India's Constituent Assembly, like Tunisia's and Indonesia's constitution-framing bodies, also functioned as a legislature. The Indian assembly, alternating between dealing with legislative matters and constitutional debates, took three years to finish its work, taking votes on many significant matters as it proceeded but in the end arriving at what Granville Austin called "consensus" but what Shibanikinkar Chaube described as "accommodation."[22] The assembly reached its decisions after extensive deliberation, including an eleven-month period of final clause-by-clause review of the penultimate draft.[23]

Most members of the assembly had been indirectly elected by provincial assemblies, which themselves had been elected in 1945 on a limited franchise. Others were nominated by princely states. Moreover, the departure of the Muslim League at the time of the creation of Pakistan limited the full range of potential difference that was represented.[24] The assembly also had the advantage that the majority of its members belonged to the Indian National Congress, and Congress leaders caucused before assembly sessions. Still, the

22. For the rationale for consensus, see Austin, *The Indian Constitution*, pp. 24, 311; Chaube, *Constituent Assembly of India: Springboard of Revolution*, 2d ed. (New Delhi: Manohar, 2000), p. 237. Austin minimizes the importance of the issues that had to be decided by voting. *The Indian Constitution*, p. 318. I shall return to this question in chapter 10.

23. For the drafting sequence, see Arun K. Thiruvengadam, *The Constitution of India: A Contextual Analysis* (London: Hart, 2017), p. 33.

24. A point emphasized to me by Ronojoy Sen.

assembly's membership spanned nearly all of the numerous caste, tribal, religious, territorial, and ethnolinguistic cleavage lines present in India. Chairing the drafting committee was B. R. Ambedkar, president of the Scheduled Castes Federation, the leading organization of ex-untouchables, a very substantial, deeply disadvantaged minority in India. His appointment was an important symbolic and unifying stroke.

With this level of heterogeneity, there was a significant range of views on many issues. On the most difficult, the status of Hindi as the national language, an uneasy compromise was worked out, but the language issue was not finally resolved until after violent protests against Hindi in Madras state (now Tamil Nadu) in 1965. Another issue, the shape of the federal system, was especially difficult, because, in addition to a sizeable number of delegates from India's princely states, most delegates had been elected by provincial legislatures and might be presumed to favor a weak center, as some provincial officials did.[25] Yet, after two and a half years of heavy deliberation, consensus on a rather centralized system was reached. In the end, the constitution as signed by 284 members of an assembly that originally had 299.

As I just suggested, India had the advantage that its national movement-cum-political party constituted a majority in the assembly, but that body did its work in the midst of the crisis over the partition of the country and the horrendous violence that followed in its wake. Crisis often produces time limits and a rush to adopt a constitution in a very short period as those time limits approach. But crisis did not have those effects in India (1946–49), Tunisia (2011–14), or Indonesia (1999–2002), proving that, with skill and credible action toward constitutional reform, crises can be calmed.[26] Haste is a ma-

25. Austin, *The Indian Constitution,* p. 200.

26. In Indonesia, the crisis was overcome early on by the guarantee of free elections, assented to by leaders of all parties, followed by the first reforms. Horowitz,

jor source of flaws in constitutions.[27] In spite of that, time limits are imposed in many cases. One rationale is to prevent anyone from using delaying tactics to prevail on contested matters.[28] But under such circumstances, delay would usually not lead to victory on a contested issue but to stalemate or postponement of the resolution of the issue.

Delay certainly can be a problem, especially if elections are coming soon,[29] but in most cases it will produce a failure to produce a constitution for the time being, whereas haste is far more likely to produce a flawed constitution then and there. In Iraq, the occupying American government pressured the constitutional committee not to take advantage of an extra six-month drafting period that the law allowed it to have,[30] and so there is no way to know whether a more complete consensus could have been reached. The fact is that it was not reached, and Sunni disaffection, already strong, accelerated as a result. It has been suggested that some Sunnis eventually accepted

Constitutional Change and Democracy in Indonesia, pp. 45–54. In India, the Congress had been planning for constitutional reform as part of its long struggle for independence and would not be deterred by the turmoil accompanying partition. Tiruvengadam, *Constitution of India,* pp. 24–29. In Tunisia, accusations about Ennahda's possible complicity in political assassinations induced the party, the largest, to accept a diminished voice in the assembly, following which others could be persuaded to return to the proceedings after a month's suspension. Stepan, "Democracy with Democrats in Tunisia," pp. 24–25.

27. Elster, "Political Psychology of Constitution Making," pp. 229, 233.

28. See Elster, "Ways of Constitution Making," p. 138.

29. See, e.g., chapter 8 on Sri Lanka.

30. It was widely thought at the time that the George W. Bush administration wanted swift completion of the constitution for domestic political reasons in the United States, in order to be able to claim progress in Iraq. When I asked two authoritative members of the Bush National Security Council about this motivation a couple of years later, they both advised me that the motive was to show progress *to Iraqis,* in the context of a situation that was deteriorating. Whatever the motive—and I do not doubt the NSC members' account—it was an unwise decision. The constitution was, in a great many ways, a poor product, the result of a very considerable missed opportunity.

the constitutional dispensation,[31] but the constitutional process certainly fueled the sense of the Sunnis that they were to be excluded from a significant role in the polity. From that sense, enhanced by the Shia bias of the regime of Nuri al-Maliki between 2006 and 2014, and a general bias toward Shia-majority rule thereafter, a great deal of violence and disintegrative behavior flowed.

There is much to be said against strict time limits. After all, failure to produce at least some parts of a constitution carries its own sanction of embarrassment and political cost. Rigid time limits may, ironically, defer the moment of earnest debate and decision until just before the expiration date, as they did, for example, in Northern Ireland in 1998. There was considerable latent agreement in Belfast in 1998, based on a shared reading of prior experience and periodic earlier discussions. For those reasons, the last-minute nature of the negotiations did not impair the coherence of the product. Had there not been the makings of a latent consensus, rushed negotiations might have had a quite different result. Where there is no prior agreement about the structure of the constitution,[32] that kind of deferral, with its shrinking of serious deliberation, is unwise.

The advantages of deliberation time in the face of severe divisions generally outweigh the advantages of very strict time limits and any risk that more liberality with time creates. An exception might be presented if the status quo were thoroughly intolerable, because of a totalitarian constitution, for example, in which case the better course might be to make an interim constitution pending completion of deliberations rather than to rush the process of creating the permanent constitution. To insure that such an interim

---

31. Haider Ala Hamoudi, *Negotiating in Civil Conflict: Constitutional Construction and Imperfect Bargaining in Iraq* (Chicago: University of Chicago Press, 2014).

32. On the impact, benign and malign, of earlier negotiations, see Donald L. Horowitz, "Eating Leftovers: Making Peace from Scraps off the Negotiating Table," in *Conflict and Cooperation*, ed. Günther Baechler and Andreas Wenger (Zurich: Neue Zürcher Zeitung Publishing, 2002), pp. 293–310.

constitution does not become permanent because of extended disagreement about alternatives, such a document should not cover everything, just enough to be serviceable for the time being. Ironically, Iraq had such a temporary document, the Transitional Administrative Law, promulgated by the Governing Council during the occupation, in 2004. Yet it still rushed to a conclusion. In general, the more time, the greater the scope for deliberation and consensus on the agreed document.

There is, however, a cynical but practical reason to fear an entirely open-ended process. A close observer of delegate behavior is convinced that, with no time pressure at all, representatives in constituent assemblies can get too comfortable and unproductive, especially if generous per diem is provided. Some informal but certainly extendable termination date may be desirable. More important would be good leadership of the constitution-making body.

There are additional reasons in favor of legislative drafting of constitutions, provided, of course, that the legislature is democratically elected.[33] A legislature is a body that sits regularly to do business apart from constitution-making. If it cannot agree on the shape of a constitution, it may not be as readily perceived as deadlocked as a specialized constituent assembly would be, and it may choose to put out such constitutional provisions as it does agree on *seriatim,* as the Indonesian supralegislative body did between 1999 and 2002. Having calmed the acute sense of crisis by running a democratic election and then making clear that the aim was a democratic dispensation and a clear rejection of the authoritarian regime, the Indonesian constitutional reformers gained time to overcome great initial disagreement on numerous questions among themselves by postponing constitutional changes until consensus was reached on

33. John M. Carey finds countries utilizing elected bodies for constitution making to be more democratic years later. Carey, "Does It Matter How a Constitution Is Created?" in *Is Democracy Exportable?* ed. Zoltan Barany and Robert G. Moser (New York: Cambridge University Press, 2009), pp. 155–77.

each. In fact, the Indonesians proceeded with constitutional change by consensus.[34] They took practically no votes and waited patiently until agreement of all factions was in place.[35] Over time, many initial positions on important issues changed, often dramatically.[36] Incremental change within a single constitutional process can mitigate problems of consensus by providing extra time for it to develop.

Interestingly enough, the Indonesians were operating under an amendment procedure under the 1945 constitution that required only a two-thirds vote of the large supralegislative body authorized to amend the constitution, which, under other conditions, might have discouraged a search for a wider consensus. In this case, it did not have that effect. Among other things, Indonesia's history of violence at times of regime change fostered a strong urge to wait patiently for consensus to develop on each issue.

To be sure, one-shot drafting may be unavoidable. In Iraq and Afghanistan, countries in which wars had just ended, there might have been an even more difficult interregnum than there was, and making a new constitution may have allayed the anxieties of the moment and prevented unilateral moves by groups to change the map by grabbing territory or declaring independence. Yet the political and institutional costs of rushed agreement in both of those countries were substantial and continuing. Efforts to overcome crises and gain time for deliberation would have been preferable to making a rushed constitution.

In some countries, such as Hungary and Chile, incremental amendments were the method of constitutional change.[37] Hanna

34. Horowitz, *Constitutional Change and Democracy in Indonesia*, pp. 74–77, 155–60.

35. The one vote they took was to expel certain unelected members, provided by the previous authoritarian regime, from the body deliberating on the constitution.

36. Ibid., pp. 55–123.

37. See Elster, Offe, and Preuss, *Institutional Design in Post-Communist Societies*, pp. 65–67; Katja Michalak and Gerald Pech, "Constitutional Design Versus Re-

Lerner has argued for even more incrementalism, in order to avoid lack of consensus. In severely divided societies, she advocates a thin constitution, the barest framework, with a large measure of ambiguity, thereby allowing a "long-term evolutionary process of collective redefinition"[38] to play out over time. Fundamental issues, she suggests, can be left to a subsequent political process. Rosalind Dixon also cautions against premature drafting if constitution makers are unable to gain the requisite knowledge to solve certain problems they confront or if they wish to leave particular matters for legislative resolution.[39]

In these limited circumstances, deferral on a few specifics can be a wise choice. The thin constitution, however, is another matter. It may also have considerable utility where dissensus, although serious, has not broken out into overt conflict (and especially not into violence); where democratic norms are strongly, even if not uniformly, grounded; where there are overarching loyalties to the state that mitigate the impact of divisions among groups; and where there are independent courts that can win respect (or at least obedience) for their efforts to fill in constitutional gaps. As a constitutional consensus is being fleshed out over the long term, implicit assumptions of majority rule and minority rights can serve as foundations for the polity. These conditions characterize the Israeli case—albeit only imperfectly with respect to the Israeli-Arab minority—and a few other countries that could afford to allow constitutional practices to evolve over time.

---

form in Emerging Democracies: Lessons from Post-Communist Transitions," paper presented at the 2009 annual meeting of the International Studies Association.

38. Hanna Lerner, *Making Constitutions in Deeply Divided Societies* (Cambridge: Cambridge University Press, 2012), p. 39.

39. Dixon, "Constitutional Design Deferred," in *Comparative Constitution Making,* ed. David Landau and Hanna Lerner (Cheltenham, U.K.: Edward Elgar, 2020), pp. 165–85. See also Allen S. Weiner, "Constitutions as Peace Treaties," *Stanford Law Review Online,* vol. 64, no. 8, November 18, 2011, www.stanford lawreview .org/online/constitutions-peace-treaties.

Unfortunately, however, a thin framework and extended incrementalism will not generally be adequate to make basic decisions. In 2005, Iraqi constitution makers deliberately left several sections blank. These dealt with important issues, such as the organization of the upper house that was to represent federal units. They were to be filled in by constitutional amendment or legislative clarification later, but a decade and a half later, these provisions had still not been drafted. It is also pertinent to recall that less detail in constitutions is associated with less durability for them.[40]

Many societies have experienced a threat of (or a history of) violence that makes establishing basic rules of the political game exigent. In these societies, if the foundations of group differences are ascriptive, there are also conflicting visions and conflicting theories about institutions for interethnic accommodation, not to mention (generally) weakly embedded democratic norms and a fragile rule of law. Participants who later gain the upper hand in politics may use the power they gain to shape the basic structures of the polity as they see fit. By themselves, majority rule and minority rights are an inadequate framework for such polities, both because unadorned majority rule can serve to exclude minorities perennially from participating in governance and because a weak rule of law is inadequate to defend minority rights. In those cases, which are numerous, incrementalism is best used to achieve consensus over a more limited time within an explicit constitutional process, rather than to avoid decisions for many years by recognizing lack of consensus at the outset. The risks of omission are too great.[41]

---

40. Elkins, Ginsburg, and Melton, *Endurance of National Constitutions*, p. 141. Extreme ethnic heterogeneity is also found to be associated with less durability, ibid., p. 138, but unfortunately the measure used for heterogeneity is fractionalization, whereas much greater threats to political stability in general (and almost surely to constitutional durability) arise from polarization, rather than fractionalization.

41. For further qualifications regarding incrementalism, see Mara Malagodi, "The Rejection of Constitutional Incrementalism in Nepal's Federalisation," *Federal Law Review*, Vol. 46, no. 4 (2018), pp. 521–40.

If the preference is for a specialized constituent assembly to draft afresh, the inclusion-consensus tradeoff poses a serious problem for deciding on the appropriate electoral system for that assembly. Ideally, such an electoral system should maximize inclusion of all ethnic and social groups in the drafting body. There is very little hard evidence on what process variables correlate with the success of constitution makers in producing either durability of the document or of democracy, but what little there is points strongly to the inclusiveness of an elected constitutional forum.[42]

Gabriel L. Negretto has studied the relation of inclusiveness to democracy by operationalizing a common distinction between constitutional processes dominated by a ruling party and those involving the agreement of two or more parties. He finds that the cooperation of freely elected representatives of two or more parties in constitution making "facilitates the implementation of liberal principles and the improvement of liberal democracy during the years of life of the new constitution."[43] (Interestingly, Negretto finds that direct citizen participation in constitutional processes does not have any such effect, a topic we shall return to in chapter 7.) An essay in the same volume contrasts Hungary's ruling-party-dominated constitutional process with Poland's, in which there were concessions to the large extra-parliamentary opposition. The inclusion of opposition concerns constrained and altered the constitution-making process in Poland and produced a more democratic result than that of Hungary.[44] Broad inclusion and agreements that reflect the

---

42. Carey, "Does It Matter How a Constitution is Created?" pp. 155–77; Elkins, Ginsburg, and Melton, *Endurance of National Constitutions*, pp. 78–79, 97–99, 139, 206.

43. Negretto, "Replacing Constitutions in Democratic Regimes: Elite Cooperation and Citizen Participation," in Negretto, ed., *Redrafting Constitutions in Democratic Orders: Theoretical and Comparative Perspectives* (Cambridge: Cambridge University Press, 2020), p. 117.

44. Gabriel L. Negretto and Solongo Wandan, "Procedural Rules and Majoritarian Politics in Poland (1993–1997) and Hungary (2010–2011)," in ibid, pages 155–74.

cooperation of political elites are likely to affect political behavior after the constitution is adopted.

If inclusiveness were the only value to be maximized, then most of the time list-system proportional representation, with large, multimember constituencies and low thresholds of exclusion, might be thought to be the best choice, for that choice would make it easiest for small segments of the population to achieve representation. But the more heterogeneous the delegates are, the more potential veto players there are and, *ceteris paribus,* the harder it is to achieve agreement.[45]

On grounds of inclusiveness, Elster argues that list PR should be the preferred system for a constituent assembly. However, for a legislature, in which the creation of durable, cohesive governments is a competing concern, Elster prefers a more majoritarian electoral system—and on this he is by no means alone.[46]

As Elster says, inclusiveness is a dominant consideration for choosing a constituent assembly, although, as just mentioned, one must be concerned about excessive polarization. For that reason, thresholds and district magnitudes would need to be calibrated carefully, in order to prevent party proliferation on the extremes of the spectrum. Hasty designs of electoral institutions in a number of constitutional planning exercises suggest that this kind of careful calibration may not be accomplished. And if it is not, stretching the party spectrum may pose a threat to consensus and compromise

45. Except, perhaps, at a very high cost in side payments involving rent seeking. For the Nigerian story, see A. Carl LeVan, *Dictators and Democracy in African Development* (New York: Cambridge University Press, 2014).

46. Elster, *Securities Against Misrule,* pp. 223, 227. See also Benjamin Reilly, *Democracy and Diversity: Political Engineering in the Asia-Pacific* (Oxford: Oxford University Press, 2006); Jean Tournon, "Représenter ou gouverner, il faut choisir," in *La Représentation,* ed. François d'Arcy (Paris: Economica, 1985), pp. 107–19, at pp. 108, 119. By "majoritarian" is generally meant the Anglo-American first-past-the-post, plurality system or the French two-round majority runoff system or the Australian alternative vote preferential system, often referred to in the United States as instant-runoff or ranked-choice voting.

when delegates to the constitution drafting body attempt to reach agreement.

Many considerations apart from inclusion become relevant for *legislative* elections. Among them are aggregation of interests, avoidance of long and dangerous hiatuses in forming governments, durability of governments, conflict brokerage, avoidance of party fragmentation in the legislature, and a strong local-district element for accountability to constituents. Yet because those who benefit from initial institutional choices tend to prefer them for subsequent choices of the same sort, switching from PR in a constitutional process to a different electoral system later may prove difficult. This is another case of possible inadvertent spillover from the constitutional process to the permanent institutions adopted in the constitutional process. Again, criteria for success in a constitutional process may suggest one institutional choice—here, PR for maximal inclusiveness—whereas criteria for success in subsequent governmental processes might commend different choices. As I mentioned earlier, a choice for constitutional process purposes that biases choices about permanent institutions during the process should be avoided. Those institutional choices should be made deliberately, based on prevailing country conditions and needs, rather than by dint of spillover from choices made for the prior purpose of organizing the constitutional body itself.

In many countries, this specific dilemma will have an answer. There is a growing body of evidence that, in countries in which minorities are geographically concentrated, plurality or majority elections may provide as much descriptive representation for those minorities in an assembly as PR does.[47] In many countries, moreover,

47. Wolfgang Wagner, "The Overstated Merits of Proportional Representation: The Republic of Macedonia as a Natural Experiment for Assessing the Impact of Electoral Systems on Descriptive Representation," *Ethnopolitics*, Vol. 13, no. 5 (2014), pp. 483–99; Sonia Alonso and Rubén Ruiz-Rufino, "Political Representation and Ethnic Conflict in New Democracies," *European Journal of Political Research*,

geographic concentration of minorities is the rule, so there may be no need for PR elections for constitutional assemblies. Where, however, groups are geographically intermixed, the preference for list-PR might well be justified.

Inclusion and consensus are not always good friends, as we have already seen. If, in a given society, inclusion requires a relatively large body, that may make consensus especially hard to reach. Worse yet, the need for both inclusion and consensus can impair the coherence and clarity of the resulting constitution. The extensive bargaining inevitable in multiparty proceedings can produce ambiguities and anomalies—institutions that do not quite fit together.[48] Standards of perfection are, therefore, inappropriate in constitutional processes that accord great importance to both inclusion and consensus, but very serious attention to both is not misplaced.

If broad inclusion can make genuine consensus harder to achieve, narrow inclusion can make it easier to achieve but less durable. In the face of what was then Malaya's recent emergence from very severe ethnic violence, an agreement on constitutional provisions bearing on ethnic interests would have been hard to achieve in the mid-1950s. As I described in chapter 4, an interethnic coalition, called the Alliance, had recently been created to pool votes for elections and had done so very effectively. This was explicitly a coalition of moderates on ethnic questions that was challenged by more radical contestants. The leaders of the Alliance were concerned about

---

Vol. 46, no. 2 (2007), pp. 237–67; Nenad Stojanović, "Do Multicultural Democracies Require PR? Counterevidence from Switzerland," *Swiss Political Science Review,* Vol. 12, no. 4 (2006), pp. 131–57; Daniel Zollinger and Daniel Bochsler, "Minority Representation in a Semi-Democratic Regime: The Georgian Case," *Democratization,* Vol. 19, no. 4 (2012), pp. 611–41; Mathijs Bogaards, "The Choice for Proportional Representation: Electoral System Design in Peace Agreements," *Civil Wars,* Vol. 15, no. S1 (2013), pp. 71–87.

48. For anomalies in the inclusion-and-consensus-driven Indonesian constitution, see Horowitz, *Constitutional Change and Democracy in Indonesia,* passim but esp. pp. 124–42. We shall examine further examples of incoherence in chapter 6.

the lingering effects of the most recent violence, an insurgency of local communists, overwhelmingly drawn from the large Chinese minority. Begun in 1948, the rebellion was mostly under control by 1956, but it had impressed upon Malay and non-Malay leaders alike the need to solidify the loyalty of the Malayan Chinese community and, therefore, the need for an ethnically accommodative constitution.[49] Equally important, however, were the legacy of the very ugly and widespread anti-Chinese violence that had occurred in 1945–46 and Malay reluctance to countenance terms of complete political equality with non-Malays, most of whose ancestors had migrated to the country under British auspices less than a century before.[50] On ethnic issues, the range of choice was narrow, and the need for compromise was exigent.

When the time came to draft the independence constitution, leaders of the coalition partners formed a committee to deal with the most serious ethnic issues. Eight members came from the Malay partner, nine from the Chinese, and six from the Indian. Led by moderates, the committee compromised on contested issues, such as language policy and the balance between ethnic preferences and interethnic equality. The leaders came from elite backgrounds and were eager to move past recent ethnic conflicts and into an independent Malaya. Even on this committee, however, there were radicals, especially among Malay members from more modest backgrounds, and outside the committee there were Chinese radicals, again from less elevated social strata. The moderate leadership prevailed, and their compromises became the basis of the Alliance memorandum

---

49. Joseph Fernando, *The Making of the Malayan Constitution* (Kuala Lumpur: Malaysian Branch of the Royal Asiatic Society, 2002), pp. 89–91. Among other studies of the communist rebellion, see Lucian W. Pye, *Guerrilla Communism in Malaya* (Princeton: Princeton University Press, 1956).

50. On the ethnic violence, see Cheah Boon Kheng, *Red Star Over Malaya* (Singapore: Singapore University Press, 1983). On the impact of the violence on the constitution, see Andrew Harding, *The Constitution of Malaysia: A Contextual Analysis* (Oxford: Hart, 2012), pp. 31–32.

to the British-appointed constitutional commission, the substance of which found its way into the constitution.[51] The more radical positions, however, survived the constitutional process and formed the basis of subsequent revisionist demands that emerged on both sides within a decade or so and, especially on the Malay side, formed the later basis of claims and policies either inconsistent with the constitutional bargains or, in some cases, profoundly amending them.[52]

For the most part, those demands came from younger Malay politicians who had played no role in the constitutional negotiation and felt that bad bargains had been struck. Some of these revisionist positions we shall examine in chapter 6. The point here is that the conciliatory inclinations of the narrow negotiating group were not wholly representative of their wider constituency on either the Malay or the non-Malay side.[53] There was no role in the process for opposition politicians, who in aggregate would win close to 50 percent of the vote (though a much smaller share of seats) in the first post-independence elections just a little more than two years away.

A more broadly composed set of constitutional negotiators would have had much more difficulty reaching agreement. As things turned out, significant areas of agreement of the top leaders, who were more attuned to the necessity of finding the middle ground, eventually came undone years after normal politics resumed. Every so often, constitution making produces what in retrospect can be seen as tragic dilemmas. This particular dilemma, featuring the felt need for narrow inclusion resulting in a defective consensus, is certainly among them.

51. See Fernando, *Making of the Malayan Constitution,* pp. 65–94; Harding, *Constitution of Malaysia,* pp. 30–33.

52. Relatively radical Malaysian Chinese claims were repelled in 1959, shortly after independence. Malay claims were received more hospitably after an ugly bout of deadly ethnic violence following elections in 1969.

53. See, e.g., Karl von Vorys, *Democracy without Consensus: Communalism and Political Stability in Malaysia* (Princeton: Princeton University Press, 1975).

In some countries, because of the presence of warfare, elections for a constituent assembly or legislature cannot be held, but there may be a strongly felt need for a new constitution to provide a fresh start. In many of those countries, as we have observed, constitution making is entangled with the peace process, which, as I have indicated, is not at all ideal. In other countries experiencing violence, however, efforts are made to produce inclusive bodies for constitution making. Yemen and Somalia, we have observed, are two such cases. In both, there was agreement on inclusive composition, but the members were appointed or coopted into the initial process rather than being elected. Inevitably, there are questions about whom such bodies really represent.

There was not much doubt about this question in Afghanistan in 2003–04.[54] There a Loya Jirga, consisting of a mix of 1,051 indirectly elected representatives and 600 representatives appointed by and mainly loyal to the sitting interim president, appointed committees that eventually reported to a second Loya Jirga, which was accorded little time to deliberate and did not take a genuine vote on contested proposals. The constitution prescribed a unitary government in an ethnically and territorially divided polity as well as a strong presidency favored by the appointed incumbent and his ethnic base.

We have already seen that time pressure can work against consensus. An elected body, rather than an appointed commission, is likely to be given more time to reach agreement. The state of the political parties also bears on the ability to arrive at consensus. The more inchoate the party system, the less experience party leaders have with each other and with their followers, and the less likely the

54. See Larry Goodson, "Afghanistan's Long Road to Reconstruction," *Journal of Democracy*, Vol. 14, no. 1 (2003), pp. 82–99; Andrew Reynolds, "Constitutional Engineering and Democratic Stability: The Debate Surrounding the Crafting of Political Institutions in Afghanistan," in *Building State and Security in Afghanistan*, ed. Wolfgang Danspeckgruber and Robert P. Finn (Boulder, CO: Lynne Rienner, 2010), pp. 36–55.

leaders are to reach agreement or, for that matter, to make or react to arguments about appropriate institutions. On the other hand, the less fixed the interests of parties are, the less the visibility of parties about the future and the greater the likelihood that a veil of ignorance will enable participants to engage in reasoned arguments about the contours of an appropriate constitutional dispensation.

If consensus is finally achieved in an elected constitution-making body, will a referendum be necessary to approve the constitution? Referenda are increasingly used for the purpose of establishing or confirming agreement.[55]

The Tunisians, it will be recalled, worked hard at securing consensus in their constitutional deliberations. Their vote was close to unanimous, but they, like others, had legally specified criteria for agreement short of consensus. The Tunisian standard to approve the constitution was a two-thirds vote of the assembly, which could be repeated once if the requisite two-thirds were not achieved on the first ballot, provided the overall drafting committee had offered some revision after the first failed ballot. A failure to achieve two-thirds on the second ballot would then trigger a referendum, in which the draft would be approved if it received merely a majority vote of those citizens participating in the referendum.[56]

This was a rare example of a referendum to approve a constitution not approved by the assembly in which it was drafted. Referenda are typically used to seal the adoption of a constitution, not

55. Ginsburg, Zachary Elkins, and Justin Blount, "Does the Process of Constitution-Making Matter?" *Annual Review of Law and Social Science*, Vol. 5 (2009), pp. 201–23, at p. 205. Still, the number of constitutional referenda in severely divided societies is not great. See Matt Qvortrup, *Referendums and Ethnic Conflict* (Philadelphia: University of Pennsylvania Press, 2014), pp. 25–44. South Africa and Tunisia both managed to avoid referenda. In each, it is certainly possible that a referendum might have revealed deep divisions on the constitution by polarized groups, as it did in Northern Ireland, as I shall point out momentarily.

56. See Bill Proctor and Ikbal Ben Moussa, "The Tunisian Constituent Assembly's By-Laws: A Brief Analysis," International IDEA, Stockholm, 2012, p. 27, citing Tunisia Constitutional Act no. 6, art. 3.

to reverse non-adoption by the drafting body. Most drafting bodies with high standards for approving constitutions do, however, have fallback provisions for the body itself if those high standards cannot be met. Sometimes these are two-thirds, sometimes simple majority. In Sri Lanka, as we shall see in chapter 8, a constitutional assembly sought consensus but needed merely a majority vote to pass the approved document on to parliament, which then needed two-thirds to pass it, even though parliament consisted of exactly the same membership as the Constitutional Assembly. So, while in many countries a majority might suffice at some stage or other, there are various voting sequences and standards.

In the study described earlier, Negretto finds no positive relationship between referenda and post-adoption democracy.[57] Indeed, there is as yet no compelling evidence of their benign effect on constitutional longevity, democracy, or intergroup accommodation, and there is serious concern that referenda may foster polarization, especially because their results may appear to create permanent winners and losers.[58] On occasion, formal demonstrations of public approval of a constitution embodying difficult interethnic compromises might make them more durable. Still, there are important qualifications.

If a constitution was created with only partial consensus, a referendum may reveal an ethnic foundation for intergroup or, for that matter, intragroup dissensus in the population, as it did in Northern Ireland. According to the best estimates, majority Protestant approval lagged nearly unanimous Catholic approval in the referendum by about 40 percentage points. After the new regime was installed, the referendum gap revealed an underlying split in Protestant opinion. This split in support for the new dispensation

57. Negretto, "Replacing Constitutions in Democratic Regimes," p. 117.

58. See Ben Reilly, "Democratic Validation," in John Darby and Roger McGinty, eds., *Contemporary Peacemaking: Conflict, Violence and Peace Processes* (Basingstoke: Palgrave Macmillan, 2002), pp. 230–41.

was replicated in opposition within Protestant ranks to the government elected after the referendum. As I mentioned earlier, this divide in Protestant opinion, blatantly obvious in the referendum results, made it very difficult for the precariously placed Protestant first minister to make concessions to Catholic members of the governing coalition and thereby to establish a genuinely functioning regime years after the new government took power. The regime has been plagued by recurrent stalemates ever since.

The Iraq constitution of 2005 was, as I also noted, overwhelmingly rejected by Sunni voters, who nevertheless did not quite have the votes required to defeat it in the referendum. There was no sense afterwards that it was their constitution.

Alternatively, the referendum may fail altogether, as it did in Kenya (2005), where those who lost in the drafting process fought successfully against ratification. The Polish referendum (1997) had a low turnout, 43 percent, which various politicians interpreted as showing lack of support for the new constitution or unhappiness with the rather ugly referendum campaign—which was "thick with insults and outright lies"[59]—or disenchantment with politics in general. Ewa Letowska provides a different explanation, that low turnout was driven by a sense that the new constitution would have no direct effect on standards of living. In fact, she contends, within a week it was clear that the new constitution was "accepted as reality."[60]

All these disparate outcomes and their interpretations, accurate or fanciful, indicate that referenda can sometimes be dangerous to the health of new constitutions and their underlying arrangements. On the other hand, where consent might be in doubt, even for a document agreed to by the then-largest party of each group, as in Northern Ireland, a referendum might still be necessary, despite the

59. Letowska, "Constitution of Possibilities," p. 80.
60. Ibid.

rift that it exposed in Protestant opinion and the difficulties in governing that rift produced.

There may be some survey evidence suggesting that African constitutions ratified by referenda have more support than those not so ratified,[61] but this relationship may simply reflect the fact that constitutional drafts that enjoy greater support tend to be submitted to referenda—an endogenous effect. If there is inadequate inclusion or no consensus, the referendum will prove divisive.[62] If, however, there are inclusion and consensus, a referendum could be superfluous. Inclusion followed by a relatively high level of consensus ought generally to be sufficient if, and *only* if, the drafting or approving body has been democratically elected, but, as I said earlier, approval in a referendum might just impart legitimacy to difficult compromises. Still, there is every reason to be skeptical of referenda results when the standard for approval on fundamental constitutional change is anything short of a strong supermajority. Unfortunately, most referenda are deemed approved if 50 percent plus one vote in the affirmative.[63]

61. See Elkins, Ginsburg, and Melton, *Endurance of National Constitutions*, p. 79.

62. But see Ian O'Flynn and Ron Levy, "Deliberative Constitutional Referenda in Deeply Divided Societies," *UBC Law Review*, vol. 53, no. 1 (2020), pp. 205–40, which advocates deliberative measures in referendum campaigns and preferential voting in order to foster moderate discourse to counter possible extremism.

63. See also Andrew Arato's well-founded skepticism of yes-or-no choices on complex packages of institutions. Arato, *Post-Sovereign Constitution Making*, p. 123.

CHAPTER 6

Consensus, Compromise, Clarity, and Coherence

Like many collective decision processes, constitution making involves multiple goals that can be harmonized only with difficulty. It will be noticed immediately that compromise can cause problems for coherence, clarity, and consensus. Compromises may seem internally contradictory. A classic example is contained in article 153 of the Malaysian Constitution, which provides for safeguarding "the special position of the Malays" and "the legitimate interests of other communities."[1] Although this clause was intended to be a balanced provision, with minimal effect on the equal citizenship rights provided elsewhere in the same document,[2] an expansive reading of one of these phrases or the other can easily impinge on the scope of what remains. Conflicting interpretations can easily make article 153 incoherent, and in fact they did exactly that, as we shall see.

A clause of this kind can produce two different kinds of disagreement. One pertains to agreement on a formulation in order

1. 1957 Constitution of Malaysia, as amended, art. 153(1). For an exposition, see Harding, *Constitution of Malaysia*, pp. 38–39, 70–79. After the formation of Malaysia, this clause was amended to extend the special position wording to "natives" of the newly incorporated Borneo states of Sabah and Sarawak.

2. 1957 Constitution of Malaysia, art. 8.

to cover over a deeper disagreement; the other relates to those who dissent from what most have agreed to.

First, those who agree to a compromise, even if they are a large majority of the assembly, can disagree about its meaning and, more significantly, its later interpretation. Indeed, many such compromises are made deliberately ambiguous, so that both sides (or all sides) can claim credit for having achieved their enactment. Greater specificity would make such varied claims impossible and so make enactment more difficult. This kind of ambiguity is innocuous if the differing subsequent interpretations are also innocuous, but it can be very dangerous to future coexistence if the differing subsequent interpretations cut anywhere near the core of the arrangements required to live together. Sometimes, the radical divergence in such views and their harmful effects cannot be foreseen, and ambiguity is embraced innocently as a way out of a logjam. This very lack of foreseeability makes it imperative not to opt for ambiguity on anything that might later lend itself to critical interpretive disagreement. It is preferable to argue about and record for posterity what is meant at the time of drafting rather than to open the way to—or, more cynically, to add an additional possibility for—disruptive disagreement, willful or otherwise, years or decades later.

Second, some members of the assembly or important constituents outside may reject a compromise, perhaps be outvoted, and later become constitutional revisionists. Compromise has to be extremely judicious and carefully worded in order not to create downstream problems of coherence and clarity, manifested specifically in problems of perverse constitutional interpretation by government officials, courts, and the public. Compromises sometimes open the way to ambiguity, but they require clarity so that they cannot be undone easily and so that actors belonging to a side that is later ascendant cannot chisel away at their meaning.

The history of article 153 is not in doubt. The problem was not ambiguity to cover disagreement but open-textured language whose meaning it was easy to misrepresent later. The cryptic phrasing comes from an earlier constitutional document of the late colonial period, the Federation of Malaya Agreement of 1948.[3] Nine years later, the report of the Reid Commission, the body appointed by the British colonial authorities to draft a constitution, stated that the privileges for Malays embodied in the special position clause should be temporary and be reviewed after fifteen years.[4] When the multiethnic Alliance coalition, which had an overwhelming majority of elected seats in the colonial legislature and would constitute the first post-independence government, objected to this time limit, it was dropped. Despite the "special position" language, the clear thrust of the deliberations was that, save four specific exceptions,[5] everyone was to have "equal rights, privileges and opportunities and there must not be discrimination on grounds of race or creed . . . ."[6] The prime minister-in-waiting, Tunku Abdul Rahman, leader of the largest party in the coalition, representing Malays, made it clear that it was not the intention of the Malays to "seize all rights for ourselves alone."[7]

Although the meaning of article 153 may have seemed settled at the time of its enactment, the consensus on it among some Malays

---

3. 1948 Federation of Malaya Agreement, art. 19(1)(f).

4. The privileges originally extended to four areas: certain lands where ownership was reserved to Malays, hiring quotas in the civil service, preferences in the allocation of taxi and road haulage licenses, and scholarships for higher education. *Report of the Federation of Malaya Constitutional Commission, 1957,* Colon. no. 330 (London: HMSO, 1957), para. 164. These should "gradually disappear." Ibid., para. 165. In the 1970s, however, a formal, full-blown program of ethnic preferences was produced for Malays and natives of the two Borneo states, who had been designated as indigenes and were therefore entitled to share in the privileges. Called initially the New Economic Policy, it has proved quite durable, in spite of criticism and changes of nomenclature.

5. See ibid.

6. The Alliance memorandum, quoted in ibid., para. 163.

7. Quoted in K.J. Ratnam, *Communalism and the Political Process in Malaya* (Kuala Lumpur: University of Malaya Press, 1965), p. 60.

was shallow.[8] With passing generations, article 153 and another provision of the Malaysian constitution, this one relating to religion,[9] have, more than a half century after their enactment, been at the center of very dangerous conflicts. When there is insufficient clarity, there is room for misinterpretation, whether willful or merely historically ignorant. Or, to put it more forcefully, when incentives for interethnic cooperation decline once a constitution is in force and it becomes expedient to deny what was agreed, greater clarity in the document can make denial harder and conciliatory constitutional bargains stickier. Constitution makers should be wary of "incompletely theorized agreements" that can cover over fundamental differences.[10] In severely divided societies, being theoryless on important institutions is to court danger.

Beginning in the 1980s, some Malay extremists, including several in the largest component of the coalition that ruled Malaysia until 2018, have contended that the "special position of the Malays" was not merely an acknowledgment that the Malays had not attained economic parity with their Chinese and Indian fellow citizens and could, on that ground, receive special help from government in the form of ethnically reserved opportunities. For those extremists, the special position clause was also intended to be a recognition of *ketuanan Melayu*, "Malay supremacy," a strong claim that diminishes

8. See ibid., pp. 59–60, 112–14; Fernando, *The Making of the Malayan Constitution*, pp. 76–84. After ethnic riots took place in 1969, the constitution was amended to allow parliament to enact restrictions that forbid public questioning of the special position of the Malays or the citizenship of the non-Malays, among other things. 1957 Constitution of Malaysia, as amended, art. 10. The Sedition Act was also so amended. Sedition Act of Malaysia, as amended, art. 3.

9. 1957 Constitution of Malaysia, as amended, art. 3(1). For the original meaning, quite clear from historical documents, and later challenges to that meaning, those intended to privilege Islam over other religions, see Dian A. H. Shah, *Constitutions, Religion, and Politics in Asia: Indonesia, Malaysia, and Sri Lanka* (Cambridge: Cambridge University Press, 2017), pp. 42–46, 59–60.

10. Cf. Cass Sunstein, *Designing Democracy: What Constitutions Do* (Oxford: Oxford University Press, 2001), p. 60.

the "legitimate interests" of the other communities and places their well-being at the sufferance of the Malays. After all, the *quid pro quo* for the clause was said to be liberalized citizenship provisions for Malaysian Chinese and Indians, many of whom were not yet citizens at the time of independence. The grant of citizenship, it is sometimes argued by those who favor an expansive reading of the special position provision, was the outer limit of generosity for descendants of Chinese and Indian "guests" who had been invited by the British during the colonial period, beginning in the nineteenth century. The sovereignty that was restored by decolonization was mainly, on this view, sovereignty for the Malays. For those who make this argument, citizenship means, implicitly and sometimes quite explicitly, second-class citizenship for non-Malays.

When the special position provision is considered in connection with its drafting history, there is clearly no support for this interpretation. But the clause on its face alone lends itself to expansion of the "special position" language at the expense of the "legitimate interests" language, or vice versa. On a matter like this, greater drafting clarity in the text could have produced less likelihood of adoption of the provision and perhaps impaired the whole structure of constitutional compromise. But this was improbable, as the Alliance and its Malay component were determined to produce a compromise. The more likely alternative is that greater textual clarity on the limited meaning of the special position provision would have produced a somewhat lower level of consensus among segments of the Malay public. And so a certain amount of apparent incoherence and less-than-optimal clarity was accepted for the sake of achieving compromise and a more or less broad consensus, at the risk, no doubt unforeseen, of interpretive difference and even serious trouble in the future. That trouble did, in fact, arrive.

There was trouble, too, over a similar compromise over the status of Islam as "the religion of the Federation," a clause, according to its proponents, that was by no means intended to create an Islamic state. On the contrary, Tunku Abdul Rahman himself stated that the intention was to create "a secular state," and the Pakistani commission member who had insisted on the clause declared it to be "innocuous."[11] The clause itself makes clear that religions other than Islam "may be practiced in peace and harmony in any part of the Federation."[12] Decades later, however, neither part of the clause retained the entire substance of its original meaning. Authoritative voices proclaimed Malaysia to be an Islamic state, and freedom of religion has been far from assured.[13] In later years, especially from 2013 to 2018, practitioners of minority religions were frequently subject to serious discrimination—and sometimes worse.[14] In retrospect, the risk of later misinterpretation, like the comparable risk in article 153, probably should not have been taken.[15]

There are comparable ambiguities in the 2014 Constitution of Tunisia, article 1 of which declares that the religion of Tunisia is Islam.[16] These words are verbatim from the secular independence constitution of 1959. The drafters have stated that this language is merely "descriptive" rather than "prescriptive."[17] Before the constitutional process, not everyone in Ennadha, the Islamic party, clearly favored a secular state. An earlier draft article, which had defined Islam as the state religion but had also described the state, confusingly, as a

---

11. Shah, *Constitutions, Religion, and Politics in Asia,* p. 46.

12. 1957 Constitution of Malaysia, as amended, art. 3(1).

13. See Patricia A. Martinez, "The Islamic State or the State of Islam in Malaysia," *Contemporary Southeast Asia,* Vol. 23, no. 3 (2001), pp. 474–503.

14. This category includes Bible seizures, removal of places of worship, and (although the culprits are unconfirmed and the cases unsolved) the organized disappearances of religious figures, one Shia Muslim and two evangelical Christians.

15. On the role of specificity in supporting the durability of constitutions, see Elkins, Ginsburg, and Melton, *Endurance of National Constitutions,* pp. 141, 208.

16. 2014 Constitution of Tunisia, art. 1. See Stepan, "Democracy with Democrats in Tunisia," pp. 28–29.

17. Stepan, "Democracy with Democrats in Tunisia," p. 29.

"civil" entity, was straightforwardly deleted after it had been heavily criticized.[18] Article 6 guarantees, in no uncertain terms, the freedom of religion but also speaks of "the protection of the sacred and the prohibition of any offenses thereto," possibly including blasphemy, a criminal prohibition of which had been deleted from an earlier draft following criticism and much soul searching within Ennahda itself.[19] (Despite the clear commitment to religious freedom in the Indonesian constitution, its Constitutional Court has upheld the validity of an earlier anti-blasphemy law, and prosecutions for that offense have proliferated since the constitutional revision.[20]) The same article 6 pledges that the state "undertakes to prohibit and fight against Takfir," meaning accusations of apostasy, which might lead to violence against anyone so accused.[21] In the face of these provisions potentially restricting speech, article 31 unequivocally provides for "freedom of expression."

As we observed in chapter 3, the Tunisian constitution overall was the result of a consensus on a mainly secular democratic regime, forged by deliberation and the actions of the Consensus Committee but supplemented by compromises along the way. The final product received close to unanimous support from secular and religious members of the assembly. Yet there is this residual, odd mix of provisions. Insufficiently developed or insufficiently articulated agreement can create ambiguity.

---

18. Monica Marks, "Convince, Coerce, or Compromise? Ennahda's Approach to Tunisia's Constitution," Brookings Institution Doha Center Analysis Paper no. 10, February 2014, p. 4.

19. Ibid., pp. 24–26.

20. Putusan No. 140/PUU-VII/2009 (Mahkamah Konstitusi Indonesia). For the religious freedom provisions, see 1945 Constitution of Indonesia, as amended, arts. 28E, 29(2). Nevertheless, the state is not wholly secular, because its foundation is said to rest on a belief in one God. See ibid., art. 29(1). For other problems of religious freedom, see Horowitz, *Constitutional Change and Democracy in Indonesia*, pp. 249–56.

21. Indeed, in the Assembly itself, a secular-leaning member had received death threats.

As the constitution developed over the course of two years, Ennahda withdrew its support for proposals to make Islam the basis of the state and Islamic law the foundation of the legal system as well as proposals to remove a guarantee of freedom of conscience from the document. After an angry reaction among secularists to an accusation by an Ennahda member of the assembly that another member was "an enemy of Islam," the party also assented to the anti-Takfir provision in article 6. All of these changes in the draft were supported by majority, albeit divided, votes by Ennahda members of the assembly.[22]

These were substantial concessions to secular ideals, but they reached a limit after the anti-Takfir provision was conceded. Left in place was "the protection of the sacred and the prohibition of any offenses thereto" in article 6. Considered in connection with article 6's guarantee of religious freedom and the guarantee of freedom of expression in article 31, this was an incoherent compromise. It was, however, a reflection of the point beyond which the most dedicated Islamists could not be pushed, once they had conceded on the three controversial provisions just described. This was especially the case after the prohibition of declarations of Takfir, for at that point Ennahda's initially strong negative reaction to the prohibition proposal precipitated a renegotiation of article 6 that created the confused product that article assuredly is.[23]

The view of article 6 as a compromise is supported by the strong vote in the National Constituent Assembly in favor of the article as a whole: 153 yes, 14 no, and 15 abstentions. That vote came near the end of the constitutional process. As the assembly moved through four drafts, various provisions reflected the rethinking of Ennahda's

22. Sharan Grewal, "From Islamists to Muslim Democrats: The Case of Tunisia's Ennahda," *American Political Science Review,* Vol. 114, no. 2 (2020), pp. 519–35.

23. Anna Guellali, "The Problem with Tunisia's New Constitution," *World Policy Journal,* February 3, 2014, https://WorldPolicy.org/2014/02/03/the-problem-with-Tunisias-new-constitution.

various segments, who during the previous authoritarian regime had not always had the freedom to deliberate together.[24] The ambiguities that remain comprise the residue of thinking that could not be dislodged, particularly in the light of the previous regime's long history of hostility to the religious piety of large numbers of its citizens.

Perhaps more deliberation and more attention to precise drafting could have narrowed the gaps within article 6 and between it and article 31, but the process had already consumed more time than originally envisioned, and feelings had become a bit raw by the time debate on article 6 had reached a sticking point. After the Egyptian coup of July 2013, it seemed increasingly dangerous to allow the Tunisian proceedings to drag on. The ultimate revision of article 6 began on January 5, 2014, and the final version was approved on January 23. Three days later, the whole constitutional process was concluded. Haste may not make waste, but it can leave ambiguities intact. These ambiguities regarding religion are, of course, especially dangerous, as we have just witnessed in Malaysia.

For Ennahda, a serious compromise concerned the structure of government rather than anything related to Islam. Because of the long history of strongman-autocratic regimes in Tunisia, Ennahda advocated a British-style parliamentary system. (Many of its leaders had been in exile in London.) Ennahda's opponents, from smaller parties, feared that Ennahda's strong electoral position, with 41 percent of the seats in the assembly and facing a more fragmented op-

24. In a sophisticated analysis, Grewal demonstrates the influence of Western democracy on those who had been exiled in Europe or America. Those in exile had had limited communication with those in Tunisia, who were imprisoned or were being closely watched by the security services. The result was limited intraparty debate before December 2011, when the regime was overthrown. Grewal, "From Islamists to Muslim Democrats." On questions of the kind raised by article 6, the party required and had vigorous debate. On others, however, such as the equality of women, little debate was needed. Ennahda quickly withdrew a clause that implied less than full equality and replaced it with an unequivocal declaration of full equality, elaborated in later drafts by strong protections for that equality. Marks, "Convince, Coerce, or Compromise?" pp. 22–24.

position, would permit it to dominate a parliamentary system. They therefore sought a balance in a strong presidency. Eventually, Ennahda was willing to support a mixed regime with a relatively weak president, but in the end it conceded a French-style arrangement, with a prime minister ("head of government") and a president with limited powers.[25] There was no real consensus on this: it was an unadorned compromise in which Ennahda made the concessions.[26]

So compromise can produce clarity, as it did in this instance, while strong attempts at consensus can leave ambiguities in place. Needless to say, ambiguities, whatever their source, are not limited to group differences over ethnicity or religion. They can involve some politically contentious questions of constitutional structure.[27] On sensitive matters agreed in a constitutional process, especially those pertaining to ethnicity or religion, clarity is an important quality.

Spain's territorial formula, or really formulae, are an excellent example.[28] The Spanish constitution, approved in a referendum in 1978, had been produced in a tumultuous process, marked by disagreements between right and left, most of which were compromised

25. 2014 Constitution of Tunisia, arts. 77–88, spelling out executive power in great detail.

26. Marks, "Convince, Coerce, or Compromise?" pp. 26–27. Cf. the Mongolian compromise on the same question in chapter 1, n. 10.

27. The 1995 Constitution of Ethiopia, art. 47(3), provides a clear process for creating new states that can automatically become members of the federation. Confronted with a strong demand from the Sidama people to separate their territory from the state in which it was embedded, the government of Ethiopia contended that this process was not sufficient but that a constitutional amendment, with more stringent procedures, would be required, because art. 47(1) lists the nine existing states of the federation and would have to be changed to list a tenth state. Yonathan Fessha, "Internal Secession and Federalism in Ethiopia," IACL-AIDC Blog, July 15, 2019. It seems obvious that the government's argument was a makeweight, but article 47 could be more explicit about the modification of subsection 1 by subsection 3. The Sidama did eventually vote overwhelmingly to secede from the state in which they were located.

28. My account of the Spanish process is drawn from Bonime-Blanc, *Spain's Transition to Democracy.*

when the two main parties were able to negotiate in those periods when quiet conditions prevailed.[29] The most troublesome issues concerned territorial autonomy, on which the right and the left did not quite see eye to eye, issues on which demands from the Basques proved particularly difficult.

After many long debates, punctuated by violence in the Basque country, what emerged was described as "a regionizable unitary state,"[30] namely a unitary state in which regional governments could be formed. Through some very convoluted processes, autonomy could be realized for communities as large as a recognized region of Spain, but the powers were fairly limited and hedged with central government controls and discretion.[31] What a region could expect by way of autonomy was hardly certain, and none of the drafters who agreed to the mix of powers and restraints was satisfied with the formula (if such complexity can be called that).[32] Yet there was, at the end, rather broad agreement on the constitution as a whole in the legislature. The Basques in parliament did not vote in favor, however, and most Basques abstained in the subsequent referendum.

Spain's most serious difficulties regarding regionalism arose four decades later. Ironically enough, the difficult demands came from Catalans rather than Basques. The problems were compounded by the central government's resort to the powers and controls it contended it possessed under the territorial formula. Andrea Bonime-Blanc put her finger on the underlying problem, which was "the mediocrity and ambiguity of the formula. Some of the provisions, often filled with superfluous detail, left substantial questions

29. See ibid., pp. 54–62.

30. Ibid., p. 84.

31. See the rather prolix provisions of the 1978 Constitution of Spain, as amended, arts. 145–57. See also ibid., pp. 81–88.

32. Bonime-Blanc, *Spain's Transition to Democracy*, p. 87.

to be resolved by future organic laws."[33] The hard-fought battles in the legislature over the territorial allocation of power had produced dual powers with uncertain boundaries that augured future conflict, as Bonime-Blanc correctly predicted.[34] Complexity resulting from compromise can result in ambiguity, and the combination can impair coherence.

Coherence, clarity, compromise, and consensus are a difficult mix to optimize, as the Malaysian, Tunisian, and Spanish examples show. Lack of clarity can facilitate achievement of consensus in the constitutional process but can foster declining consensus over time and can help to undo important compromises. Multiple compromises can aid in producing agreement on the document as a whole, but at the expense of clarity and coherence. If three of the four are achieved, the one likely to suffer is coherence of the constitutional scheme, which can sometimes be suffused with contradictions and provisions that point in different directions. This is a tendency exacerbated by the presence of many hands in drafting or drafters who are aiming in different directions.

There are several audiences for constitutional drafters to consider. Two of the most important are politicians and judges.[35] Politicians may be the bigger threat, but judges can be their collaborators or enablers. Drafters who distrust the interpretive fidelity of judges, as Rosalind Dixon points out,[36] tend to write lengthy, quite specific

33. Ibid. Pages 86–87 refer to possible contradictions between articles 148 and 149.

34. Ibid., p. 90.

35. On the willful misinterpretation of Burundi's constitution by its president in order to secure a third term, see Ken O. Opalo, "Constitutional Protections of Electoral Democracy in Africa," in *Annual Review of Constitution-Building Processes: 2015*, ed. Bisarya, pp. 15–30, at p. 19. On the interpretive laxity of judges, see Shah, *Constitutions, Religion, and Politics in Asia*, pp. 173–203.

36. Dixon, "Constitutional Drafting and Distrust," *International Journal of Constitutional Law*, Vol. 13, no. 4 (2015), pp. 819–46.

constitutions in order to dictate subsequent judicial interpretation. The drafters of India's constitution distrusted judges and produced a comprehensive document. South Africa's drafters, by contrast, trusting a newly created constitutional court, wrote more sparingly. Efforts to tie the hands of judges through specificity may achieve the opposite of their intended result. The more specific their language, the more that judges may find that some unforeseen situation—which, had they foreseen it, the drafters might have included in the provision at issue—is excluded by the very specificity of the language used by the drafters.[37] Since drafting based on distrust can actually engender untrustworthy interpretation, Dixon urges drafting in a relatively open-textured, framework-oriented way.

The problem is different, as Dixon acknowledges, when compromise has been negotiated to protect people against action by their opponents and, we may add, when the rule of law is not reliably established. In those circumstances, specificity is demanded. It is not surprising, as Yash Ghai points out, that many Asian and African constitutions are suffused with detail.[38]

One somewhat unconventional way to attain specificity is by embedding the aims of the provision explicitly in the text. With ethnic compromises in severely divided societies, clarity can become an overriding objective. But, of course, fidelity to any compromise can be difficult to achieve if followers are determined not to adhere to the consensus achieved by leaders or if later generations decide to undo it because their commitment was not forged in the experience of accommodation that accompanied constitution making. In severely divided societies, reneging on fundamental bargains is hardly unknown, as balances of power among ethnic groups and parties

---

37. Dixon points to the maxim of statutory interpretation that states that if one thing is mentioned in a law, others are, by implication, excluded: *expressio unius est exclusio alterius*.

38. Ghai, "A Journey Around Constitutions: Reflecting on Contemporary Constitutions," *South African Law Journal*, Vol. 22, no. 4 (2005), pp. 804–31.

change and some actors decide to use their advantage to defect from the constitutional consensus.

A common aphorism states that one generation should not dictate to the next. On many matters, this is true. But when political commitments have been made and relied upon, and the next generation of one side in a conflict decides to unsettle them, a different principle comes into play: mutuality. If a formula has been found for peaceful accommodation of ethnic claims within an agreed set of constitutional provisions, the reliability of commitments becomes exceptionally important. This is particularly the case if the claims of the defectors are ethnically skewed and disruptive, as they often are.

Of course, if the constitution contains *so much* clarity—or, really, specificity—that, as conditions change, the provisions have become too rigid or demonstrably unfair, it may be time for some redeliberation and renegotiation. That is a different matter from the opportunistic reneging just described. Of course, durability, standing alone, is not the highest goal, particularly in severely divided societies; conflict reduction and democracy are. Some constitutions that endure can lose their integrity as they are undermined along the way on crucial points previously agreed.

I have already suggested that a mix of arguing and bargaining is desirable as well as inevitable in constitutional processes. Arguing implies exposure of the implications of alternative choices respecting institutions and formulations to describe constitutional choices. Arguing assumes the possibility of persuasion. Persuasion can create agreement—even consensus—and, hopefully, commitment to what has been agreed. Furthermore, arguing is also important because the careful choice of institutions can help severely divided societies cope with their problems and because, if everything is left to bargaining, a stronger party may prevail over a weaker one.

On one set of issues, excessive bargaining can easily produce incoherence. That bargaining concerns the main political institutions put in place to govern severely divided societies. There are divergent approaches to institutional choice. One, called consociational, is based on elaborate minority guarantees: proportional participation in an inclusive government, maximal cultural autonomy, proportional financial allocations, and even a minority veto on ethnic issues. Another, generally referred to as centripetal, is predicated on the need for incentives, usually in the electoral system, to produce a politics of moderation and compromise and a voluntary interethnic majority-coalition government, rather than a mandatorily inclusive government not limited to moderates and not deriving from a preelectoral interethnic coalition.[39] Mixing the two approaches can sometimes create an incoherent hybrid, in which one institution can work against another. We shall see an example of this shortly in the case of Fiji.

More generally, all institutional choices are related to others in a constitution, and coherence among them must be a prominent goal of a constitutional process. If drafting is done by a commission, legislature, committee, or constituent assembly and then reviewed by another body, perhaps a legislature or legislative committee, there is a strong need for great care when the later body reviews the work of the earlier, lest two conflicting objectives be imported into the product. Often it seems that when a commission or other body spends a great deal of time studying and deliberating about institutions for a new constitution and then presents a fully elaborated document for review by an assembly or legislature, the reviewing committee to which it is assigned may be accorded relatively little time to study the proposals and may do so in the absence of those who prepared them. Such a reviewing body may make major changes it regards as

39. On the two approaches, see Arend Lijphart, *Democracy in Plural Societies* (New Haven: Yale University Press, 1977); Donald L. Horowitz, "Constitutional Design: Proposals Versus Processes," in *Architecture of Democracy*, ed. Reynolds, pp. 15–36. See also Horowitz, "Conciliatory Institutions and Constitutional Processes in Post-Conflict States," *William and Mary Law Review*, Vol. 49, no. 4 (March 2008), pp. 1213–48.

essential or changes it conceives of as minor tweaks to mitigate some discontent. In fact, however, such changes may introduce serious incoherence into the document. Ironically, this can happen when the reviewing body finds the text generally acceptable and so spends much less time reviewing its implications than the original drafters did creating it.

A serious problem arises when the reviewing body, assured of majority support, neglects the interests—or sets out to impair the interests—of a group whose support is not necessary to the majority in favor of the draft being reviewed. Closed-door negotiations to review a draft, especially when the review is rushed, create dangers of neglect of this kind or of outright rent seeking, in addition to the danger of provisions that do not work well together.

Consider the creation of the 2010 Kenyan constitution.[40] The background to the new constitution was the horrific ethnic violence that followed the 2007 national election, in which the chair of the electoral commission announced the winner before he had any idea who the actual winner was and after which an independent commission of inquiry concluded that the commission had failed miserably in performing its duties.[41] An attempt to adopt a new constitution had failed in a referendum in 2005, when more than half of the political elite organized against it. Following the 2007–08 violence, politicians agreed to produce a new constitution, under procedures

40. See Charles O. Oyayo and Nana Poku, *The Making of the Constitution of Kenya* (New York: Routledge, 2018); Eric Kramon and Daniel L. Posner, "Kenya's New Constitution," *Journal of Democracy*, Vol. 22, no. 2 (2011), pp. 89–103; Christina Murray, "Kenya's 2010 Constitution," in *Constitution Making*, ed. Sujit Choudhry and Tom Ginsburg (Cheltenham, U.K.: Elgar, 2016), pp. 707–48. (In late 2009 and early 2010, I was a member of a committee that reviewed several drafts by bodies described in the text. The committee was organized at the initiative of the International Development Law Organization in Rome. In several memoranda, our group did suggest some redrafting, but none of our work concerned constitutional process.)

41. Report of the Review Commission on the General Elections Held in Kenya on 27th December, 2007, Nairobi, September 17, 2008.

established by a Constitution of Kenya Review Act 2008, and they kept their word, but the manner in which they did so was flawed.

The process involved a Committee of Experts consisting of six Kenyans and three foreigners, operating under directions from the legislature. The CoE was to harmonize previous constitutional drafts, identify contentious issues, conduct a public consultation, and then present a new draft constitution to a parliamentary select committee of twenty-seven members who were to resolve contentious issues and return the draft to the CoE for a revision based on the new agreement. That version was then to be approved or amended by parliament and finally submitted to a referendum. "In the new process," comments Christina Murray, a member of the CoE, "legitimacy was to be secured primarily through the credibility of decision-making by the [two parties that were] coalition partners."[42]

In the first phase, the CoE engaged in a very modest amount of deliberation. It had been enjoined by the statute that created it to harmonize the provisions of earlier drafts, the last of which had failed in the referendum of 2005.[43] This role, of course, limited the CoE's ability to consider many matters afresh. It was appointed in February 2009 and published its draft in November of that year. The draft was a great improvement on the existing constitution, containing as it did rights provisions and checks and balances. Once the 2009 draft was published, there was then a one-month period for public review and comment, by the end of which the CoE had received 39,439 written submissions containing 1,732,386 recommendations.[44] The CoE took a mere three weeks to review submissions (obviously, highly selectively), following which it submitted its report to the multiparty Parliamentary Select Committee, which had jurisdiction to review and amend the draft.

42. Murray, "Kenya, 2008–2010," p. 10.

43. Constitution of Kenya Review Act, 2008, sec. 23.

44. Report of the Committee of Experts on Constitutional Review, Nairobi, January 8, 2010, p. 5.

That review allowed three weeks but actually was finished in less time.[45] During that brief period, the PSC made very significant revisions to the revised CoE draft, including a change from a mainly parliamentary system, eliminating the prime minister altogether, to a presidential system, with strong powers for the chief executive of the kind that autocratic Kenyan presidents had previously enjoyed, but with new safeguards. (A strong presidency was a high priority for the incumbent and his party, and they later utilized the Provincial Administration, now called the National Administration, to escape some of those safeguards.[46]) The PSC also altered the powers of the upper house that was to represent the forty-seven counties that enjoyed new, devolved powers, and it changed revenue arrangements. It eliminated an Ethics and Anti-Corruption Commission, added eighty new legislative seats, mainly to rectify malapportionment,[47] and revised and removed a number of rights provisions in the CoE draft. All that and more in about two weeks of intensive closed-door negotiation!

The new draft then returned to the CoE, which was accorded an additional three weeks to do some redrafting, but it was warned not to tamper with the "deals" to which politicians had agreed in the PSC.[48] Those deals between former opponents were sufficient to secure passage in the required referendum but, in certain respects, perhaps sufficient also to assure the opposition of a prominent ethnic group whose support was not necessary to victory in the referendum to follow. According to the Hansard of the meeting between the PSC and the CoE, important deals pertained to the additional

---

45. The PSC discussions ended later than contemplated, but they had actually started later as well.

46. Mai Hassan, "Continuity Despite Change: Kenya's New Constitution and Executive Power," *Democratization*, Vol. 22, no. 4 (2015), pp. 587–609.

47. Many of the public recommendations that were submitted to the CoE had actually expressed a preference for fewer seats. Report of the Committee of Experts on Constitutional Review, January 8, 2010, p. 10.

48. Murray, "Kenya's 2010 Constitution," p. 716.

legislative seats and the limited functions to be accorded to the upper house, a compromise between those who wanted no such house and those who wanted one.[49] The shift to a strictly presidential system was also subject to considerable logrolling.[50] It was clearly favored by the sitting president, but in the end also by his opponent in the most recent presidential election, who managed to secure acceptance of considerable devolution.[51] Their agreement made the PSC deal possible.

Three weeks later, the CoE submitted a slimmed-down revision of the whole constitution to the National Assembly, which, for thirty days, entertained a plethora of amendments, not one of which passed. The constitution was approved in a referendum three months after that.

One important prohibition is found in the constitution. As mentioned, the constitution devolves power to forty-seven counties, but it prohibits the formation of ethnically based or regional parties.[52] Counties are, therefore, to be governed by members of the main national parties, and the Senate, which is to represent county interests, is expected to do so through those same parties. That local or ethnic-minority interests can be protected in this way is highly problematic.[53] Many counties are ethnically plural, and Kenya has,

---

49. Hansard, *Verbatim Record of Committee of Experts on Constitutional Review Meeting with the Parliamentary Select Committee Held on 16th February 2010*, Nairobi, 2010, pp. 47, 64–66, 101.

50. Abrak Saati, "Technocratic, Representative, and Participatory Constitution-Making in Kenya," paper presented at the American Political Science Association annual meeting, 2019, p. 17.

51. And also softened his opposition to a strong presidency that he probably thought might be his after the next election. On the PSC deals, see Kramon and Posner, "Kenya's New Constitution."

52. 2010 Constitution of Kenya, arts. 91(1)(a), 91(2)(a).

53. Indonesia, too, devolved power to regions but prohibited ethnic and regional parties and raised the national threshold for representation in order to limit the number of parties, thereby depriving some local communities of representation by two parties (one of them Muslim, one Christian) that were strong at the local

before and after the adoption of the 2010 constitution, experienced bouts of ethnic cleansing and violence at the local level.[54] Some local chief executives have attempted to homogenize their counties.

In addition to conflicts over local ethnic disputes concerning who belongs in a local area, there is a serious risk deriving from the fact that the 2010 constitution requires a successful presidential candidate to secure, in addition to an overall majority, one-fourth of the votes cast in at least half the forty-seven counties. This centripetal provision was added by the Parliamentary Select Committee at the same time as it rejected the CoE proposal for a semi-presidential system with a mainly ceremonial president.[55] In the 1992 election, when territorial distribution of the vote for president was required in five of the eight provinces, there had been considerable violence and ethnic cleansing against groups of people unlikely to vote for a particular presidential candidate in certain provinces. Counties are much smaller units and much easier to cleanse, at least sufficiently to reduce votes for opponents. In view of Kenya's then-recent history of ethnic violence connected with the 2007 election, prominently including targeting so-called settlers of Kikuyu origin in the Rift Valley, too little consideration was afforded by the PSC to the likely ethnic dynamics of devolution in the light of constitutional provisions for electing the president.

I recognize that I have veered off from considerations of process to matters of conflict reduction, but not to advocate here one view

level but too weak nationally to survive the higher threshold. See Horowitz, *Constitutional Change and Democracy in Indonesia*, pp. 187, 202.

54. Gabrielle Lynch and David M. Anderson, "Democratization and Ethnic Violence in Kenya," in *Democratization and Ethnic Minorities*, ed. Jacques Bertrand and Oded Haklai (New York: Routledge, 2014), pp. 83–102; Ngala Chome, "Violent Extremism and Clan Dynamics in Kenya," *Peaceworks*, no. 123, U.S. Institute of Peace, Washington, DC, October 2016.

55. Report of the Parliamentary Select Committee on the Review of the Constitution on the Reviewed Harmonised Draft Constitution, Kenya National Assembly, Nairobi, January 29, 2010, p. 9.

of conflict reduction measures over another. Rather, my point is only that the process can have profound effects on the interrelation of provisions intended, as territorial distribution of the vote is, for broad electoral appeals to facilitate conflict reduction. And I have mentioned the interconnection of only three sets of quite fundamental changes in the constitution that may not quite cohere and, at worst, may facilitate violence: provisions about parties, devolution, and presidential electoral requirements. But, of course, at the PSC stage, coherence was not the highest priority: the deal was.

Notice how little time was devoted to multiple changes that were made in a draft that had taken many months to produce: a brief period of straightforward negotiation by the Parliamentary Select Committee, followed by reconsideration by the CoE, which decided that some of the PSC changes were not in conformity with the law governing the creation of the new constitution but did indeed leave the main elements of the PSC deal in place. This stunted process after the conclusion of the longer process in the CoE's first round was conducive only to bargaining and inadequate for deliberation. It is notable that members of four of the five largest ethnic groups later voted in favor of the constitution in the referendum, while the fifth, the formerly ascendant Kalenjin under the presidency of Daniel arap Moi (1978–2002), campaigned and voted against it. The PSC deal was adequate to join former Kikuyu and Luo opponents together in a strong coalition in support of the constitution, but certain aspects of the new dispensation alienated Kalenjin.[56]

At the PSC stage, it appears that Kalenjin did not formally oppose the draft, but former president Moi and the leading Kalenjin politician, William Ruto, campaigned vigorously against it at the

56. Interestingly enough, however, in the 2013 election, the previous uneasy coalition, led by Kikuyu and Luo, did not survive. A Kikuyu presidential candidate and a Kalenjin vice-presidential candidate (William Ruto) teamed up to defeat the same Luo presidential candidate who had lost the 2007 election and had concurred in the final version of the 2010 constitution that Kalenjin had opposed.

referendum stage. The reasons were quite similar to, but perhaps a bit broader than, their opposition to the 2005 draft. Kalenjin favored devolution to provinces, large units in which their interests could be defended, especially in the Rift Valley province, more effectively than in multiple counties where Kalenjin reside but might form only a minority in some. They also preferred a parliamentary regime, rather than a strongman presidency they would not be likely to control. Both of these were reasons for Kalenjin to dislike where the PSC had come down. But the major reason concerned the provisions relating to land and fears about their position in the country.[57]

Land had been a favorite currency of patronage during successive Kikuyu and Kalenjin presidencies. The Kalenjin are rural people, apprehensive about the security of their possession of land. In 1992–93, a significant number of non-Kalenjin were evicted violently from the Rift Valley, where Kalenjin are concentrated and consider themselves to be indigenous occupants threatened especially by Kikuyu "guests." After the violence, patterns of land ownership were apparently altered to the advantage of Kalenjin who were in a position to buy land from those unable to return to it.[58] The post-electoral violence of 2007 was, in some ways, a repeat performance, except that now a Kikuyu president had succeeded Moi and created fear among Kalenjin that the government would punish them and ignore the interests of "the rightful owners of the land" in favor of "outsiders" in need of land.[59] During the regime of President Mwai Kibaki,

57. For discussions of this aspect of ethnic politics and the constitution, I am indebted to close observers in Kenya and elsewhere. Certain Christian groups also opposed the constitution for quite different reasons.

58. Gilbert M. Khadiagala, "Constitutional Design and Conflict Management: Kenya," paper presented at the conference on Constitutional Design and Conflict Management, University of Texas, May 2011, p. 10.

59. Gabrielle Lynch, *I Say to You: Ethnic Politics and the Kalenjin in Kenya* (Chicago: University of Chicago Press, 2011), pp. 198–204; David Anderson and Gabrielle Lynch, "Autochthony, Indigeneity, and the Politics of Identity on Mount Elgon, Kenya," paper presented at the conference on Democratization and Ethnic Communities, University of Toronto, April 17–18, 2009.

beginning in 2002, Kalenjin had felt poorer, less respected, and more vulnerable to usurpation of land by some of Kibaki's Kikuyu followers than they had been under Moi's presidency,[60] when some politically influential Kalenjin had acquired valuable tracts of land. In 2010, they feared being left out of the emerging governing coalition that was apparently solidified in the PSC deal, which would leave them even more vulnerable to land grabs and to what Gabrielle Lynch identifies in her work on the Kalenjin as a strong feeling of status reversal from the period of Moi's ascendancy.[61]

The 2005 draft constitution rejected in the referendum of that year had contained a chapter on land that Kalenjin found quite dangerous. The government was accorded broad powers over land allocation and regulation. One provision declared that the government "shall prescribe minimum and maximum land holding acreage in arable areas."[62] In the CoE, there was a brief but unsuccessful attempt to modify the breadth of this power.[63] The 2010 draft had the same provision, but without the qualification pertaining to arable land, substituting the phrase "private land,"[64] a change made by the CoE.

Kalenjin opposition to the 2010 constitution proceeded from a by-then durable sense of ethnic bias against their group. In 2005, they had already seen the final draft produced by Attorney General

60. For these sentiments, see Lynch, *I Say to You*, pp. 195–97 et passim. See also the caustic and pointed remark of the chair of the CoE in the foreword to that body's final report: "Such opposition was to be expected from the owners of obscenely vast tracts of land acquired fraudulently and corruptly through abuse of office by previous regimes." Final Report of the Committee of Experts on Constitutional Review, Nairobi, October 11, 2010, p. 9.

61. Lynch, *I Say to You*, p. 195.

62. Republic of Kenya, Proposed New Constitution of Kenya, August 22, 2005 [Wako Draft], Kenya Gazette Supplement, no. 63, art. 86(1)(l).

63. Some of the resistance to modification derived from the role of H.W.O. Okoth-Ogendo, a respected expert on land law at the University of Nairobi, in framing the original provisions of the chapter in the 2002–04 period.

64. 2010 Constitution of Kenya, art. 68(c)(1).

Amos Wako as allowing "further Kikuyu encroachment onto land in the Rift Valley" by opening up "unutilized arable land."[65] The change in wording to "private land" in 2010 was not reassuring. Complaints about loose drafting that could enable the state to seize private land featured prominently in the campaign by land owners in the Rift Valley. The rectification of what were called historical injustices in land allocation was seen as aimed at those who had acquired land under the Moi regime. A year earlier, some Kikuyu politicians were heard to vow that power should never again fall to a hostile regime.[66] The mix of Kikuyu resentment, constitutional provisions that would reduce Kalenjin power to defend their interests,[67] and the apprehended insecurity of land title all fed "an ever-evolving persecution complex"[68] among Kalenjin that alienated them from the new constitutional dispensation.

And so a process with little real deliberation, culminating in a quick deal, had two potentially adverse consequences. In future presidential elections, a presidential electoral formula requiring distribution of the winner's vote at the county level risked facilitating further ethnic cleansing. The design of devolution and the open-ended land clauses that seemed aimed at reducing the advantages of an ethnic group already experiencing a bout of extreme defensiveness risked further destabilization of the sort Kenya had recently experienced. The PSC may not have experienced open dissensus, but this was far from a process geared toward broad consensus.[69]

---

65. Gabrielle Lynch, "The Fruits of Perception: 'Ethnic Politics' and the Case of Kenya's Constitutional Referendum," *African Studies,* Vol. 65, no. 2 (2006), pp. 233–70, at pp. 258, 259.

66. See Lynch, *I Say to You,* p. 223. Such statements recall the oathing that took place in the late 1960s that was intended to solidify Kikuyu determination not to let power pass from Kikuyu to Luo (or any other) hands.

67. Specifically, devolution to counties. Ibid., pp. 186, 213.

68. Ibid., p. 212.

69. The threats to Kalenjin landholding interests did not materialize, at least in the short run. See Catherine Boone et al., "Land Law Reform in Kenya: Devolution, Veto Players, and the Limits of an Institutional Fix," *African Affairs,* vol. 118, no. 471

Now turn briefly to Fiji (1997), which went through a simplified version of a similar process, with a legislative committee reviewing an elaborate commission report on a new constitution, thereby introducing two major anomalies into the draft constitution. In the Fiji Parliamentary Select Committee, too, there was negotiated agreement between politicians of different groups—a well-intended agreement, perhaps, but one that adversely affected some central features of the constitutional design.

The Fiji Constitution Review Commission was appointed in March 1995 and rendered its 790-page report, including a draft constitution, in September 1996. The commission consisted of a Fijian member, an Indian (that is, Indo-Fijian) member, and a chair from New Zealand who had previously served as archbishop and then governor-general of that country. The commission was supported by a very able senior staff. Commission members were few, but they were in touch with members of their communities in Fiji as they deliberated on the document to be presented.

(2019), pp. 215–37. But another threat did. Perhaps surprisingly in the face of Kikuyu-Kalenjin animosities, the ruling party's successful ticket in 2013 and again in 2017 included as vice-president the same William Ruto who had opposed the 2010 constitution. The widely accepted idea was that Ruto would be the designated successor to the Kikuyu president, Uhuru Kenyatta, in 2022. Kalenjin had supported the ticket in both previous elections, on the understanding that the favor would be returned when, after two terms, Kenyatta was no longer eligible for reelection. By 2020, however, doubts about the succession appeared as Kenyatta distanced himself from Ruto. Speculation arose that the deal would not be honored and that Kikuyu would not support any non-Kikuyu for president. Cf. the oathing referred to in note 66. The result was a revival of serious tension between the two groups. Narrelle Gilchrist, "Succession Politics and the Renewed Threat of Ethnic Violence in Kenya," www.lawfareblog.com/succession-politics-and-renewed-threat-ethnic-violence-Kenya, March 20, 2020. The danger of ethnic violence is omnipresent. In 2017, during a divisive local election campaign, there were incitements to killing in the ethnically mixed Rift Valley. It was one thing to have a powerful presidency and county-level devolution when Kalenjin were included in the regime, but quite another if they were not.

Among the commission's many recommendations was one for a new electoral system, based on an Australian model, designed to foster interethnic accommodation between the two largest ethnic groups, Fijians and Indians in Fiji. To make the new electoral system work as intended, the commission recommended that Fiji dramatically reduce the number of legislative seats in which only members of only one ethnic group were qualified to stand for election and only members of the same group were qualified to vote for candidates of that group. This type of arrangement is usually called reserved seats with communal rolls. Fiji had never elected all candidates on a common electoral roll, with any candidate of any group qualified to run in any seat and any voter of any group qualified to vote for any candidate running in a constituency in which the voter was registered. To facilitate the creation of interethnic coalitions that could pool their votes and elect moderate candidates, the commission proposed that there should be forty-five such open seats and, for a transitional period, a reduced number of ethnically reserved seats, twenty-five to be exact, for a total house of seventy. For the rest, Westminster rules for forming governments would apply. The largest party or coalition would ordinarily form the government after the election. It was anticipated by the commission that the government would be a coalition and that its composition would be multiethnic.

By Fijian standards, these were major changes in reserved seat arrangements, but the original impetus to create a new constitution had come from a de facto interethnic coalition,[70] which had expected

70. Technically, there was no interethnic "coalition," but, in the 1990s, a Fijian-party minority government was being supported by an Indian party in opposition on condition that a constitutional review be launched, as indeed it then was. The expectation was that these two parties would cooperate in elections that followed, which they later did, but rather poorly and ineffectively, for reasons that need not detain us here.

to benefit from any changes. So, although the commission's specific proposals were not anticipated, the idea of parties lining up to contest seats together was not far-fetched under the circumstances, and it was carefully developed in the commission report.[71] When the report was submitted to parliament, it was, like the Kenyan report, sent to a parliamentary select committee for review.

A sticking point revolved around the electoral provisions. The crucial talks were conducted principally by a Fijian member of the ruling party and an Indian member of the opposition. Fijians were especially fearful of losing seats reserved to them and their voters. Indians, too, were unsure of being on the winning side under the new system. Although they had long favored open seats, they wanted some assurance that they would not be a minority in perpetual opposition.

So, while Fijians preferred no open seats, Indians were happy to have all forty-five open seats, but they wanted a guarantee that they would be in government. Accordingly, there was a deal. The two sides agreed to reverse the commission's seat apportionment. Adding a seat for a total of seventy-one, rather than the commission's seventy, it was agreed that there would be forty-six reserved seats and only twenty-five open ones. In the open seats, but in those alone, votes could be pooled by coalition partners across group lines to achieve the commission's desired effect on intergroup moderation and compromise. (In fact, only some of these were truly ethnically heterogeneous and conducive to pooling votes across

71. Towards a United Future: Report of the Fiji Constitution Review Commission, 1996, Parliament of Fiji, Parliamentary Paper No. 34 of 1996 (Suva: Government Printing Department, 1996), pp. 304–64. (In the early stages of its work, I was a consultant to the commission, and I recommended an electoral system, a version of which the commission later recommended. With the help of Australian advisors, the Fiji government implemented that system but significantly modified it in certain ways, some of which are described below. The system as implemented and its electoral results proved controversial for reasons different from those germane to this discussion. I have written elsewhere in response those controversies.)

group lines.) There was later a minor dispute about how many reserved seats each group would be allocated, but in the end no dispute about reversing the commission's allocation. And then, in order to be sure that Indians would be in government, just in case they were not in the winning coalition, it was agreed that any party with as little as 10 percent of the seats would be entitled to sit in the cabinet.

The deal was the result of a private conversation between a Fijian in the ruling party and an Indo-Fijian during a grog session.[72] The Indo-Fijian asked for places in government so as to facilitate interethnic rule, presumably to guard against an unfavorable electoral result. In return, he offered to agree to fewer open seats and more reserved seats, thereby allaying Fijian apprehensions about open seats. The Fijian thought this a sensible exchange. Out of this conversation grew the reversal of the proportion of open and reserved seats and the provision for cabinet access based on the 10 percent standard. The PSC accepted the deal, put it on paper, and passed it on to the legislature. Two bowls of grog, and the deal was done.

In the end, this exchange became the basis of two amendments that the legislature made to the commission's plan. Both produced criticism from the most knowledgeable people concerned with creation of the constitution, because they undermined the constitutional plan.

The 10 percent cabinet membership provision would allow an extremist party with a small fraction of support into a cabinet designed to foster interethnic moderation, and it was not popular with those who understood the commission's approach to intergroup accommodation. Professor Yash Ghai, who had represented the two Indian parties before the commission, criticized it for its likely effect

72. Grog is a common beverage in Fiji prepared by mixing water with powder derived from the kava plant. My account here is based on interviews I conducted in Suva in 1999.

on a cabinet intended to be composed of moderates dedicated to interethnic accommodation.[73]

More broadly and more sharply, Alison Quentin-Baxter, the senior legal counsel to the commission, who was most heavily involved in drafting the commission report and the proposed constitution, found both changes by the PSC to be in derogation of the central intentions of the commission in proposing the electoral arrangements, in particular its recommendations that "The primary goal of Fiji's constitutional arrangements should be to encourage the emergence of multiethnic government," and that "The people of Fiji should move gradually but decisively away from the communal system of representation."[74] The hope of a multiethnic coalition had been based a preponderance of open seats that the PSC deal drastically reduced. In 2002, Quentin-Baxter published an article on her constitution-drafting experience, in which she criticized the PSC's changes. The commission, she wrote,

> saw each part of the Constitution as load-bearing. All its parts were essential to carry the weight of the structure as a whole. Accordingly, the Commission recommended that approximately two-thirds of the seats should be open to candidates from any community, elected by the voters of all communities, but, as a transitional measure, approximately one third of the seats should be reserved for particular communities. Neither the Government, nor the Opposition members of Parliament, were ready to contemplate such a large departure from the existing political culture. The 1997 Constitution reverses the [commission's] recommended proportions of communal and open seats, but seeks to compensate for this timidity by introducing, against the [commission's] recommendation, the con-

73. Yash Ghai, "The Implementation of the Fiji Islands Constitution," in *Confronting Fiji Futures,* ed. A. Haroon Akram-Lodhi (Suva: University of the South Pacific Centre for Arts and Culture, 1998), pp. 21–49, at pp. 33, 36, 41. This criticism highlights the hazards of adding a consociational guarantee into a system designed to produce centripetal incentives for moderation.

74. *Towards a United Future,* Recommendations nos. 1, 4, p. 673.

> troversial provision that all parties with ten percent or more of the seats in the House of Representatives are entitled to be represented in the Cabinet. This retention, and even accentuation, of conflicting electoral incentives threatens the stability of the whole Constitution.[75]

The constitution did indeed prove unstable in the end, for the government elected under it, whose complexion would almost certainly have been different under the earlier allocation between open and reserved seats, was overthrown in a paramilitary putsch in 2000. Only years later was the constitution itself superseded by one drafted under the auspices of a military-dominant regime.

What needs to be stressed here is that review processes in legislatures are likely to be less deliberative than when they themselves act as drafting bodies, particularly if reviews are conducted hastily and secretively. Legislators acting as reviewers of a draft that is the product of a deliberative process, as the Kenyan and Fijian ones were, are likely to be oriented toward deal-making, as they seek to adjust the constitution to their interests and get it over the finish line. In the course of focusing on particular provisions that some prefer and others do not, they may easily see the makings of a deal by which they can accommodate each other and allay their separate concerns about prospects under the new constitution. Ironically, as the Fiji case especially shows, major incompatibilities can be introduced into the text by gestures of mutual goodwill. Bargaining in circumstances in which the effects of a deal cannot be scrutinized carefully makes review processes more prone to hazards of anomalies, inconsistencies, and unseen problems imported into the text.

It is not, of course, that there is no bargaining in legislative proceedings at the earlier drafting stage. As I have said earlier, there is and very often needs to be. But the focus on the big picture that

75. Alison Quentin-Baxter, "Making Constitutions, from the Perspective of a Constitutional Adviser," *Victoria University of Wellington Law Review,* Vol. 33, nos. 3/4 (2002), pp. 661–96, at p. 685 (footnotes omitted).

occupies drafters at that stage also—and, one hopes, principally—inclines participants to deliberation about what institutions would serve the country well, be publicly acceptable, and not impair the coherence of the constitutional plan. When it comes to the final stages, when the general outlines of the constitution seem clear, and especially when time is limited, politicians are likely to focus on gains they might make and losses they find it hard to accept. By then they have more visibility about how the new arrangements will probably advantage and disadvantage them. And if the effective body of decision makers is a small and secretive one, deals may be easier to consummate at the expense of others or of the constitutional design.

The elected body, of course, must have the last word if there is no referendum, which is all the more reason for lack of haste in its deliberations and those of its committees that review constitutional drafts. The review, if it is brief, may have rough edges and usually could benefit from a review of its own, by the legislature in public, or at least it ought to have a consultant at the table who is familiar with the drafters' original intention, so as to minimize potential inconsistencies. Otherwise, compromise to serve particular political interests of the moment can easily defeat coherence.

All constitutional bodies must make room for negotiation leading to compromise. Yet, as we have just seen, there are hazards to secret bargaining at the end of a constitutional process. And there are other hazards as well. Two kinds of bargaining can be distinguished, and both can be essential. Logrolling can be described as the exchange of incommensurables. A wants this, and B wants that, where this and that bear no formal relation to each other. William H. Riker has asserted that this kind of exchange helped consummate agreement at the American Constitutional Convention in 1787.[76] Logroll-

76. William H. Riker, *The Art of Political Manipulation* (New Haven: Yale University Press, 1986), pp. 89–102. Riker's view on this is not, however, universally accepted.

ing can be hazardous if the downstream returns to A prove later to be more favorable than are those to B, prompting grave discontent with the bargain.[77] A different kind of bargaining is also common in severely divided societies. It is typified by the Malaysian special position clause, in which more recognition for the Malays produces less for the non-Malays and vice versa. This is negotiating over interests that seem entirely commensurable, and can become zero-sum, and it is very common in fashioning provisions relating to cultural issues, such as language or religion, as well as territorial arrangements for regional autonomy, or federalism, or economic interests that are correlated with ethnic or other group interests. Each type of bargaining is thus prone to a hazard specific to its subtype.

Of course, there is also what negotiation specialists sometimes call by various names and prefer when it is possible. This is the agreement that takes what appear to be conflicting demands of the parties and creatively produces a supervening formula that attends to the underlying interests involved (regardless of the specific demands). In that way, the agreement is said to create additional shared value rather merely splitting some difference or facilitating an exchange. This type of compromise is, unfortunately, unusual but not unknown. In Sri Lanka, for example, the demand of the Tamil minority for territorial autonomy proved to be attractive to provincial authorities in the Sinhalese south of the country, as we shall observe in chapter 8.

As we have seen with the Malaysian special position clause, there is no optimal answer to the problems that can arise when open-textured language is adopted on the basis of an unambiguous understanding at the outset that can be denied or degraded by interested contenders at a later date. Apart from inserting explicit language in the provision about its meaning, the best that can be

77. For a Malaysian example of discontent from disparate downstream returns, see Horowitz, *Ethnic Groups in Conflict*, pp. 582–85.

hoped for is a deliberative process that creates a high level of commitment to the consensus that emerges among participants, coupled with strong leadership that publicizes the contours of the agreement. Also helpful is a clear and accessible historical record, available to a fair-minded judiciary, assuming that violations are justiciable.[78] Even then, an agreement can prove fragile later. In any case, agreement at the time on such sensitive issues is by no means assured, as a multitude of failed constitutional processes shows.[79]

78. See Ginsburg, *Judicial Review in New Democracies.*

79. See, e.g., David Landau, "Constitution Making Gone Wrong," *Alabama Law Review,* Vol. 64, no. 5 (2013), pp. 923–80.

CHAPTER 7

External Advice and the Participation Imperative

Many forces combined to propel the increase in external advice in democratization and constitutional renovation. The proliferation of newly independent countries after World War II; promotion of human rights by the United States and other Western governments beginning in the late 1970s;[1] the interest of the United Nations in mitigating conflict and genocide; the concern of the World Bank with the rule of law and anti-corruption measures in order to facilitate international investment and economic growth; an array of NGOs dedicated to improving international regimes regulating environmental, humanitarian, or other transnational problems: these and similar state and nonstate actors helped to create networks or "epistemic communities" working across borders and engaged in "prescriptive discourse."[2] With the Third Wave of Democratization, new networks

---

1. Joel Barkan, "Can Established Democracies Nurture Democracy Abroad? Lessons from Africa," in *Democracy's Victory and Crisis,* ed. Alex Hadenius (Cambridge: Cambridge University Press, 1997), pp. 371–403.

2. The last phrase is from Yves Dezalay and Bryant G. Garth, "Legitimating the New Legal Orthodoxy," in *Global Prescriptions: The Production, Exportation, and Importation of a New Legal Orthodoxy,* ed. Dezalay and Garth (Ann Arbor: University of Michigan Press, 2002), pp. 306–34, at p. 311. On networks and communities, on which there is a large literature, see, e.g., Anne-Marie Slaughter, "Breaking Out: The Proliferation of Actors in the International System," in ibid., pp. 12–36; Kathryn

and new organizations began to discuss standards and norms and to prescribe new norms, even "fundamental principles,"[3] concerning rights, governmental structures, legal regulation, and constitutional processes. Of course, the diversity of legal and political systems—not to mention particular circumstances and events that trigger decision points—defies the application of standardized principles, and third-party experts, whether engaged through organizations or individually, encounter domestic clients who must assess the advice they receive and forecast its likely impact and desirability.

The Third Wave ushered in a succeeding wave of foreign experts crossing oceans to counsel constitutional reformers. The American Bar Association created the Central and Eastern Europe Law Initiative, which sent many lawyers and judges to that region. For example, the professor of American constitutional law Herman Schwartz chaired a group of twenty-five experts who worked in Czechoslovakia before its dissolution. Some such foreign experts were quite bold in their proposals. In Bulgaria, a complete draft submitted by a representative of the U.S. Chamber of Commerce was, unsurprisingly, modeled on the United States Constitution. Ethnocentrism is to be expected in such projects. If experts arrive with little knowledge of the country in which they must work, they may carry clauses of the constitutions with which they are familiar, to dispense as needed.[4]

Sikkink, "Transnational Advocacy Networks and the Social Construction of Legal Rules," in ibid., pp. 37–64.

3. Elizabeth Heger Boyle and John W. Meyer, "Modern Law as a Secularized and Global Model: Implications for the Sociology of Law," in ibid., pp. 65–95, at p. 76.

4. Even earlier, at the time of decolonization in Asia and Africa, from the 1940s to the 1960s, a few American lawyers participated in constitution making for newly independent countries they did not know well, and their proposals rested on imported provisions that may not have been wholly apt for—and were rejected by—the receiving country. See, e.g., Mary Dudziak, "Working Toward Democracy: Thurgood Marshall and the Constitution of Kenya," *Duke Law Journal*, Vol. 56, no. 3 (2006), pp. 721–80. More often, as I have noted, eminent British and Commonwealth constitutional lawyers chaired or sat on constitutional commissions at the

Provision merchants of this kind were not and are not confined to those traveling from American shores.

There is less missionary boldness in constitutional advice today than in the heady days after 1989. On the whole, there is more expertise about the countries to which numerous foreign NGOs send staff than there was then—although this is variable—and there is more reluctance to prescribe whole constitutions *a priori* or even specific provisions on a wholesale (as opposed to an interstitial) basis. There are, however, a few general rules of the constitution-making enterprise that are widely shared in the international NGO community that has emerged in recent decades. These rules are very frequently, nearly universally, advocated. Some have to do with what is regarded as the standard equipment of democracy, while many others concern constitutional process rather than content.

In constitutional processes, a paradigm case was the making of the South African constitution, in which a "globalizing constitutionalism" encountered the commitments of a liberation movement and produced some significant compromises. The result, described in a fascinating way by Heinz Klug, was "a hybridized incorporation of global standards and the local formulation and production of global options," with certain ambiguous matters left to be resolved by the internationally recommended and newly adopted institution of a rather powerful constitutional court.[5]

In spite of the frequently articulated aim to recommend "international best practice," however that may be determined (or imagined), the record of international advice shows a mix of standardized recommendations and varied recommendations. What drives the mix are, on one side, convictions about appropriateness

---

time of decolonization, but typically they had somewhat better information about their own colonies.

5. Klug, "Hybrid(ity) Rules: Creating Local Law in a Globalized World," in *Global Prescriptions*, ed. Dezalay and Garth, pp. 276–305, at pp. 279, 297.

and considerations of efficiency and, on the other, a need to accommodate local conditions.

Judicial review for constitutionality is now a standard piece of internationally imported equipment, sometimes implemented in its original American incarnation, through the ordinary courts, but more often in recent years in the Austrian version of a separate constitutional court, to which constitutional questions can be referred.[6] This recommendation fits well with the desire of political incumbents to seek assurance that, should they lose power, their downside risk will be limited, because they have purchased "insurance."[7] Bills of rights are similarly uniformly recommended and usually adopted, sometimes with qualifications that reflect the ambivalence of aspiring rulers about the future application of rights guarantees against themselves.

For our purposes, because it affects the selection of constitution makers, the most important near-uniformity of recommendations about institutions, rather than about processes as such, concerns electoral systems. Ben Reilly has pointed out that, in UN-conducted elections (and in many others), the recommendation has been for list-system proportional representation "in its simplest closed-list, large-district form," sometimes with the whole country as a single constituency.[8] This practice, he explains, reflects the desire to avoid the task of demarcating constituencies, as we have already seen in the case of Iraq. As Reilly emphasizes, it also reflects the low prior-

6. See Horowitz, "*The Federalist* Abroad in the World," pp. 502–32, at p. 515; Donald L. Horowitz, "Constitutional Courts: A Primer for Decision Makers," *Journal of Democracy,* Vol. 17, no. 4 (2006), pp. 125–37.

7. Ginsburg, *Judicial Review in New Democracies,* pp. 25, 64.

8. Reilly, "Timing and Sequencing in Post-Conflict Elections," in *Building Sustainable Peace: Timing and Sequencing in Post-Conflict Reconstruction and Peacebuilding,* ed. Arnim Langer and Graham K. Brown (Oxford: Oxford University Press, 2016), pp. 72–86, at p. 79; Reilly, "Political Parties and Post-Conflict Peacebuilding," *Civil Wars,* Vol. 15, no. S1 (2013), pp. 88–104, at pp. 95–96. Tim Sisk has made similar points. Sisk, "Power-Sharing in Civil War: Puzzles of Peacemaking and Peacebuilding," *Civil Wars,* Vol. 15, no. S1 (2013), pp. 7–20, at p. 16.

ity accorded to the building of political parties that can aggregate interests and can furnish a link between voters and their elected representatives. So administrative efficiency trumps important issues that, one suspects, may not even get debated. Guidelines from the Organization for Security and Co-operation in Europe affirm the right of minorities to form political parties, and so, with elections configured as Reilly describes them, providing very high degrees of proportionality, they can easily produce ethnically polarized results.[9] This form of PR may also produce a significant number of small parties, some far away on the ends of the spectrum from others, making any agreement difficult.

These practices make it obvious that external actors have interests of their own, a point that has been made many times.[10] Given a choice and a heavy agenda back home at the office, they may well opt for efficiency over competing concerns. Such actors are often hard pressed to maintain a consistent position, sometimes because the same organizational actor offering advice may consist of multiple people with a variety of inclinations, or because that actor's interests may have changed over time, or because organizational actors on the same side of advice-giving have different missions which produce conflicting advice, even in a single country.[11]

9. Reilly, "Political Engineering and Party Politics in Conflict-Prone Societies," *Democratization*, Vol. 13, no. 5 (2006), pp. 811–27. For a critique of American policy for its tolerance and even encouragement of regimes founded on ethnicity and ethnic differences, see Lise Howard, "U.S. Foreign Policy Habits in Ethnic Conflict," *International Studies Quarterly*, Vol. 59, no. 4 (2015), pp. 721–34.

10. See, e.g., William Safran, "Ethnic Conflict and Third-Party Mediation: A Critical Review," in *Ethnonationalism in the Modern World*, ed. Daniele Conversi (London: Routledge, 2002), pp. 184–205; I. William Zartman and Saadia Touval, "International Mediation," in *Leashing the Dogs of War: Conflict Management in a Divided World*, ed. Chester A. Crocker et al. (Washington, DC: USIP Press, 2007), pp. 437–54.

11. I can testify from personal experience in Bosnia at the end of the 1990s that the High Representative for Bosnia and the head of the OSCE office there had very different interests and inclinations. Within each of these bureaucracies was a variety of personalities and also opinions about particular matters of substance and about

The best example of conflicting advice is provided by the way the internationally negotiated Bosnian constitution contained in the Dayton Accords has been treated by international bodies since they were signed in 1995. That constitution is replete with minority guarantees for the Serbs and Croats of Bosnia-Herzegovina. Subsequently, international actors, even those charged with overseeing compliance with the constitution, have soured on it, mainly because it allows Bosnian Serbs the luxury of noncooperation and appeals to ethnic sentiment. Among those charged with assuring compliance, there is considerable sympathy for civic rather than ethnically based institutions and generally against ethnic particularism. The compliance with which these actors are concerned relates not to Dayton but to a wider body of international norms they are keen to uphold. They generally feel closer to the Bosniak preference for a civic polity than to the guarantees afforded Serbs and Croats at Dayton. The Venice Commission, an international body of jurists that was not involved in the original negotiations, has repeatedly condemned aspects of the constitution for their allegedly undemocratic character, and internationally appointed judges have produced judgments at odds with what was agreed at Dayton and far more congenial to Bosniak than to Serb aspirations.[12] International actors disdain the consociational Dayton Accords but applaud the consociational Northern Ireland Agreement and try to persuade Greek and Turkish Cypriots to emulate its consociational character. The general dangers of contradictions such as these have been well spelled out by Christine Bell.[13]

Despite these problems, there is an important place for external advice in constitutional processes. Because constitution drafters so often come to the table without significant experience or prior

---

the deference that should be accorded to the preferences of local actors. Harmony did not always prevail.

12. See Christopher McCrudden and Brendan O'Leary, *Courts and Consociations: Human Rights versus Power-Sharing* (Oxford: Oxford University Press, 2013).

13. Bell, "Introduction: Bargaining on Constitutions," pp. 28–31.

reflection on the issues at stake,[14] they can benefit from advice concerning procedures, organization, and personnel, as well as models from which they might consider borrowing institutions. But, as I have said, external advisors often have their own agendas and biases.[15] They may have only sketchy knowledge of the country that is the object of their attention, although, on this, standards have improved somewhat over the years. Their time horizons also may be different from those of the drafters. They may wish to settle conflicts quickly and move on, whereas drafters, who must live with the consequences, may want more durable solutions.[16] Countries that have had little experience with constitutions intended to be taken seriously after adoption, and are therefore inadequately attuned to the importance of the exact words that they use, will, however, need help in considering alternative choices and formulations. Expert advice, external or internal, may prove invaluable.

A veritable alphabet soup of national and international organizations is now available to service constitutional processes. Together, they form a policy community or network, especially when it comes to process. Although they vary in their origins, expertise, and precise mission—and many utilize sophisticated experts in their work—most such organizations sing from a remarkably harmonious hymnal. Their voices exalt a certain version of a recommended process, and proponents of that process can be surprised and disappointed when constitution drafters neglect it.[17] The cardinal

14. According to numerous oral accounts, the Iraq constitution drafters, for example, had very little idea of some important features of their task and yet were time-limited in completing it.

15. For a skeptical statement about the role of such advisors, see Mark Tushnet, "Observations on the Politics of 'Best Practices' in Constitutional Advice Giving," *Wake Forest Law Review,* Vol. 50, no. 1 (2017), pp. 101–16.

16. Andreas Mehler, "Introduction: Power Sharing in Africa," *Africa Spectrum,* Vol. 4 (2009), pp. 2–10, at p. 4.

17. There are now "handbooks" and "practical guides" to constitution-building processes that reflect current conventional wisdom, some of them essentially

principle is extensive public participation at all stages of the process. A corollary is that the process must be transparent. We have already seen that a strong case can be made for secrecy in at least some deliberations, but what of thoroughgoing public participation?

The most influential case for public participation was made by Vivien Hart, who cited several examples of participatory processes in the last two decades of the twentieth century, none more influential than the South African process, which for Hart "became a full-scale demonstration of participatory constitution-making."[18] For her, a constitution is not "a contract" but "a conversation,"[19] and the right to public participation in constitution making is said to be enshrined in international law—a claim that is far from established.[20] Following Hart, others have argued that the constitutional process must be accessible and highly participatory at all stages. Constitu-

---

cookbooks for "best practices" that are easily accessed. Some, however, are more nuanced and sophisticated. These provide real options to decision makers.

18. Vivien Hart, "Democratic Constitution Making," United States Institute of Peace, Special Report no. 107, July 2003, p. 8.

19. Ibid., p. 3.

20. Hart discovered this right in a law review article declaring the "emerging" existence of an international law "entitlement" to democratic governance. See Thomas M. Franck, "The Emerging Right to Democratic Governance," *American Journal of International Law,* Vol. 86, no. 1 (1992), pp. 46–91. A general right to democratic governance, even as embellished by international conventions cited by Hart, is still unrecognized, and Franck himself was unwilling to say there is an international law right to public participation in constitution making. Thomas M. Franck and Arun K. Thiruvengadam, "Norms of International Law Relating to the Constitution-Making Process," in *Framing the State in Times of Transition: Case Studies in Constitution Making,* ed. Laurel Miller (Washington, DC: USIP Press, 2010), pp. 3–19. For a critique of an international-law "right to democracy," see Donald L. Horowitz, "Self-Determination: Politics, Philosophy, and Law," in *Ethnicity and Group Rights,* ed. Ian Shapiro and Will Kymlicka (New York: New York University Press, 1997), pp. 421–63, at pp. 450–51. For an example of some of the mischief that can be caused by international law ostensibly created by the "hardening of norms" produced by the practices of NGOs, see the enthusiastic discussion of those norms in Ian Johnstone, *The Power of Deliberation: International Law, Politics, and Organizations* (Oxford: Oxford University Press, 2011), pp. 160–70, a discussion that neglects the absence of democratic accountability of the NGOs involved.

tional drafters, they say, must reach out to the public, educate it, and attend to its preferences. There will be, it is asserted, "democratic empowerment" and greater legitimacy for the constitution if the public takes "ownership" of the document by being actively engaged at every stage of its creation.

It is difficult to find anyone in the organized third-party advisor community who openly dissents from this prescription or even speaks seriously about important tradeoffs of participation against other values, such as the time available for deliberation, or potential pitfalls, such as the ability of authoritarians to bring out crowds to coerce constitution drafters.[21] Interestingly enough, there is little or no evidence of dissent from the advisor community when public participation is completely absent as external interveners put together a coalition government, often with a new constitution, between a sitting regime and rebels—and commonly only a fraction of rebel groups—who have been fighting against it. But eliminate a background of civil war, and intensive and extensive citizen participation suddenly becomes the *sine qua non* of democratic constitution making. The idea has caught on, one suspects, because it seems to be a universally applicable solvent: it travels well regardless of the peculiarities of any given country, and its ostensibly democratic pedigree is difficult to dispute.

A review of dozens of publications from the organized community reveals a startling similarity of formulations. Here is a selection:

> 1. Perhaps the most important assertion to have arisen from constitutional assistance practice to date is the notion that broad-based "ownership" of constitutions, based on inclusive discussion and consensus-seeking elites, ordinary citizens, and vulnerable groups may be the important factor in ensuring that all parties continue to comply with the letter and spirit of the resulting text.
>
> . . . .

21. For this pitfall, see Landau, "Constitution Making Gone Wrong," pp. 954–57.

This understanding is embodied in references to a participatory constitution making as a "transformational exercise," which, crucially, not only illuminates "the basis of democratic governance" but also raises familiarity with "relevant international principles and standards."

2. A participatory constitution-making process is one in which the people are educated about the process and the choices being decided, and are given a free, fair and genuine opportunity to directly express their will in a secure forum that is facilitated by those tasked with analyzing and incorporating the people's views into the final constitution. Importantly, such a process requires substantially more time than a closed, elite-driven constitutional review—two years is not uncommon. . . . A transparent constitution-making process is one where the public is aware of what is happening at each stage of the process.

3. The experience of other transitional societies is clear. Popular participation in and acceptance of the basic pillars of the new order are critical to its success and longevity. The creation of a foundational document that . . . is based on popular input and consensus may well be the optimal way of whittling away support for the insurgents . . . and stabilizing [in this case] Iraq.

4. It is important to give people opportunities at different points to participate in and contribute to the process, and to assure them that their views are valued and demonstrate how their recommendations have influenced decisions.

5. Regardless of how the constituent assembly is formed [whether by appointment or election], the interim government should create mechanisms for the . . . people to participate throughout the constitution-drafting process in order to ensure the legitimacy of the new constitution.[22]

---

22. Sources for the five identified quotations are, in sequence: (1) Rhodri Williams, "Constitutional Assistance and the Rule of Law in Post-Conflict Transitions," Folke Bernadotte Academy, Swedish Agency for Peace, Security and Development, Sandöverken, Sweden, September 2013, pp. 19–35; (2) Jason Gluck, "Constitutional Reform in Transitional States: Challenges and Opportunities Facing Egypt and Tunisia," USIP Peace Brief no. 92, Washington, DC, April 29, 2011, p. 4; (3) "Iraq: Don't Rush the Constitution," International Crisis Group Middle East Report no. 42, Brussels, June 8, 2005, p. 1; (4) Francesca Binda et al., "Democracy in the Making: Key

After unverified assertions of this sort, it is easy to agree with Laurel Miller's judiciously understated conclusion that "the practical purposes of soliciting participation remain underspecified."[23]

Constitutional advice organizations usually express few official views on whether a constitutional assembly should be elected or appointed—indeed, they rarely discuss elections to the relevant body as a crucial form of public participation[24]—or on any other important process issues, but they reiterate the participation mantra. The focus on public participation can preempt serious discussion of appropriate processes apart from public participation. Again, public participation falls under the rubric of "best practices" to guarantee a constitution that is "owned by all" the people.[25] A pocketful of standard practices is helpful to have if knowledge of the particular country and its problems is in short supply because the need for assistance has arisen suddenly and urgently, but borrowing "off the peg models" can be hazardous.[26]

Options in Iraq's Democratization Process," Policy Options on Democratic Reform Series, International IDEA, Stockholm, 2005, p. 7; (5) "Planning for Syria's 'Day After': Security, Rule of Law, and Democracy," Public International Law and Policy Group, March 2012, p. 10. See also the eight benefits listed in Jason Gluck and Michele Brandt, "Participatory and Inclusive Constitution Making," USIP, Peaceworks series no. 105, 2015, pp. 11–15.

23. Miller, "Designing Constitution-Making Processes: Lessons from the Past, Questions for the Future," in *Framing the State in Times of Transition: Case Studies in Constitution-Making,* ed. Miller, pp. 601–65, at p. 636.

24. See, e.g., the lengthy document by Interpeace, "Constitution Making for Peace," April 6, 2015, https://constitutionmakingforpeace.org/book/2-2-public participation/.

25. See, e.g., Commonwealth Human Rights Initiative, "Best Practices of Participatory Constitution Making," www.humanrightsinitiative.org/programs.ai/const/india/practices.htm. In the field of constitution making, the phrase *best practices* is usually used by one organization because they are so considered by another. In this field, as Georg Simmel stated long ago, "Institutions in competition with each other tend to resemble each other."

26. Robert Goodin, "On Constitutional Design," ARENA Center for European Studies, Oslo, Working Paper 97/26, 1997, n.p.

Four qualifications are necessary in order to avoid misunderstanding and misrepresentation about the need for participation right at the outset. These will not obviate the criticism that the intense participation assertions require, but they will make clear what I am not saying.

First, of course the public has to be informed and provided an opportunity to make its views known,[27] particularly through organizational representatives, and to receive periodic reports of progress. The need for constitution makers to report periodically and to engage with the public along the way can help deter rent-seeking private deals. The public also has a strong role to play in discussions of any constitutional drafts, some of which may prove controversial and require public explanation, clarification, and debate if they are to be approved, whether by referendum or otherwise.[28] Public discussion with drafters can actually play a more helpful role once there is a draft to discuss. That, however, is hardly the same as producing a lengthy, intensively participatory constitution-making exercise in which an undifferentiated public "takes ownership" of the process

27. An experienced external commission member reports seeing some internal commission members change views as they saw more of the country and listen attentively. The same is attested by the chair of the Kenya commission of 2000 to 2005. See Jill Cottrell and Yash Ghai, "Constitution Making and Democratization in Kenya (2000–2005)," *Democratization*, Vol. 14, no. 1 (2007), pp. 1–25, at p. 21. Yash Ghai also notes that civil society played a major role in getting a constitutional process started in Kenya. "Civil Society, Participation, and the Making of Kenya's Constitution," unpublished paper, n.d. There is no case for hermetically sealing a committee or an assembly. But "public ownership" of the process, according to its advocates, amounts to a far more extensive, time-consuming, high-cost enterprise altogether.

28. Alison Quentin-Baxter was, as mentioned earlier, senior legal counsel (and principal drafter) for the Fiji Constitution Review Commission that reported in 1996. After that constitution came under challenge some years later, she argued that a major defect of that constitutional process was the failure to translate the document into local languages and to engage the public and those most influential in shaping public opinion in serious explanation of the provisions of the new dispensation and of what they were intended to achieve. Quentin-Baxter, "Making Constitutions," pp. 683–84.

(whatever that means) and participates at every stage, right from the beginning.

Second, nothing I say here concerning this kind of extensive public participation in constitutional processes is intended to disparage deliberative democracy as such. There may well be a helpful place for direct engagement of the public in mitigating conflict in severely divided societies,[29] but direct participation that outweighs representation—and in some versions implicitly or explicitly supersedes political representation—for purposes of constitution making can be dysfunctional to constitutional processes, particularly because of the important role that politicians must play in these events, as described in earlier chapters.

Third, public participation becomes more important if a constitution-drafting commission or other unelected body is given authority to draft a constitution that will not be vetted thoroughly by a democratically elected legislature or constituent assembly—always an unwise process—but will go directly to a referendum or be approved without even a referendum. In such a case, the public has not been represented through elections in the pre-referendum process, and a referendum process itself hardly qualifies as a substitute for representation.

Fourth—and crucially—direct public *participation* is not synonymous with *inclusion,* for inclusion of all relevant groups can and should be achieved through representative democracy. Elections, rather than mass meetings to educate the public and receive repeated feedback, assure inclusion. In severely divided societies, the public is often represented by ethnically based political parties. In these circumstances, but not these alone, the public is likely to seek and prefer participation through parties it trusts to represent

29. See esp. John S. Dryzek, "Deliberative Democracy in Divided Societies: Alternatives to Agonism and Analgesia," *Political Theory,* Vol. 33, no. 2 (April 2005), pp. 218–42.

its interests. The advocacy literature on public participation does not acknowledge the problem of fitting public participation together with party representation, and it very often mistakenly conflates direct public participation with inclusion, sometimes combining them in the same phrase. This is an important point I will return to shortly.[30] Moreover, when the literature speaks of the "public," it more often speaks of members of the public as undifferentiated individuals than of the public as affiliates or members of groups and organizations that have some role in representing them.

There is indeed a tension between the unexamined direct-democracy assumptions of intensive public participation and the necessity for political parties in a modern democracy, as there is between direct democracy and representative democracy through elected representatives in general.[31] Parties and representation are generally absent from the literature on participation in constitution making. Yet parties are ubiquitous in constitutional processes, and they are inordinately important for their outcomes. As I said earlier, politicians and political parties are the most likely defectors from constitutional commitments, and they need to be among the most important participants in public, as well as private, discussion.

To take seriously admonitions favoring extensive public participation at every stage of a constitutional process in a severely divided society is to risk dangerous ethnic polarization in the process and

30. For an example of the conflation, see Susanna D. Wing, *Constructing Democracy in Transitioning Societies of Africa: Constitutionalism and Deliberation in Mali* (New York: Palgrave Macmillan, 2008). The thesis of the book is that Mali's constitutional process was exemplary because of its participatory nature, but then the author writes that "while the participant lists include a broad range of social groups, they are limited to a narrow range of individuals, namely members of an elite class, predominately male." Ibid., p. 70. This may be elite inclusion, but it is not widespread participation.

31. For a case study of the alienation of party leaders from a highly participatory process, see Alicia L. Bannon, "Designing a Constitution Drafting Process: Lessons from Kenya," *Yale Law Journal*, Vol. 16, no. 8 (2007), pp. 1824–72.

to risk amplifying majority voices over those of minorities.[32] In severely divided societies, intensive public participation also risks disproportionate activity on the part of extremists, whose public submissions may make compromise more difficult in the constitutional process. In South Africa's constitutional process, as we have seen, the breakdown of the first phase of prenegotiation in the CODESA process was followed by a less publicly visible process than the one that had pushed negotiators to stake out extreme positions. Public participation can polarize rather than legitimize.

And then there are the herculean administrative problems. Uganda's commission (1995) received 25,547 submissions; Kenya's (2009), 39,439 during a thirty-day period;[33] Ghana's (2010), more than 70,000.[34] The most ardent proponents of intensive participation assume, generally without discussion of the issue, that drafters or their staffs can manage the task of reviewing and aggregating thousands of public submissions, oral and written, into a coherent set of inputs and can then integrate them with proposals that emanate from government, political parties, and experts. In some countries, however, the problems of dealing with submissions has undermined the legitimacy of the constitutional body or created insuperable conflicts among the parties to the process.[35] Where procedures for

32. Cf. Jonathan Wheatley, "The Disruptive Potential of Direct Democracy in Deeply Divided Societies," in *Direct Democracy and Minorities*, ed. Wilfried Marxer (Heidelberg, Germany: Springer Verlag, 2012), pp. 64–73, which deals only with referenda.

33. Although some sources say (merely!) 26,451 submissions.

34. Coel Kirby and Christina Murray, "Constitution-Making in Anglophone Africa: We the People?" in *Growing Democracy in Africa: Elections, Accountable Governance, and Political Economy*, ed. Muna Ndulo and Mamoudo Gazibo (Cambridge: Cambridge Scholars Publishing, 2016), pp. 86–113, at p. 102.

35. In Rwanda (2003), only 7 percent of responses to public questionnaires were reviewed, which gave rise to inferences of manipulation. Angela Banks, "Expanding Participation in Constitution Making: Challenges and Opportunities," *William and Mary Law Review*, Vol. 49, no. 4 (2008), pp. 1043–70, at 1063–67. In Zimbabwe's

handling public submissions do not break down, they are likely to detract from the time needed to diagnose problems requiring constitutional attention and then to judge among a variety of methods for dealing with them. Processing submissions requires staff and expertise that are frequently absent in the quantities required to do the job well, and they pose serious opportunity costs in the allocation of time and energy.

There are inevitable time-management choices to be made in constitutional processes. Serious, sustained attention to widespread and frequent public participation, especially in time-limited processes, will inevitably come at the expense of internal deliberation and consensus formation,[36] consultation with experts, reconciliation of the demands of competing group and party representatives, and (potentially) the need for an internally coherent set of institutions.[37] Even if the advocates of intense public participation were right about its benign effects on the legitimacy and democratic character of the resulting constitutions, why would participation alone be given pride of place in third-party recommendations about process, ahead of inclusion by representation, deliberation time, careful drafting, institutional choices, and all the other ele-

---

post-2009 constitutional process, a dispute arose over how much weight to give to the many public submissions, a subject generally not discussed in the participation advocacy literature, which refers to public "ownership" of the process. The party of Robert Mugabe preferred to rank submissions by the number of times they were raised during meetings, whereas the opposition favored "an approach based on the quality of those submissions." The dispute caused a suspension of the constitutional negotiations. Agence France Presse, May 12, 2011.

36. See David Sally, "Conversation and Cooperation in Social Dilemmas," *Rationality and Society*, Vol. 7, no. 1 (1995), pp. 58–92.

37. A number of writers have contended that the proliferation of conflicting voices might impair the coherence of the resulting constitution. See Ginsburg, Elkins, and Blount, "Does the Process of Constitution-Making Matter?" p. 214; Roberto Gargarella, "Constitution Making in the Context of Plural Societies: The 'Accumulation Strategy,'" in *Constituent Assemblies*, ed. Elster et al., pp. 13–30, at p. 23. This risk was indeed evident in provisions of the crowd-sourced draft of Iceland, discussed below.

ments that create a suitable product? The answer to this question is hardly obvious.

Contrary to the extraordinary claims of the intensive participationists, the creation of contextually apt, democratic, workable institutions is the *sine qua non* of a constitutional process, and it is the likely criterion on which public judgment will ultimately rest. Andrew Reynolds has made a case for a "contingent theory" of constitutional design that places emphasis on the context.[38] There is nothing contingent or contextual about the uniform prescription for extensive public participation. As I have suggested, political elites are the ones who derail most constitutional understandings. They threaten constitutional democracy when they are insufficiently committed to democratic institutions, and it is supremely important that a constitutional process be geared to producing institutions to which they are attached.[39] Public disaffection, needless to say, is a major impediment to democracy, but popular participation in constitution making cannot assure either the absence of disaffection or the creation of institutions that command the assent or acquiescence of those with the power to disrupt democracy on behalf of their own publics.

Members of the public also have to make assessments of their own about whether and how to participate in public education and feedback exercises. There are, after all, disincentives for citizens to become sufficiently knowledgeable about constitutional issues to discuss them in ways that will be useful to drafters. The literature in economics on rational ignorance suggests strongly that, for most citizens, these disincentives will prevail on so specialized a subject.[40]

---

38. Reynolds, *Designing Democracy in a Dangerous World* (Oxford: Oxford University Press, 2011), pp. 181–82.

39. The Kenya process of 2000–04 was a model of public participation, but that was not sufficient to overcome the opposition of sitting politicians, who later defeated the draft in a referendum.

40. See Guido Pincione and Fernando R. Tesón, *Rational Choice and Democratic Deliberation: A Theory of Discourse Failure* (Cambridge: Cambridge University Press, 2006).

The only economist to have confronted this specific question—at least the only one to the best of my knowledge—appears to agree.[41] If this is correct, many public submissions may be unhelpful, although some may certainly be knowledgeable and useful. In a Nepalese constitutional process that had gone on for nearly a decade, surveys of the most important problems facing the country ranked failure to finalize a constitution near the bottom, mentioned by only 11 percent of respondents. Asked whether a federal state should be created—the question debated over two years by two successive constituent assemblies—"Don't know or can't say" led the responses by far, at 45 percent. And of those who had an opinion, the rights of minorities and marginalized communities, crucial questions in Nepal, ranked fourth in importance at merely 11 percent. Both lack of knowledge and lack of liberality were prominently on display.[42] Revealingly, as I have suggested, proponents of the participation mantra generally discuss none of these problems.

The claims of the intense participationists are not supported by any evidence of results regarding the subsequent legitimacy of the constitution, the democratic character of the dispensation, or a decline in violent conflict. The matter is hard to study because of the confounding influence of so many variations in constitutional process—as mentioned previously, by one count eighteen main permutations; by another, nine—and because serious efforts at engaging the public can sometimes be difficult to distinguish from window-dressing.[43] Jennifer Widner has found that representativeness of a

41. Stefan Voigt, "The Consequences of Popular Participation in Constitutional Choice: Towards a Comparative Analysis," in *Deliberation and Decision*, ed. Anne van Aaken et al. (Aldershot, U.K.: Ashgate, 2004), pp. 199–229, at pp. 205–6.

42. Sudhindra Sharma and Team Members, "Nepal Contemporary Political Situation Opinion Survey, Main Findings," February 1, 2015; "Himalmedia Public Opinion Survey 2015," www.nset.org.

43. For sources, see Horowitz, *Constitutional Change and Democracy in Indonesia*, pp. 12–13; Miller, "Designing Constitution-Making Processes," p. 637.

constitutional process is positively related to a reduction in violence in the five years following ratification of a new constitution in Africa, but she finds no evidence that public consultation is so related.[44] These results are consistent with the finding, described earlier, that inclusion of all groups, which can be accomplished through a representative process, is more important than extensive public participation is. A study by Abrak Saati comparing twenty participatory processes with twenty-eight nonparticipatory processes in post-conflict countries beginning in 1985 found no consistent effects of participation on democracy scores, either up or down, in the years following conclusion of the processes.[45] Democracy values for both types of process were similar at two different times of post-adoption measurement.

In an extended study of participants and nonparticipants in Uganda's constitutional process of the 1990s, Devra C. Moehler concludes that participation did not affect the legitimacy of the resulting constitution for those who participated; they "were no more supportive of the constitution than those who did not participate."[46] Partici-

---

44. Jennifer Widner, "Constitution Writing and Conflict Resolution," *The Round Table,* Vol. 94, no. 381 (2005), pp. 503–18, at p. 517.

45. Saati, *The Participation Myth: Outcomes of Participatory Constitution Building Processes on Democracy* (Umeå, Sweden: Umeå University Department of Political Science, 2015), pp. 109–35, esp. p. 122. Cf. Joanne Wallis, "How Important Is Participatory Constitution-Making? Lessons from Timor-Leste and Bougainville," *Commonwealth and Comparative Politics,* Vol. 54, no. 3 (2016), pp. 362–86. Wallis contrasts outcomes in two cases, one only lightly participatory, one heavily so, and attributes a range of successful outcomes to the more participatory case of Bougainville. The problem is that the other elements, including elements antecedent to participation, such as one-party domination of the process, were vastly less favorable to democratic outcomes in Timor-Leste than in Bougainville, and so the attribution of favorable results to differences in participation is unreliable. Lower levels of participation were, almost surely, the result of one-party domination of the Timorese process, which, unsurprisingly, produced unfavorable outcomes.

46. Devra C. Moehler, *Distrusting Democrats: Outcomes of Participatory Constitution Making* (Ann Arbor: University of Michigan Press, 2008), p. 39.

pation did, however, appear to teach participants to form opinions about the constitutional process, but this finding is qualified by the fact that leaders in particular regions influenced the way in which citizens viewed the constitution.[47] Most people had never read or seen a copy of the document, and 54 percent agreed that "the constitution is too complicated for most people to understand."[48] Most relied on local experts and had no other sources of information or skills of evaluation.[49] Although participation in Uganda's process does seem to have produced both more democratic attitudes and more distrust of government, on the whole the study reinforces what is known about the role of opinion leaders and about the rationality of citizens who decline to invest excessively in a complex subject that culminates in a one-time event. Susanna Wing's study of the Malian National Conference likewise reports that participants refused to vote on the choice between a supreme court and a separate constitutional court for judicial review, on the ground of lack of expertise. And they were members of the elite.[50]

There is one and, to the best of my knowledge, only one aggregate-data study that asserts a positive association between citizen participation and democratic outcomes.[51] As I mentioned in chapter 5, a study by Gabriel Negretto finds no such association.[52] As we shall see shortly, the study asserting a positive association has been superseded by the later work of two of the authors, so

47. Ibid., pp. 144, 155–57.

48. Ibid., p. 161.

49. Ibid., pp. 162, 165.

50. Wing, *Constructing Democracy in Africa*, p. 71.

51. Todd Eisenstadt, A. Carl LeVan, and Tofigh Maboudi, "When Talk Trumps Text: The Democratizing Effect of Deliberation During Constitution-Making, 1974–2011," *American Political Science Review*, Vol. 109, no. 3 (2015), pp. 592–612. The article was expanded into a book, *Constituents Before Assembly: Participation, Deliberation, and Representation in the Crafting of New Constitutions* (Cambridge: Cambridge University Press, 2017).

52. Negretto, "Replacing Constitutions in Democratic Regimes."

there is now no study with such findings. But, for the moment, let us stay with the assertions of the first of the two studies.

While the study at first speaks extensively of participation, direct input from "ordinary citizens" that "visibly influenced debates,"[53] and public engagement along the lines of the theory of deliberative popular democracy—as opposed to representative democracy[54]—the operationalization of its causal variables and its coding turn out to be very different. The authors speak of distinctions between "decreed" or "imposed" processes, on one side, as against "polyarchic" or "popular" processes, on the other. Decreed or imposed processes, by which the authors mean elite-driven processes, were found to produce undemocratic polities, whereas polyarchic processes tend to produce democratic results, as measured by Polity scores. The problem for the study is that their category of polyarchic processes embraces those involving elected representatives, whether or not there has been extensive citizen participation of the sort recommended by scholars and practitioners, such as those quoted above.

When the authors did their coding, polyarchic processes were said to include "systematic civil society input OR strong transparency OR specially elected drafters 'freely and fairly' elected."[55] Note the disjunctive in the coding. The authors were actually measuring three different attributes of the process: direct citizen participation of a certain sort; secrecy or transparency; and the presence of a democratically elected—that is, representative—constituent assembly. For them, any one of the three variables counts as popular participation. But the kind of participation they initially set out to test is the more

53. Eisenstadt et al., *Constituents before Assembly*, p. 29.

54. Which, said the authors, could be "broadly inclusive but entail little meaningful participation" by citizens. Ibid., p. 31.

55. Eisenstadt et al., "When Talk Trumps Text," p. 59; Eisenstadt et al., *Constituents Before Assembly*, p. 30 (capitalization of the disjunctive in the original of both versions).

limited sort, the direct citizen engagement championed by Vivien Hart and the advocacy literature that followed.[56] Despite challenging the democratic adequacy of merely representative democracy and purporting to test for the superior democratic results of citizen participation, the authors' conception of participation ends up including representation through elections as well as citizen input through civil society organizations. With, however, one exception: in the first tests they conducted of what they call the "convening stage," the earliest part of the process, before deliberations begin, there were eighteen cases in their much larger sample that had had "citizen involvement." In those cases, there was a small but statistically significant increase in democracy three years later.[57] In the debate and ratification stages, however, citizen involvement was found to have no such effect. The study as a whole conflates direct citizen *participation* with *inclusion* through representation, thereby making unclear exactly what it is finding. Ambitious though it is, this effort brings to mind entreaties against "conceptual stretching,"[58] with its inevitable costs in accuracy.

This, however, is not the conclusion of the story. In the end, the authors were not oblivious to the issue of conflation, which, as mentioned previously, is common in discussions of "participation." Remarkably, within two years, using a larger data set, two of the authors had rethought the matter and published (in a different journal from the one in which they had published their earlier findings) a startlingly different finding. In the more recent article, they conceded explicitly that they had indeed earlier "conflated together as one variable" inclusion with participation. When the two variables

56. See, e.g., *Constituents Before Assembly*, pp. 56–61.

57. Ibid., p. 40.

58. Giovanni Sartori, "Concept Misformation in Comparative Politics," *American Political Science Review*, Vol. 64, no. 4 (1970), pp. 1033–53, at pp. 1033–36.

were disentangled, they found that "inclusion is what matters" for democratic outcomes. Inclusion of social groups shows a statistically significant relationship to democratic outcomes, while citizen participation does not.[59]

Despite the absence of evidence for the hypothesis linking participation with democratic outcomes, interest in that hypothesis has not abated. There has been a certain fascination with Iceland's crowd-sourced experiment in constitution making in 2012. Iceland's constitutional committee convened a forum of 950 people drawn randomly from the census, but a high refusal rate skewed participation upward in socioeconomic terms. This body then designated twenty-five members for a constitutional council, again biased upward. After judicial invalidation of the initial designation, parliament redesignated the same twenty-five people. The council received 3,600 comments from the public, many suggesting constitutional provisions, and it utilized some 10 percent of them, mainly related to rights provisions—a not surprising result, since Iceland's constitution dated to 1944, and there had been a worldwide profusion of rights adoptions in the years since. The draft constitution produced by the council was approved in a referendum by a 64 percent majority—with, however, only a 49 percent turnout. Even after editing by the Venice Commission, the quality of the document was poor, and it was very complex. Parliament never approved, or even took up, the draft. The unexamined assumption of the exercise was that constitutions should, to the maximum extent possible, be designed without participation by experts, politicians, or organized

59. Todd A. Eisenstadt and Tofigh Mabouti, "Being There Is Half the Battle: Group Inclusion, Constitution-Writing, and Democracy," *Comparative Political Studies,* Vol. 52, nos. 13–14 (2019), pp. 2135–70, at pp. 2149–50. Negretto, "New Constitutions in Democratic Regimes," p. 17, n. 25, has criticized this article for continuing to conflate the two independent variables in their coding.

groups of any kind.[60] It did not require an experiment to refute this proposition.[61]

Public participation at various stages can be helpful in a constitutional process, but a certain type of extensive participation, beginning at a certain time, is assuredly not the gold standard for a legitimate process or a democratic outcome. Extensive public participation, especially at the inception of a process, can have crucially important costs, measured in delay that produces a fading prospect of what could have been a constitutional consensus, a megaphone for ethnic or other political extremists, and a serious reduction of deliberation time for those engaged in seeking consensus and compromise.

Participation is more likely to be helpful not at the beginning of the process but when there are actually constitutional proposals to

60. To their credit, Eisenstadt et al. decisively rejected such assumptions, even when they argued for extensive citizen participation in constitutional processes. See *Constitutions before Assembly,* pp. 148–50. Other treatments of the Icelandic and similar experiments run the gamut. See Carlos Bernal, "How Constitutional Crowdsourcing Can Enhance Legitimacy in Constitution-Making," in *Comparative Constitution Making,* ed. Landau and Lerner, pp. 235–57; Björg Thorarensen, "Why the Making of a Crowd-Sourced Constitution in Iceland Failed," www.constitutionnet.org/news/why-making-crowd-sourced-constitution-iceland-failed; Mark Tushnet, "New Institutions and Mechanisms for Making Constitutional Law," in *Democratizing Constitutional Law,* ed. Thomas Bustamante and Bernardo Gonçalves Fernandes (Basel: Springer, 2012), pp. 167–83; Hélène Landemore, "Inclusive Constitution Making: The Icelandic Experiment," *Journal of Political Philosophy,* Vol. 23, no. 2 (2015), pp. 161–91; Alexander Hudson, "Does Public Participation Really Matter? The Case of Iceland's Crowd-Sourced Constitution," unpublished paper, University of Texas Department of Government, May 11, 2015; Thorvaldur Gylfason, "Chain of Legitimacy: Constitution Making in Iceland," in *Constituent Assemblies,* ed. Elster et al., pp. 138–60.

61. For a cogent critique of citizens' assemblies and their lack of accountability to voters (and the difficulty of joining widespread participation with deliberation), see Silvia Suteu and Stephen Tierney, "Squaring the Circle: Bringing Deliberation and Participation Together in Processes of Constitution-Making," in *The Cambridge Handbook of Deliberative Constitutionalism,* ed. Ron Levy et al. (Cambridge: Cambridge University Press, 2018), pp. 282–94.

discuss.[62] Periodic dialogue between citizens and constitution makers, especially including explanations of what the latter are attempting to achieve, is more useful than one-way submissions from the public before the formal process begins or before anything has been decided. When a draft of the Indian constitution was circulated, hundreds of comments poured in, from members of provincial assemblies and executives, government ministries, members of the public, even from members of the constituent assembly itself. These produced multiple amendments to the draft, then amendments to the amendments, and revisions to the draft right up to the conclusion of the assembly's work.[63] This was a far more effective way of involving the public than a pre-deliberation participation exercise would have been.

There are still articles being crafted, handbooks being published, and advice being pressed earnestly upon constitution makers that widespread public "ownership" is crucial to the success of constitutional processes. But there is no convincing evidence that this is so, much evidence that it is not so, and every reason to emphasize other aspects of processes that compete for time and attention with extensive citizen participation exercises but are more likely to be associated with good results. Skeptics, who continue to believe that participation by which the public "takes ownership" of the constitutional process in order to give it legitimacy is the exclusive path to constitutional success should consider the immediate effects of the Indian Constitution, "a document with alien antecedents that was a product of elite consensus, [that] became part of the experience of ordinary Indians in the first decade of independence."[64] Inclusion through representation (albeit, regrettably, with only indirect

62. See Abrak Saati, "Constitution Building and the Sequencing of Political Participation," *Journal of Politics and Law*, Vol. 10, no. 3 (2017), pp. 13–25, at p. 22.

63. Chaube, *Constituent Assembly of India*, 2nd ed., pp. 107–10.

64. Rohit De, *A People's Constitution: The Everyday Life of Law in the Indian Republic* (Princeton: Princeton University Press, 2018), p. 4.

elections) and long deliberation to forge agreement were far more important in producing a constitution owned by the public. There is an important role for the public in feedback and dialogue, but it is very different from the "ownership" beginning on day one that proponents advocate. Ownership by the public is a chimera. Whatever happens, for better or for worse, the politicians will own it, and they need to be accountable for it.

CHAPTER 8

Consensus and Defection

The Case of Sri Lanka

Any idea that very extensive public participation has a uniformly favorable benefit-cost ratio can be dispelled by considering Sri Lanka's aborted constitutional reform process that began in late 2015 and ended in 2018. It is worth studying that process as an example of a case in which an extended effort at public consultation at the outset of the constitutional reform took considerable time, revealing wide differences of opinion on badly needed constitutional changes. The public consultation certainly had no beneficial impact on the outcome, which was determined by politicians defecting from commitments they had earlier undertaken.[1] Sri Lanka illustrates the importance of leadership and timing and the uses of momentum for change, all of which can bear on outcomes in which real consensus is emerging.

To understand the failure of constitutional revision in Sri Lanka, a brief excursus into the background of the country's problems is necessary. Sri Lanka's constitutional history reflects its history of

1. Unless otherwise specified, my account of the Sri Lankan developments is based on a series of interviews and conversations with participants in the Constituent Assembly and its Steering Committee, as well as experts and close observers of both. All such interviews and conversations were conducted under an assurance of confidentiality, meaning no individual identification or attribution.

ethnic conflict. The British commission that crafted its independence constitution rejected demands from its Tamil minority[2] for equality of legislative representation and generally provided few minority protections, save for a general nondiscrimination clause.[3] Beginning in 1956, conflict between the Sinhalese majority and the Tamils was greatly aggravated by the electoral victory of a coalition of Sinhalese parties that had advocated an official language policy of "Sinhala Only."[4] Only with an amendment passed in 1987, under pressure of civil war, was Tamil recognized in the constitution as an official language.[5]

This symbolic exclusion of the Tamils was followed by extensive discrimination in selection and promotion in the public services and in higher education. It was also punctuated by periodic outbreaks of serious violence directed against Tamils, in 1956, 1958, 1977, and 1983,[6] the last following guerrilla attacks on soldiers that marked the beginning of the long war that ended only in 2009.

The early responses of Tamils to political exclusion and violence took the form of demands for federalism. The logic was that if Tamils were to be excluded from power in the central government, at least they might govern in the main areas of the island in which they were concentrated—principally in the north and east—and which

2. There are actually two Tamil minorities in Sri Lanka, a group of "Sri Lankan Tamils" of about 12 percent, who arrived on the island, on average, about a millennium ago, and a smaller group of Tamils whose ancestors were recruited from India, during British rule, to work on tea estates. When I speak of Tamils, I refer to the first group, rather than the second. The two groups tend to be geographically and socially separate.

3. 1948 Constitution of Ceylon, art. 29. See generally Rehan Abeyratne, "Uncertain Sovereignty: Ceylon as a Dominion, 1948–72," *International Journal of Constitutional Law*, Vol. 17, no. 4 (2020), pp. 1258–82.

4. For this period, see W. Howard Wriggins, *Ceylon: Dilemmas of a New Nation* (Princeton: Princeton University Press, 1960).

5. 1978 Constitution of Sri Lanka, amendment 13.

6. I have described these events at various points in Donald L. Horowitz, *The Deadly Ethnic Riot* (Berkeley: University of California Press, 2001).

they claimed as "traditional homelands." The Tamil Congress, which had been the principal party representing Sri Lankan Tamils, was eclipsed by an organization called the Federal Party after the first stirrings of anti-Tamil discrimination by Prime Minister S.W.R.D. Bandaranaike in the 1950s. (In keeping with what I suggested earlier about foreign models, some in the Federal Party were especially keen on the Swiss example.) A variety of devolution schemes were proposed from time to time but often rejected. Even those that were implemented provided weak powers to districts and provinces and reserved control in the central government.

Tamil demands were also rebuffed in proceedings that resulted in a new constitution in 1972. That constitution accorded a "foremost place" to Buddhism, the religion of most Sinhalese; it declared Sri Lanka to be a "unitary state" and gave constitutional status to Sinhala as the official language.[7] This was majoritarianism with a vengeance. The 1972 constitution was superseded by a constitution passed in 1978, which created a new semi-presidential system that featured a strong president. While the new dispensation had some more liberal elements,[8] it did little to reverse the Tamils' sense of exclusion.[9] Within a few years, the country was in a civil war initiated by Tamil separatists, punctuated by lengthy but unsuccessful negotiations for peace.

In 1999–2000, a very serious attempt to produce a new constitution was led by President Chandrika Kumaratunga of the Sri

---

7. 1972 Constitution of Sri Lanka, arts. 2, 6, 7. Previously, Sinhala had been declared the official language by statute enacted in 1956; in 1958, the Tamil Language Special Provisions Act had been passed, allowing for official use of Tamil for certain administrative and educational purposes.

8. Particularly the protection of fundamental rights, which were, for the first time, made justiciable; the safeguards for judicial independence; and the electoral system for the president, which gave minorities the potential to decide a race between two Sinhalese candidates, a potential that would only be realized thirty-seven years later, as I explain below. On that electoral system and its conciliatory potential, see Horowitz, *Ethnic Groups in Conflict*, pp. 639–43.

9. For a helpful critique, see DeVotta, *Blowback*, pp. 143–44.

Lanka Freedom Party (SLFP), who had courageously explained to the country the need for an end to the "unitary state" conception in the constitution and for devolution. The opposition United National Party (UNP), led by Ranil Wickremesinghe, was not unequivocally in support. What killed the project, however, was a revolt in the president's own party. That revolt had been led by her own prime minister, the future president, Mahinda Rajapaksa. Sinhalese-Buddhist opinion was opposed to federalism, which the president was accused of promoting, and in the end Wickremesinghe, too, opposed the president's efforts.[10] This was, on Kumaratunga's part, a brave, concerted attempt to deal with Sri Lanka's ethnic problems through constitutional means.

When efforts at constitutional reform resumed in 2001, Kumaratunga was still president, but the former opposition UNP, led by Wickremesinghe, controlled parliament. Intensive negotiations were held with the rebel Tamil Tigers, and both sides agreed that federalism needed to be on the agenda. Over time, however, the Tamil Tigers put forward proposals that suggested they were interested in a federalism that would be the prelude to a confederation or to the independent Tamil state for which they had been fighting—and with no real minority safeguards at that.[11] The negotiations thus failed, and the war went on for a total of twenty-six years, culminating in a victory for the government in a brutal final campaign in 2009.[12]

---

10. See ibid., pp. 182–83.

11. Edrisinha, "Debating Federalism in Sri Lanka and Nepal."

12. For a good chronology, see Neloufer de Mel et al., "Ethnopolitical Conflict in Sri Lanka: Trajectories and Transformations," in *Handbook of Ethnic Conflict*, ed. Dan Landis and Rosita D. Albert (New York: Springer, 2012), pp. 93–118. See also V. K. Nanayakkara, "From Dominion to Republican Status: Dilemmas of Constitution Making in Sri Lanka," *Public Administration and Development*, Vol. 26, no. 5 (2006), pp. 425–37; Jayadeva Uyangoda, "Sri Lanka's Conflict: Role of the State," in *Internal Conflicts: A Four State Analysis*, ed. V. R. Raghavan (New Delhi: Vij Books, 2013), pp. 219–44.

The war ended during the regime of the autocratic and pro-Sinhalese president Mahinda Rajapaksa. Sinhalese triumphalism was much in evidence in the first few years after the war, and Tamils were a deprived, in some ways occupied, population.[13] Before the 2015 presidential election, however, Rajapaksa's Sri Lanka Freedom Party (SLFP) split, and a new coalition between a portion of his party and the opposition United National Party (UNP) emerged to contest the presidential and then the parliamentary elections. With the strong backing of civil society groups and of the minorities—namely, Tamils and the Muslim population (the latter almost 10 percent of the population),[14] whose joint support provided the margin of victory—Rajapaksa's former cabinet colleague Maithripala Sirisena defeated him. Months later, the coalition also won a new parliamentary majority, led by the UNP's Ranil Wickremesinghe, who became prime minister once again. Because Tamil and Muslim support was crucial to the election results—Rajapaksa had won about 58 percent of Sinhalese votes in the presidential election—the new government had a mandate to reduce the impact of majority domination and particularly to ameliorate longstanding Tamil grievances. The election campaign had provided impetus for reform. It had assuredly created what has been called by Bruce Ackerman a "constitutional moment."

This was among the best opportunities for constitutional amelioration of ethnic grievances since independence sixty-seven years earlier. Besides its strong majority in parliament, the new coalition government could count on the moderation of Tamil demands. In a

---

13. When I drove north from Kandy to Jaffna in 2014, five years after the end of the war, I passed multiple military camps, including two in Jaffna, in the Tamil heartland, and several war monuments extolling, in Sinhalese-Buddhist terminology, the valor of the military heroes they celebrated. No official sign of reconciliation was evident anywhere I looked.

14. Tamils are mainly Hindus. Sri Lankan Muslims are usually Tamil speakers, but they generally do not identify with Tamil aspirations for territorial autonomy, because they fear Tamil domination in areas where the two groups are intermixed.

new constitutional dispensation, the Tamil National Alliance (TNA) seemed willing to leave in the text phrases specifying that Sri Lanka is a "unitary state" and according Buddhism a "foremost place," provided that there were provisions for substantial devolution and for a strong anti-discrimination clause reflecting credible guarantees of equality.[15] In fact, the TNA had reconciled itself to the foremost-place clause much earlier and to a unitary-state clause somewhat more recently.

Defying Tamil radicals, the TNA also seemed as if it might be willing to abandon earlier Tamil demands for a unit merging the Northern and Eastern provinces, where most Tamils reside, though it had not explicitly said so during the process. The Northern province is more than 90 percent Tamil, but the Eastern province has a Tamil plurality of only 40 percent. In that province, the Muslim minority of 37 percent and the Sinhalese minority of 23 percent have long been apprehensive about a Tamil-dominated regional government if both provinces were to be combined. And, of course, although Tamil parties never acknowledged it, governing the two provinces together, with unhappy Sinhalese and Muslim groups turned into smaller minorities in the merged unit, would be a very difficult task.

After the presidential election, parliament passed, with but a single dissent, a constitutional amendment clipping the extensive powers of the president, which it was widely thought had long been exercised autocratically.[16] Constitutional reformers, who had been contemplating reversion to a parliamentary system, saw the amendment as an essential interim step, although others entertained a suspicion that the newly elected president might just relish a second term. Thereafter, the first step taken on more wide-ranging consti-

15. More about these possible concessions when we discuss the reports that emerged from the Steering Committee of the Constitutional Assembly.

16. 1978 Constitution of Sri Lanka, amendment 19. At the time, it was anticipated that a new constitution would probably produce a parliamentary, rather than presidential, regime.

tutional reform, in December 2015, was to set up a Public Representations Committee on Constitutional Reform, composed of politicians, academics, and lawyers of all major ethnic groups. Public consultations were prioritized. In multiple sessions, the committee listened to the public and also explained the workings of the constitutional process. Most of its members were appointed by political parties, and they tended to adhere to the views of their parties in the report the committee prepared. Following the script of the extensive public participation school, the committee visited every district in the country.

When the Public Representations Committee published its report in May 2016, it had received 3,655 submissions.[17] In a survey conducted in October of that year, however, it emerged that only 1.1 percent of the population was "extremely aware" that a constitutional process was underway, while 21.9 percent were "somewhat aware"; nearly 25 percent did not know that any such process was taking place. Just short of 70 percent of Sri Lankans had not even heard of the Public Representations Committee, and 76.8 percent had not heard of the Constitutional Assembly that had been created to recommend reforms.[18] This was the result in a country with a literacy rate of 92 percent, one of the highest literacy rates among developing countries in Asia. Yet, even here, extensive public participation had not produced public "ownership" of the constitutional process. For the most part, it was organizations and interest groups that had made their views known.[19]

The same survey established, with predictability of the kind that would not have eluded members of the assembly in the absence of public consultation, that on the key questions of constitutional

17. Report on Public Representations on Constitutional Reform, Colombo, Public Representations Committee, May 2016.

18. Topline Report, "Opinion Poll on Constitutional Reform," Colombo, October 17, 2016.

19. Report on Public Representations on Constitutional Reform, p. vii.

design and ethnic politics, Sri Lankans were still strikingly divided, and particularly so by ethnic group. Public participation had certainly not produced guidance for drafters or provided decision makers with information they did not already have. On key issues such as the place of Buddhism in the constitution and the terms and scope of devolution, the Public Representations Committee had likewise found its interlocutors among the public divided,[20] as the committee itself often was. Although it sensed among the public a desire for peace and ethnic reconciliation, the multiple options the committee presented included both divisive and conciliatory possibilities.[21]

While the committee was engaging the public from December to May, discussions moved slowly for the creation of a body to consider a new constitution. The Constitutional Assembly, which was composed of all members of parliament—a reprise of a previous constitution-making procedure[22]—was not appointed until March of 2016, fourteen months after the presidential election, seven months after the parliamentary election, and three months after the public representations process had begun. The resolution to create the CA had been passed in January, and the delay in appointing the body was due to disagreements, particularly among SLFP members, about whether an entirely new constitution was needed.

When the report on public representations appeared, the government paid little attention to it. The report's recommendations, phrased in the alternative, often followed party lines, with Rajapaksa's followers dissenting from liberal formulations. An unfortunate byproduct was that enemies of the constitutional reform proj-

---

20. Ibid., pp. 16–18, 47–51.

21. E,g., ibid., pp. 18–19, on religion. For more constructive alternatives, see Benjamin Schonthal and Asanga Welikala, "Buddhism and the Regulation of Religion in the New Constitution: Past Debates, Present Challenges, and Future Options," CPA Working Paper on Constitutional Reform no. 3, Colombo, July 2016.

22. In accordance with our discussion of attractive and aversive precedents in chapter 2.

ect could pick out options on controversial subjects from the public representations report that were unlikely to be incorporated in the constitution and then tar the reform project with the most radically unpleasant possibilities. To make things worse, the government took no stand at this point on any concrete possibilities. In fact, it made no attempt to persuade the public about what was necessary. The Public Representations Committee, having labored mightily and rendered its report, never met the public again.

The CA's work was divided between a Steering Committee, which took on the most controversial issues, and subcommittees for the remainder. The Steering Committee was appointed by the prime minister and consisted of himself and twenty additional members from all parties in parliament. The committee took it for granted that Rajapaksa's followers would oppose any reforms. The CA, identical to the composition of parliament, including the Sirisena wing of the SLFP, nevertheless would have more than the two-thirds needed to get a new constitution approved by that body, especially if it could count on the support of the TNA, representing the Tamils, and a smaller Sinhalese party, which at that stage proved to be accommodating to constitutional changes. Accordingly, the Steering Committee concentrated on various alternative formulations on the most difficult issues, canvassing the range of options on each and searching for consensus among what began as the strong majority amenable to constitutional change.

At first, prospects seemed good. Not only was the prime minister to chair the Steering Committee, but the president appeared to confidants eager not to allow the ethnic problem to be passed to the next generation. The prime minister proved early on to be supportive but not proactive. After the early stages, he appeared only rarely, was apparently prioritizing economic issues in his daily work, and seemed reluctant to take on Sinhalese Buddhist extremists. For his part, the president had not appointed the members of the committee and played no significant role in its work. The prime minister's view on reform—and, even more, the president's—may have been affected by SLFP members who had come over to the governing alliance but were not enthusiastic about constitutional change for interethnic accommodation. Neither leader began a serious program of public outreach. If they were not supportive, the project could not succeed.

A government victory in 2009 over the Tamil Tiger rebels in their violent quarter-century quest for separatism and then the defeat of a Sinhalese chauvinist autocrat by a fragile interparty coalition in 2015 opened the way to reconsider the full spectrum of Sri Lankan political institutions: the controversial constitutional place of Buddhism, the majority religion; the perennial desire of Tamils for the devolution of power to minority areas; the need to rethink or replace the existing presidential system and the electoral systems for the executive and legislative branches; and measures to restore the badly damaged rule of law. Several of these issues were contentious along ethnic lines, and for many of them there were multiple options to be considered, on some as many as six.[23] Among them, as we have seen, was the description of the state (was it to remain "unitary"?); possible modification or qualification of the "foremost place" accorded to Buddhism; specific guarantees of ethnic equality; and the extent of power to be devolved to provinces, at the moment carefully circumscribed by the central government. The Constitutional Assembly was bound to produce recommendations by a majority vote, to be followed, as indicated, by parliamentary approval by a two-thirds vote, and a referendum with a majority requirement, but accompanied by the expectation that if more than half of the Sinhalese majority did not vote for the proposal in the referendum, a new constitution could be stillborn.

23. Asanga Welikala, "As Sri Lanka Strives Towards Its Third Republican Constitution, Social and Political Divisions on Fundamental Constitutional Issues May Derail the Reform Process," August 2016, available at www.constitutionnet.org/news/sri-lankas-search-constitutional-consensus-amid-social-and-political-divisions.

The Steering Committee identified a cross-ethnic consensus on most issues that could pass, in the face of some segments that were determined to prevent anything from passing.[24] In the worst case, party discipline could do the rest. Sri Lanka is one of those cases in which consensus or compromise could prevail among people in the middle of the spectrum but might not eliminate the need for vote counting in the end. There is, however, no doubt that the Steering Committee was oriented toward securing consensus, not some midpoint between two opposed positions. The CA took no votes.

Not all of the omens were unfavorable. The Constitutional Assembly had solicited the views of the chief ministers of provinces in the southern, heavily Sinhalese-Buddhist part of the country on the subject of devolution, which was a crucially important demand of the Tamils in the north and east. The chief ministers, a critical constituency whose own power would be enhanced by the likely devolution proposal, proved to be favorable toward it. A minor Sinhalese-based party, the Janata Vimukthi Peramuna (JVP), despite a previous record of anti-Tamil positions, was also mostly favorable. Support from UNP members of the Steering Committee was not problematic. Some SLFP members of the committee were not convinced, however, that a wholly new constitution was required. Still, with support from the leading Tamil party as well, a strong majority was within reach. In the middle of the Constituent Assembly process, there was a dispute in the expert committee about whether to submit a draft constitution, because some experts objected to a draft that they had not produced. And so, in the first instance, an interim report, replete with multiple options, was tendered to parliament by the Steering Committee in September 2017.

That first interim report of the Steering Committee was the product of some forty-four meetings of that committee, and it was

24. I have verified this sense of the proceedings from two participants and inferred it from conversations with a third.

ready long before it was submitted. By the end of 2016, some SLFP members of the committee started to back away from what had been agreed, manufacturing delays by raising the need for party approval and other excuses. Only after many months did the SLFP members give their assent, but they appended a memorandum to the report that indicated a great many reservations about options described in that report.

What had begun to happen has a long history in Sri Lanka, as I intimated in chapter 1. An accommodation with the Tamils is proposed and (usually) agreed by Sinhalese leaders of either the UNP or SLFP, who understand the need to meet or at least accommodate Tamil demands. Sinhalese extremists oppose the accommodation. If SLFP leaders are the accommodationists, the UNP opposes it, and the reaction of SLFP leaders is to abandon the agreement. If, however, UNP leaders are the accommodationists, they then hear from their backbenchers that, because SLFP opponents will use the accommodation against them, so that maintaining the agreed accommodation will render reelection very difficult, at which point UNP leaders abandon the idea.

The former scenario goes back to 1957, when Prime Minister S.W.R.D. Bandaranaike was considering concessions on the use of the Tamil language;[25] the latter dates to 1968 and the abandonment of the district councils devolution scheme taken up by Prime Minister Dudley Senanayake and the Federal Party.[26] Subsequently, each major Sinhalese party has alternated in thwarting plans to

25. DeVotta, *Blowback*, pp. 98–101. Later that year, Bandaranaike agreed to what was called the Bandaranaike-Chevanayakam Pact with the leader of the Tamil Federal Party. The pact would have alleviated several Tamil grievances, but Bandaranaike abandoned it under pressure from Buddhist clergy. In 1959, Bandaranaike was assassinated by a Buddhist monk.

26. On those two sequences, see DeVotta, *Blowback*, pp. 102–08, 133–34. The district councils scheme was abandoned by Senanayake when backbenchers of his party assessed that it would damage their reelection chances. I was in Colombo at this time and observed the quick erosion of support within the UNP.

accommodate Tamil aspirations, depending on who was proposing the plan.

In 2016–18, followers of defeated former president Rajapaksa were the first to become hostile to the new constitutional ideas. That hostility then spread to SLFP members in Sirisena's camp, fearful that their endorsement might have adverse political consequences for them. Similar fears appear to have animated the reticence of both President Sirisena and also of Prime Minister Wickremesinghe and to have spread in turn to members of the JVP, who also began to waver, in spite of their previous understanding of the need for a new constitutional settlement. During the post-2015 period, former president Kumaratunga was aligned with the forces favoring a new constitution, but even her advocacy and long leadership of the SLFP were not enough to convince Sirisena of the advisability of carrying the project forward. Accordingly, it met the habitual fate of such projects in Sri Lanka.

If rushed constitution making is generally a bad idea, an equivalent problem can arise when momentum for constitutional change is allowed to dissipate. As mentioned, the first interim report of the Steering Committee was sent to parliament in September 2017,[27] well over a year after the CA's subcommittees had rendered their reports and two and a half years after the presidential election of 2015 and the great optimism the election result had produced about dealing with major problems confronting the country. Much had changed. SLFP members of the CA had raised doubts and, according to multiple accounts, engaged in delaying tactics. The government had failed to take a position on the constitution it envisioned. By 2017, the president and the prime minister were locked in a public feud that rendered a unified position impossible. The two had come from different parties, very different backgrounds, very different

27. Constitutional Assembly of Sri Lanka, Interim Report of the Steering Committee, September 21, 2017.

positions on some of the issues involved, and multiple possibilities to run afoul of each other. Former adherents of the Rajapaksa faction had restored connections with President Sirisena and may have been pulling him away from his coalition with the UNP.[28] Both of the crucial politicians seemed, for their own reasons, to have withdrawn from leading the process.

When the interim report arrived in parliament, it reflected fundamental divisions that gravely threatened the constitutional renovation project, although in fact there had been more consensus in the Steering Committee early on than the report reflected. Like the Public Representations Committee report, it contained a variety of alternative formulations rather than recommendations it was prepared to defend.

On the other hand, the report contained the seeds of an agreement that might well have passed, had the political leadership not disappeared. Sinhalese radicals had demanded a reaffirmation that the state was "unitary." The committee did better than that. One of its formulations was that Sri Lanka was "one undivided and indivisible country," with "specific provisions" to be included "to prevent secession" but also provisions for "[m]aximum devolution."[29] The result was a potential accommodation of Sinhalese and Tamil positions, if judicious selections were made from the menu the report provided. The same possibilities were evident with respect to religion. Buddhism was to be given "the foremost place," and the state

28. Sirisena later dismissed Wickremesinghe from the prime ministership and appointed former president Rajapaksa to that position. When Rajapaksa could not demonstrate that he had the confidence of a majority in parliament, Sirisena dissolved parliament and scheduled new elections, an action found by the Supreme Court to be in excess of his authority. Sampanthan v. Attorney General, FR Application no. 351/2018 (Sup. Ct. Sri Lanka, 2018). Wickremesinghe therefore resumed the position of prime minister, with the support of a majority. See Mario Gomez, "The Courts Respond to Executive Tyranny in Sri Lanka," iconnectblog.com/2019/01.

29. Constitutional Assembly of Sri Lanka, Interim Report of the Steering Committee, p. 1.

would have the duty "to protect and foster the Buddha Sasana,"[30] as in the existing constitution, but with provision for all religions to enjoy certain rights specified in the constitution, also as in the current document. An alternative formulation would have substituted for the reference to other rights specified in the constitution a clause firmly guaranteeing adherents of other religions that they would be treated with "honor and dignity and without discrimination, and guaranteeing to all persons the fundamental rights guaranteed by the Constitution."[31] A second chamber was to be created to represent the provinces, which were to be the principal receptacles for devolved power. The second chamber would share with parliament the power to approve constitutional amendments, which would require a two-thirds vote of both houses, but in that version, it would not necessarily have a role in approving ordinary legislation. Again, there were alternative formulations proposed.[32] Most of these formulations were not straight compromises but statements that might have satisfied both sides—that is, elements of a genuine consensus.

The reaction of the parties to these proposals, some of which, as I mentioned, were among the options most favorable to minority (especially Tamil) concerns—by contrast to other stated options that were less favorable—suggests that a new constitution could have emerged had there been leadership available for the cause. As I mentioned, the SLFP and the JVP published annexed observations that contained disagreements, many of which could have been compromised.[33]

Most revealing were the extraordinary reactions of the TNA, the main Tamil party, which restated a number of its standard

30. The Buddha Sasana refers to the practice and doctrine of the Buddhist religion.

31. Constitutional Assembly of Sri Lanka, Interim Report of the Steering Committee, p. 3.

32. Ibid., p. 20.

33. Ibid., Documents 1A and 1B, respectively, attached to the report.

positions, capped by the following striking concession: "In the interests of reaching an acceptable consensus, the TNA will be willing to consider agreement with the main principles articulated in the interim report if the same are acceptable to the two main parties."[34] That statement reflected the consensus that had emerged in the Steering Committee months earlier. The Tamils were ready for a new constitution, even with a version of a foremost place for Buddhism but with serious protections for minority rights, an indivisible state but with substantial devolution, and—although the TNA members of the committee did not explicitly concede this much—without a possibility for merging the Northern and Eastern provinces. Discussions in the Steering Committee just before the first interim report was tendered indicated that there was still a consensus to be had.

The same was true in the following two months. In November 2017, the Steering Committee asked its committee of experts to prepare a draft constitution. Some disagreements among the experts delayed the completion of the draft, but these did not concern party-political positions, and not all experts participated in producing the draft. The drafters utilized reports of subcommittees as well as the interim report and the deliberations of the Steering Committee.

In December, however, local council elections were announced; they were to be held in February 2018. From then on, prospects for a new constitution became bleak. By that time, the president's party and the prime minister's party had ended their alliance. Nevertheless, the experts' draft,[35] completed in mid-2018, had secured unanimous—but, by then, merely nominal—agreement in the Steering Committee. SLFP members were backing out and delaying presentation of the draft, which was interrupted further by a truly major

34. Ibid., Document 1C, attached to the report.

35. Actually, there had been two experts' drafts, one by six experts and one by two others. For the details, see the speech in parliament by the Tamil co-chairman of the Steering Committee management committee, July 20, 2018, reprinted in DBSJeyaraj.com.

constitutional conflict between the president and the prime minister.[36] Once that dispute had been resolved, the draft was presented as if it were another interim report, although it was a nearly complete article-by-article proposed constitution.[37] More than a year had passed since the experts had been charged with preparing the draft.

The draft was a remarkably liberal document, replete with justiciable rights. In the very first article, it elided the "unitary state" language problem by providing Sinhala and Tamil substitutes that did not have identical meanings and that undoubtedly would have been replaced later with an agreed formulation. At the same time, the draft referred to the state as "consisting of the Center and the Provinces," thus suggesting the upgraded importance of the provincial level of government but carefully avoiding endorsement of anything resembling federalism and clearly ruling out advocacy or activity toward secession.[38] Buddhism was assured "the foremost place," but with guarantees of equality, including equal opportunity in government employment,[39] thereby promising redress of a Tamil grievance going back to the 1960s. (An anti-discrimination commission had been discussed by members of the Steering Committee and might well have been added along the way, had prospects for the draft not soured by then.) The Directive Principles of State Policy ordered the state to "refrain from promoting ethnonationalism" and to promote instead "civic nationalism and patriotism based on the most enlightened religious and secular principles" as well as "fundamental human rights and cosmopolitanism."[40] That even nominal approval

36. For details of the dispute, see note 28 of this chapter.

37. Constitutional Assembly of Sri Lanka, Report Prepared by the Panel of Experts for the Steering Committee, tabled in Parliament, January 11, 2019.

38. Ibid., arts. 1, 4.

39. Ibid., arts. 8, 14, 16, 40(2). Although they would have preferred a guarantee of a secular state, Tamil members had judged that the "foremost place" provision had rarely done much actual damage in the past and could be conceded if the remaining provisions were acceptable.

40. Ibid., art. 68(2).

was given unanimously to this language was, to put it mildly, very surprising for a Sri Lankan constitutional assembly—even though directive principles are generally, albeit not universally, considered to be nonjusticiable and even though much of this verbiage would have been unlikely to survive in the end.

In governmental structure, the draft went far toward devolution. It also went beyond the 2015 amendment that reduced presidential powers, instead creating a parliamentary system with a mainly ceremonial president elected by parliament, but it limited the power of parliament to legislate on any subject within the provincial list,[41] reaffirming the devolution of police powers to the provinces, a commitment that had been made but not enforced in an earlier constitutional amendment.[42] The draft also proposed a second house for the legislature to represent provincial interests. That house would consist of five members from each province, drawn from its provincial governing council.[43] Special two-thirds requirements of both houses would be required to enact laws relating to provincial councils or to amend fundamental rights provisions in the constitution or alter the powers of provinces; in all such cases a public referendum would be needed as well.[44]

Provinces would be permitted to merge and form a single provincial government—a longstanding Tamil demand—but only with the consent of voters of both provinces in a referendum.[45] That provision was obviously intended to insure that the Eastern Province, with its large Sinhalese and Muslim populations, not be merged into a single Tamil-dominated province, meaning that such a merger would never happen.

---

41. Ibid., art. 244(2).

42. Ibid., art. 277. Compare 1978 Constitution of Sri Lanka, amendment 13.

43. Constitutional Assembly of Sri Lanka, Report Prepared by the Panel of Experts for the Steering Committee, art. 161.

44. Ibid., arts. 132, 145.

45. Ibid., art. 237(3).

I have enumerated these provisions at some length in order to demonstrate how far the drafters had gone, with the assent of the Steering Committee, to satisfy minority aspirations. Had the constitutional process continued, some of these provisions, such as the article allowing provincial mergers, might have been struck or substantially modified.[46] But even with significant modifications, this draft would have created a foundation that would have made it difficult for any government to maintain a posture of ethno-religious exclusivism—provided, of course, that the courts and other enforcement bodies proved faithful to their constitutional missions, which the courts, at least, had recently shown their willingness to do.

Appended to the report was a section on "Political Party Representations in the [earlier] Interim Report of the Steering Committee,"[47] which laid out their previous reservations to the draft. As I said previously, these consisted, in the main, of points that could have been amended for the sake of consensus or compromise. The SLFP wanted much of the language of the existing constitution restored, including the article stating that Sri Lanka was simply a "unitary state," and it wished to preserve the existing provision privileging Buddhism without new qualifications respecting guarantees for other religions. In the end, however, it seems likely that the explicit guarantee of equality would have been added. There were also objections to limits on national legislation concerning matters on the provincial list and others concerning the provincial councils and the selection process for members of the second house.

Remarkably, however, there were no objections to creation of the second house as such or to devolving power to the provinces. Devolution was not a subject on which there had been serious disagreement in the Steering Committee. Perhaps this is a testament

46. As I have pointed out, merger of the Northern and Eastern provinces was opposed by both Sinhalese and Muslim minorities in the Eastern province.

47. Constitutional Assembly of Sri Lanka, Report Prepared by the Panel of Experts for the Steering Committee, Schedule I.

to the enthusiasm for devolution among Sinhalese chief ministers in the southern provinces, but more generally it is notable how few and how specific the dissents were. These were correctly interpreted as reneging on earlier commitments, but they mainly reflected the changes in the party-political alignments that had impaired the coalition that came to power on a wave of reforming enthusiasm of 2015. Still, by the time the draft was submitted, the process was effectively on its deathbed.

The Tamil National Alliance members had made enormous concessions, which risked their electoral future in competition with those with more extreme agendas for the Tamils. The TNA was closer to the prime minister's party than to the president's party but was let down by both. In fact, as the process went on, it became clear that none of the three leading Sinhalese politicians was ready for the new constitution. Rajapaksa was ready only to stigmatize it as a disaster for Sri Lanka, which he did explicitly in a newspaper article. Moving away from the coalition formed in 2015, Sirisena seemed to be not much interested in the constitutional project. After his dispute with Sirisena began in 2016, Wickremesinghe appeared to want to be sure that SLFP members were in agreement with the changes, and he seemed concerned about Sinhalese Buddhist extremists. In the course of the process, neither the president nor the prime minister had taken a public leadership role in the constitutional reform program.

In cases in which extremists dispute the agenda for intergroup accommodation, that agenda needs strong leadership. Going all the way back to 1958, as we have observed, Sri Lanka has had a long history of Sinhalese leaders who reneged on agreed changes needed to accommodate Tamil interests, when opposition competitors or extremists threated electoral retaliation. This time the constitutional project was stymied even before those threats had materialized in full.

The coup de grâce was provided by local council elections, which were held in February 2018. Rajapaksa had organized his own party, the Sri Lanka People's Front (SLPP, Sri Lanka Podujana Peramuna), to compete against Sirisena's faction of the SLFP, Wickremesinghe's UNP, and other parties. At odds with the prime minister, Sirisena chose to campaign for Rajapaksa, thereby splitting the vote of his erstwhile coalition and enabling the victory of Rajapaksa's candidates in a large number of councils—225 out of 341—on fewer votes than the total won by the UNP and the SLFP rump allied with it. Three years had passed since the Sirisena-Wickremesinghe coalition victory, and much time had been lost at every step in the process. With Rajapaksa's comeback, the process was dead and buried.[48]

The only possibility for change in the near term is through *seriatim* constitutional amendments, but those are most unlikely to produce a package of reforms comparable to the one that arrived at the mortuary in 2019. It is quite true that the nineteenth amendment had made important changes, and rule-of-law institutions had reasserted their independence in the post-2015 period.[49] Reduced presidential powers were redistributed among a legislature, a Constitutional Council, and a judiciary that had become subservient to the president but soon exhibited a revived dynamism. These changes should certainly not be minimized, but they did not extend to ethnic or religious issues, or to devolution, and they had been achieved during an interparty honeymoon period that followed the 2015 election. That honeymoon did not survive the whole period of constitutional deliberation, during which the two major political leaders

48. For the details, see Asanga Welikala, "An Anatomy of Failure: the 2014–18 Sri Lankan Constitutional Exercise in Context," *Annual Review of Constitution Building Processes: 2017* (Stockholm: International IDEA, 2018), pp. 80–94.

49. I am grateful to Mario Gomez for reminding me of these developments. Gomez, "Constitutional Change and Institutional Resilience in Sri Lanka," unpublished paper, Colombo, 2020.

made clear by their quiescence that they had not committed themselves to thoroughgoing constitutional revision in earnest.[50] In any case, most of the changes wrought by the nineteenth amendment were undone in 2020 by a twentieth amendment, passed after the return of Rajapaksa and his brother to power.

Interestingly enough, as late as August 2019, the then-prime minister, Wickremesinghe, seemed inclined to try to resurrect the constitutional project, at least rhetorically, for a constitutionally deprived audience that would vote again in a presidential election in three months, with a parliamentary election to follow later. Speaking in the Tamil heartland, he reaffirmed the need for a new constitution, with devolution and guarantees that "Tamils could live as equal citizens," explaining his earlier reticence as part of an effort to listen to others, on the way to a consensus, and he suggested that a path to a new constitution lay with the core of the draft that had been submitted to parliament.[51] Faced with a Sinhalese-Buddhist-majority electorate in the country as a whole, this was a faint effort at artificial respiration, one that merely asked the minorities to wait for just one more electoral cycle, the thirteenth since things started to go badly wrong in 1956.

It would not take long for decisive disappointment to set in. In the presidential election of November 2019, Gotabaya Rajapaksa, brother of the former president and former defense minister, won a decisive victory. Within months, the new president was complaining that he was hampered in the performance of his duties by the nineteenth amendment, which, as we have observed, crimped presidential powers. In the presidential election, Tamil and Muslim minorities again voted heavily for the more moderate UNP-supported

---

50. For later developments in the Sirisena-Wickremesinghe-Rajapaksa triangle, see Mario Gomez, "The Courts Respond to Executive Tyranny in Sri Lanka," iconnectblog.com/2019/01.

51. "UNP, JVP, YNA Want Executive Presidency Abolished, Only UPFA Divided, Says PM," *The Island* (Colombo), August 19, 2019.

candidate, but the Sinhalese electorate was more united than it was at the last election, now in support of a candidate regarded as very unfriendly to minority aspirations.[52] With brother and former president Mahinda Rajapaksa then appointed as prime minister, and with the landslide victory on their part in the 2020 parliamentary elections, Sri Lanka's politics took a very different turn. With an array of presidential powers reinstated and Sinhalese Buddhist partisans in charge, it seemed unlikely that the country would soon return to a conciliatory constitutional project.

Serious agreement was the objective of the Sri Lankan process while it lasted. The aim of the procedure used by the Steering Committee was to search for appropriate answers that took account of the interests of majorities and minorities and to find formulations that could command the assent of the committee. In that sense, it was a consensus-seeking exercise. The co-chairs of the Steering Committee's management committee, one Sinhalese and one Tamil, had worked with the experts to produce language in accordance with the discussions in the committee. No votes were taken as the participants accommodated each other. Had political rivalries external to the committee not had reverberations inside it—especially ones with the effect of substituting a first interim report for a genuine draft and then delaying the actual draft constitution—there would have been a real chance of major constitutional change, a very encouraging development for a country as profoundly divided as Sri Lanka. But the falling out of Sirisena and Wickremesinghe opened the prospect of a revived opposition and caused a reversion to old, ingrained Sri Lankan habits of reneging on promises to the Tamil minority.

---

52. The increased vote for another Rajapaksa presidency was very likely the result of heightened concerns for physical security after a very serious and deadly attack by radical Islamists on churches and hotels earlier in the year. Gotabaya had presented himself as the security candidate, pointing out that the previous regime had failed to act on intelligence warnings before the attack.

Among individual members of the Constituent Assembly, their agreement held only so long as the agreement of other members held. Once the leaders fell out and the prospect arose that SLFP members of the coalition might move back toward the Rajapaksa position, the consensus proved unstable. In short, there could be no consensus without a *strong* consensus, one that removed the threat of electoral attacks on the draft from those who defected. Unanimity, or something close to it, would have had real utility. It was the right standard under the country's circumstances. Had the draft been presented a year or perhaps even two years after the 2015 presidential election, constitutional change would have been far more likely.

Public participation in Sri Lanka had little impact, except to tell politicians that the public did not know much about the process but was divided on questions of constitutional change. Once that task was accomplished, the Public Representations Committee, exhausted and finished with its intensive work, was never called back to duty. Intensive participation at the outset merely consumed time.

At later stages, public participation might really have been helpful, but not quite in the way most participationists envision. They tend to think that public ownership of the process entails having the public become educated about the process and the issues and then communicating its wishes to the drafters. Instead, just as I argued in chapter 7, once a draft was in place, there might well have been a dialogue in Sri Lanka between those responsible for crafting the constitutional compromises and the public to be affected by them. The drafters, politicians from various parties—including, notably, the president and the prime minister—could have explained to the public the need for agreement across group lines, set against the terrible quarter-century of war and the sixty years of overt interethnic hostility and periodic violence. Proponents could have answered questions about the moderate nature of the changes contemplated. In doing this, they might have secured more consent from the public and simultaneously helped their chances for reelection, at the same time as the public could have registered any doubts about the agreements in progress, some of which might have been remedied or compromised in the draft. This kind of feedback would have constituted a reciprocally beneficial engagement between the crafters of consensus and the public to which it was accountable. But without the political commitment from the top in the first instance—which, of course, such a participative process could also have solidified had it existed—public participation turned out to be superfluous. The indispensable missing element of "ownership" was that of the political leadership.

CHAPTER 9

Shaping a Process

In earlier chapters, there has been much discussion of multiple trade-offs, so it might be thought that constitutional process is simply a muddle. To that discussion, I have, in still other chapters, added concerns about how to structure the engagement of the public and how to arrange the timing of deliberations so that they do not run up against imminent elections that provide a megaphone for backlash and the defection of leaders. In a substantial number of cases, of course, free choice of process may be limited. Many events can create great urgency for constitution making and even point to a single far-from-optimal process as preferable under the circumstances. A stalemated war, or the absence of any legitimate authority to convene a process, or the lack of a minimally serviceable, preexisting constitution with which to work: any of these may heighten the urgency of the situation. Even so, adjustments may be possible to enlarge the scope of inclusion, extend the time for deliberation, and aim for something more than a quick deal.

When these constraints are not present and the scope for choice is wide, there is no single metaprocess, an agreed, legitimate way to choose a sensible process. Random forces—the interests of particular politicians or social segments, unusually persuasive individuals, an authoritarian ruler, colonial traditions, successful insurgents, or foreign advisors—may manage to influence the choice. The pre-process process, so to speak, remains underorganized and understudied.

If the outset of discussions on an appropriate process is characterized by serious disagreement, muscling through one or another option in the face of opposition is quite unwise. During the Egyptian Arab Spring, after Hosni Mubarak was ousted, legislative elections were held—rather prematurely, as a plethora of poorly organized, anti-Islamist parties faced a well-organized party of the Muslim Brotherhood and another party supporting Salafism.[1] Once the results were in, disputes broke out among the parties about how to structure the constitutional process. The Islamist majority prevailed in these disputes, precipitating a walkout by their secular opponents from multiple parties. The unresolved character of the disputes poisoned the process of creating a democratic constitution that could attract adherents across the political spectrum, and divisions among civilians paved the way for a military intervention that would be received with relief by secularists.[2] A preconstitutional process, with time for party development, would have been a good idea, but the risk was that the military might have used that time to reinforce its position.

In some of the most seriously conflicted countries, innovative preconstitutional processes have been established to create a later opportunity for serious constitution making. In Yemen, as we have seen, a year-long dialogue allowed delegates to express grievances and aspirations and then formulate constitutional recommendations—

1. This is a case where the anti-Islamist parties had inadequate time to reorganize or coalesce and, in some cases, little incentive to do so, as each of several parties had a leader who aspired to be a presidential candidate. Under these conditions, the electoral results were practically foreordained.

2. On the conflict over the process rules and its effects, see Tereza Jermanová, "Before Constitution-Making: The Struggle for Constitution-Making Design in Post-Revolutionary Egypt," *Acta Politica*, Vol. 55, no. 4 (2020), pp. 648-69. See also Jason Brownlee, Tarek Masoud, and Andrew Reynolds, *The Arab Spring: Pathways to Repression and Reform* (Oxford: Oxford University Press, 2015), pp. 109–17.

prematurely, as it turned out—to be forwarded to a drafting committee. Serious deliberation can be useful even at the preconstitutional stage.

In many instances, we have witnessed procedural stumbles produced by arbitrary deadlines, or bad advice, or the interests of powerful actors, resulting in constitutions with major omissions, or defects, or in some cases no constitution at all. Most of these stumbles could have been remedied, and a better result could have followed. There is a case to be made for a stronger focus on appropriate processes, a focus that continues as the process unfolds, even in the face of idiosyncratic, country-by-country constraints.

Whatever the precise procedure adopted, the criteria of inclusion through elections, a high level of consensus across groups, and adequate deliberation time ought to travel well unless constitution making must take place in a crisis atmosphere that cannot be abated. We have observed that longer constitutions tend to be more durable, and it is probable that substantial deliberation time, especially if it leads to widespread consensus, will produce a longer constitution. If there is a high level of agreement, there will be less need to omit important provisions.

Defection over time is a problem that cannot always be avoided, especially if, subsequently, returns from the agreed arrangements disproportionately favor one group over another or if later generations prove to be far less attached to those arrangements than were those who created them.[3] But the strong attachment of the drafting generation should offer some protection against premature abandonment.

Because all polities need a coherent set of institutions, a strong dose of appropriate expertise on the substance of the institutions

3. On the latter condition, see Donald Rothchild and Philip G. Roeder, "Power Sharing as an Impediment to Peace and Democracy," in *Sustainable Peace: Power and Democracy after Civil War*, ed. Roeder and Rothchild (Ithaca: Cornell University Press, 2005), pp. 29–50, at pp. 38–39.

to be adopted is also needed. As Elster warns, "There is a risk that some countries may adopt constitutionalism à la carte—adopting elements from several models, without making sure that they can work effectively as a whole."[4]

If these are the main procedural criteria, there are further questions that require attention. If the constitution-making body is large and heterogeneous, should it avail itself of an expert drafting commission appointed to produce a draft (with or without alternative options) for the larger body? And how should the larger body organize itself when it is not sitting in its plenary capacity? Should it sit as a single committee consisting of members of all parties and ethnic groups or in multiple functional committees that are equally inclusive but specialized by subject matter? What rules should govern the work of the drafters? The need for a coherent product suggests an answer to both questions.

An expert commission is more likely to produce a constitution whose parts fit well together.[5] Such a body may also be less afflicted with some of the dysfunctions of multiparty negotiations in heterogeneous societies. Of course, the larger assembly or legislature is unlikely to be shy about rejecting what it cannot abide in the draft submitted to it, but at least that draft may have a starting advantage. Creating such a body, therefore, is often a sensible choice, but it is not free of hazards, and it ought to have thoroughgoing consultations with the larger body, both before it begins to sit separately and during its sessions as well.

---

4. Jon Elster, "Making Sense of Constitution-Making," *East European Constitutional Review*, Vol. 1, no. 1 (1992), pp. 15–17, at p. 16.

5. Christina Murray has suggested to me the utility of having drafters attached to each of the committees into which the larger body may be divided. This would require horizontal coordination among drafters attached to the various committees. As mentioned previously, earlier and later (usually more authoritative) drafters need to be in contact, so that the earlier can explain to the later the thinking that informed its draft.

If there is no amendment process in the existing constitution that can provide appropriate leeway and standards for replacing it, then new procedural rules need to be drafted. These rules need to reflect the kind of process that is envisioned. That requires careful thought about the process at this stage, more careful thought than is often given to putting the process in place. Rules that restate standard procedures for producing ordinary legislation are not likely to be appropriate.

If the constitution is part of the transition from an authoritarian regime that is still in power, that regime can more easily scuttle a draft it dislikes that comes from a small expert body than it can a draft that has been crafted by a large elected assembly, which will be in a position to fight against the regime if a usurpation of authority occurs. This fear is not hypothetical. A military government in Fiji in 2012 did exactly that: it seized and destroyed printed copies of the draft about to be circulated by a commission it had appointed, and it then proceeded to start over again. In contrast, communist regimes in Eastern Europe after 1989 had no choice but to negotiate with opposition bodies.

Even if drastic action to reject a draft is not taken, a coherent plan produced by those delegated to do the initial drafting can be made incoherent when the reviewing body gets to make changes, especially, as we have already discovered, when the changes are the result of hurried bargaining within parliamentary select committees that are sometimes appointed to review commission drafts. If the draft is by a commission, it is far preferable that it render its report to a large constituent assembly than to a small committee, in which behind-the-scenes deal-making can introduce inconsistencies into a carefully drawn proposed constitutional plan and rent seeking can produce exclusion of disfavored groups. Staged processes have advantages, but they will work better if the drafters are well integrated into an unhurried deliberative process at the review stage, so that they can explain the relation of one provision to another and the probable consequences of what may seem to be small alterations that can change, even change profoundly, the structure of resulting constitutional incentives and guarantees.

Needless to say, there is no surefire way to prevent bargaining after hours and the presentation later of consummated bargains as mere improvements in the product, even if they entail trades that merely secure private or segmental advantage. To reduce the chances, the best thing one can do is to focus on real deliberation—meaning serious discussion, argumentation, and persuasion in larger bodies—to make it harder to sell such claims. I reiterate that compromise of all conflicting interests may be the only way to secure assent—even then there may also be dissent and the need for voting—but compromise, as defined earlier, in an inclusive setting is not the same as rent-seeking deals.

Here there is a role for the public, which can be mobilized to evaluate what has been done at the last minute behind closed doors. For this to happen, however, there needs to be a pause after at least some of the last steps in the process, rather than a rush to finish the job, which is the more usual way that multistage review processes are concluded.

Similarly, the issue of a single committee versus multiple committees bears on the likelihood of a coherent product. Delegating particular problems to an array of committees or subcommittees specialized by subject matter gives rise to the possibility that one or more of them will not produce any agreed proposals at all. Multiple committees also maximize the chance that the proposals emerging from the various committees will not fit together well, unless there is some active, overarching structure linking them. In its first four-year process, from 2008 to 2012, which ended in failure, Nepal used the functional committee format, and some committees did not report. During the abortive Czechoslovak negotiations of 1990, ten committees of experts were given a list of central government powers that had been agreed in principle and were asked to develop them into a coherent proposal. No such proposal emerged, even after a working group of the committees had been created. Indonesia used a single highly inclusive committee for all issues, and its members were in fairly constant contact with their colleagues in the same party, as well as in other parties. That committee managed to have intensive discussions on all issues and to sense where obstacles to agreement lay, without taking votes that could have locked participants into hard-and-fast positions. In the end, many positions in Indonesia did in fact change over time in response to frequent discussions.

Of course, processes need to be congruent with problems. Perhaps a few homogeneous countries can live with some standard version of parliamentary or presidential institutions and their electoral and judicial appurtenances. In these cases, if the problem is simply the public acceptability of a new set of institutions, then elected politicians or an elected constituent assembly can produce them in relative openness, with a good bit of public input and feedback, and the draft can be ratified in a referendum. If, however, the problem is the difficult one of crafting arrangements that will enable groups in conflict to share power in a country that needs both conflict reduction and democratic government, then ordinary majoritarianism, even with a decent separation of powers, will not be adequate, because it will usually exclude minorities from power. A heavy dose of expertise is called for, and often an expert body of drafters needs to be commissioned to study and work toward devising a consistent plan to create an arrangement that will not produce zero-sum results among groups.

As I said earlier, a careful process is often not planned. Some constitutional processes take place in the midst of ongoing violence, in which case, unfortunately, they may be conflated with a peace process or, as in Yemen, fail when they are overcome by warfare. Many processes are too rushed; many decision makers are too inexperienced and inexpert; many groups have conflicting objectives; and many actors prefer a private deal to a plan that might provide fewer certain benefits. Many processes, controlled by authoritarians, purport to produce a reform but take advantage of the opportunity to create constituent assemblies that can "step outside the constitutional framework in order to achieve [undemocratic] goals that they lacked the power to achieve within it."[6]

The stakes can be high, as the long-term consequences of failed or stalemated arrangements in Cyprus, Bosnia, Yemen, Afghanistan, and Iraq and failures to produce completed constitutions in Sri Lanka and Somalia, among others, show. Above all, actors in severely divided societies need to expend time and effort seeking a consistent constitutional plan to create institutions that will mitigate their conflicts.

Given the diversity of starting conditions and of attractive and aversive memories of earlier processes, very detailed *a priori* prescriptions are not in order. Still, it is possible to recognize some processes that are inapt. We have seen in Iraq that a profound failure of inclusion (and after-hours dealing when some of the excluded are finally included) can exacerbate already hostile and violent intergroup relations. Afghanistan had a hasty, half-hearted attempt at inclusion, but without elections, as well as a failure of deliberation and a cooked-up consensus masking rancorous divisions.[7] Inadequate inclusion and inadequate consensus are often the result of rushed processes. They certainly were in these two cases. And rushed processes invariably produce inadequate deliberation, usually accompanied by a failure of expert advice, either because appropriate advice on institutional design was not present, as in Iraq, or was ignored, as on some points it was in Afghanistan.

---

6. Landau, "Constitution Making Gone Wrong," p. 961. For this reason, Landau is more favorably disposed toward legislative constitution making.

7. J. Alexander Thier, "The Making of a Constitution in Afghanistan," *New York Law School Law Review*, Vol. 51, no. 3 (2006–07), pp. 557–79; Barnett Rubin, "Crafting a Constitution for Afghanistan," *Journal of Democracy*, Vol. 15, no. 3 (2004), pp. 5–19.

Many conspicuous failures involve bad timing. Premature ventures into constitution making, especially those that occur while warfare is ongoing, are unlikely to produce durable institutions. We have observed in Yemen that the proposed division of the north into four provinces was resented by Houthi rebels, who sensed an attempt to divide their region and who then accelerated their violence. The premature character of the Yemeni proceedings was also attested by the incomplete representation of the south, which was experiencing a secessionist movement of Hiraaks, many of whom failed to attend. Similarly, Somalia's wartime experience left it with a constitution that was far from complete because it was far from agreed. The Somali process was begun at a time when there was widespread violence, and it was finished at a time when significant parts of the country's territory were not under government control. Under the circumstances, constitution making could scarcely be done democratically.

It is important to know when not to engage in constitution making. If warfare signals that the time is not ripe, or if there is time only for a rushed process but some interim framework is needed, it is preferable not to try to produce a definitive document. Insofar as it takes account of group grievances but makes no final determinations regarding arrangements to redress them, a Yemen-like dialogue process could produce a sketchy, minimally serviceable, explicitly temporary, written code of governance. Such a document might limp along for an interim period and yet be recognized as obviously incomplete and lacking in sufficient legitimacy to become a genuine constitution, so that when an opportunity comes for democratic constitution making the chance can be seized. As I have pointed out, the Transitional Administrative Law was well suited to perform such a role in Iraq. Tunisia, too, adopted the Law on the Provisional Organization of Public Authorities shortly after its Constituent Assembly had been elected to draft the new constitution, and Indonesia utilized the formally democratic provisions of the constitution that had been perverted by the previous authoritarian regime. Such options can—and did—serve to eliminate the need for undue haste.

Timing within the process is also important. Excessive haste may mean inadequate consideration of institutional alternatives and may result in low standards for agreement, such as merely 50 percent plus one. Losing momentum early on by front-loading an extensive canvass of public opinion and participation is risky, especially if, in severely divided societies, public opinion is divided and extremists can use the time to emphasize or exacerbate public displays of division, including displays on the streets. Near the end of the process, as drafts are circulated, visibility of interests and how each has fared in the process thus far is heightened. At that point, sending careful drafts to small groups that have inadequate time for deliberation and have, perhaps, no access to explanations for features of drafts of which they are doubtful creates risks—of incoherent amendments or amendments that embody deals that exclude certain disfavored minorities. If those bodies can then secure overwhelming support when there is no referendum scheduled or can organize that support in a referendum, there will be no further correction of what they have done. The possibility of poor integration of the stages of a process is a real danger.

So, too, is neglect of the integrity of the bodies intended to assure compliance with the constitution. Deficiencies of commitment, manifested in constitutional violations, are not uncommon even in some countries with quite durable constitutions, including some created by the processes recommended here. In every process, attention must be paid to likely downstream difficulties by the careful design of electoral commissions, anti-discrimination commissions, anti-corruption commissions, and courts so that gains in the constitution are not erased by bias or corruption in enforcement. Commitment is more credible if well-constructed bodies backstop promises. These instruments may be able to deter or thwart partial or total defection from constitutional norms. In constitutional processes, it is easy to concentrate excessively on the symbolic changes produced, to the detriment of hard work on enforcement institutions.

It is important to acknowledge the difficulty of conjuring such institutions into existence. It will almost surely be easier to revive a rule of law whose custodians have, for a time, been politically coopted or displaced by more pliable functionaries than it is to create one from scratch. Hard though it is to develop or redevelop, a reliable rule of law can be crucial in backstopping and even in engendering commitment. If enforcement can be expected, actors will be more cautious about the commitments they undertake as well as more cautious about defecting from those commitments.

In severely divided societies, where one side is aiming at exclusion of, or maintaining a superior position to, another that is seeking full inclusion, compromise can be insuperably difficult. Typically, every change will be scrutinized for its ethnic effects, and ethnic entrepreneurs may interpret any concessions as fatal to the interests of their group. Then, mobilization of moderate group leaders and careful preparation of the populace for changes are usually required. Imperfectly committed leaders are a real danger. Good chances to create constitutions that mitigate conflict must not be missed, because repeated failures condition subsequent processes for failure and lower the threshold for failure, as Sri Lanka's multiple failures over many decades indicate. After the change to a moderate, multiethnic government in the 2018 elections, Malaysia missed several chances for constitutional amendments and corrections of ethnically biased policies and institutions because of fear of backlash and difficulties of finding the two-thirds needed for constitutional change.[8] Disillusion among the government's supporters followed, and in 2020 the government fell after legislators from the ruling coalition

8. For the main tasks, see Donald L. Horowitz, "Malaysia's Road to Democratic Reform," www.eastasiaforum.org, August 26, 2018.

abandoned it and joined with the former opposition. Many other, similarly riven countries—Somalia, Yemen, South Sudan, Comoros, and Rwanda among them—have tried and failed to produce fair and durable dispensations over the years.

If a process fails or cannot be convened, resort might be had to constitutional and legislative amendment. The stillborn constitutional process in Sri Lanka after 2018 has given rise to alternative reform proposals. Although, as I have indicated, there were the makings of a benign outcome in Sri Lanka by 2016–17, the country has, at other times, had a fundamental disagreement about whether it should be a purely majoritarian state, with an assumption of Sinhalese Buddhist hegemony at the expense of Tamil, Muslim, and Christian minorities or a pluralist state in which provision is made for minority accommodation. The existing constitution leans heavily toward the former, whereas the government that came to power in 2015 was to produce a new constitution along the lines of the latter. Since those efforts came to naught, some scholars and participants in the failed exercise have argued for compromise through ordinary legislation, with small changes followed by larger changes, when feasible.[9] Much more ambitiously, others have called for working to modify the Sinhalese Buddhist worldview, with its historical assumptions of ethnic primacy, through emphasis on virtues immanent in the local tradition, so that changes that seem impossible today become conceivable in the future.[10] As long-term strategies, these ideas may be sensible, but Sri Lanka has long waited for ethnic accommodation through constitutional change, and the wait has been costly in lives and in many other ways, including economic

9. Asanga Welikala, "The Idea of Constitutional Incrementalism," Centre for Policy Alternatives, Colombo, Working Paper on Constitutional Reform no. 14, January 2017.

10. Gehan Gunatilleke, "The Constitutional Practice of Ethno-Religious Violence in Sri Lanka," *Asian Journal of Comparative Law,* Vol. 13, no. 2 (2018), pp. 359–87.

development. Many severely divided societies need serious constitutional remediation in the short term.

That brings me back to the question of timing. This is an issue at the beginning of a process and after it has gone on for quite a while. A single sentence of admonition may be helpful, but it is sometimes hard to apply: Do not squander momentum (Sri Lanka 2015–16), and do not adhere to rigid deadlines (Iraq 2005; Nepal 2012 and 2015).

CHAPTER 10

Processes, Good and Not So Good

Some final words by way of synthesis, but assuredly not *the* final word. I begin by searching for evidence of durable democratic commitment and for conditions that may have abetted the creation and endurance of what I have portrayed as some of the more successful deliberative processes. In doing this, I elaborate on elements of those processes discussed in earlier chapters and contrast them with elements found in the less successful processes also described previously. As I review these processes, I highlight the role of intentionality, of choice rather than forces beyond anyone's control.

Although severely divided societies have a special need for a deliberative process by which they can choose appropriate institutions for conflict reduction, what those institutions are is a separate matter from the choice of process as such. As I have said, a major criterion in any country for a process that stands a good chance of producing democratic outcomes is the likelihood that the process will generate commitment by participating politicians. Continuation of that commitment will depend, in some measure, on how the institutions adopted actually function. A good process should help in choosing appropriate institutions as well as generating commitment, whether or not those politicians are acting in a society characterized by serious ethnic (or ethno-religious) divisions.

It would be valuable to have had before-and-after surveys of participants in constitutional processes to gauge their democratic commitment and the extent to which the process might have caused a change. Unfortunately, there is no survey evidence at all to gauge durable democratic commitment on the part of actual participants in the Indian, Indonesian, and Tunisian processes that I have identified as inclusive, deliberative, and consensus-driven. The best evidence is their behavior after the process concludes as well as the persistence of democracy in the years following, which we shall come to shortly. There are, however, a few surveys of lower-level politicians in Indonesia and Tunisia in the years after constitutional adoption that shed some light on questions of commitment.

A 2017–18 survey of provincial legislators in Indonesia produced considerable evidence of democratic commitment. These politicians emphasized procedural and representative aspects of democracy, consisting of free elections and legislative "checking functions," in contrast to the view revealed in surveys of mass publics, in which respondents tended to see democracy as a system that delivers economic welfare, "equity," and similar outcomes. There were some illiberal views among the legislators, but none advocated authoritarian governance. According to the investigators' measures, 38 percent of the legislators were clear liberal democrats, while another 47 percent leaned in that direction; the comparable numbers were markedly smaller among citizens at large. The results, conclude the investigators, provide evidence of the legislators' "greater acculturation of democratic ideals and principles,"[1] a conclusion that is somewhat remarkable in view of the noticeable (but far from total) decline in democratic practices in the few years preceding the survey. And in spite of their more limited liberalism, a different survey of citi-

1. Edward Aspinall, Diego Fossati, Burhanuddin Muhtadi, and Eve Warburton, "Elites, Masses, and Democratic Decline in Indonesia," *Democratization*, Vol. 27, no. 4 (2019), pp. 505–26.

zens in 2018 confirmed what previous surveys had revealed—that Indonesians are overwhelmingly satisfied (by a margin of 65 percent) with their democracy.[2]

An as-yet unpublished survey of Tunisian politicians at various levels of the political system shows clear majority support for democracy, respect for the rights of political opponents, and the need to compromise with them.[3] A 2018 survey of two thousand Tunisian candidates for local election asked the candidates whether they agreed or disagreed with three statements designed to elicit the depth of their support for democracy: (1) democracy and human rights "should never be sacrificed" for the sake of security or fighting terrorism; (2) local councils should "frequently consult citizens" even if consultation "slows down decision-making"; and (3) "only the voters should have the power to remove councilors," and then only through the medium of elections. The first question received approximately 47 percent agreement, in spite of its "never" wording and the incidence of terrorist attacks in Tunisia in preceding years. The second received approximately 80 percent agreement, and the third 77 percent agreement. More than 78 percent of respondents gave affirmative answers to either two of the three questions or to all three.[4] Cynics might conclude that the candidates merely knew

2. Christine Tamir and Abby Budiman, "Indonesians Optimistic about Their Country's Democracy and Economy as Elections Near," *Fact Tank*, Pew Research Center, April 4, 2019. By even larger margins, as high as 92 percent, but with the median from 2006–19 in the high 70s, Indonesians affirm that democracy is the best form of government for the country. See Aspinall et al., "Elites, Masses, and Democratic Decline in Indonesia," p. 508, Figure 1.

3. Tunisian Elite Survey conducted in 2019 by Youssef Chouhoud, M. Tahir Kilavuz, and Matt Gordner. The politician respondents comprise a subsample of a larger group that was surveyed, and they include a large fraction at leadership levels in their parties. The responses are surprisingly positive in view of the interparty suspicion visible at the outset of the constitutional process.

4. Alexandra Blackman, Julia Clark, and Aytuğ Şaşmaz, "Tunisian Local Election Candidate Survey," Democracy International, Bethesda, Maryland, July 2018, pp. 13–14.

the right answers, but more confidence than that is warranted if we consider the divided responses to the first question.

Interestingly, this survey coincided with an Afrobarometer sampling of the Tunisian population in which there was a generally modest decline in support for democracy expressed by respondents. The most dramatic decline was in the proportion expressing a preference for democracy: only 46 percent support, down from 56 percent in 2013 and 57 percent in 2015. Nevertheless, respondents rejected specific authoritarian alternatives, often by strong majorities, and they expressed support for the supremacy of law and the accountability of politicians to the people, the latter even at the expense of not "getting things done." There was disappointment with Tunisia's actual democracy: 33 percent said it was "a democracy with major problems," and another 29 percent denied that it was a democracy at all.[5] These were not really surprising numbers; they likely reflect disappointment with Tunisia's post-constitutional legislative immobilism, deriving from its fragmented legislature and resulting inability to govern effectively.[6]

A different survey of the population conducted a few months later reported somewhat different results. A majority of 51 percent of respondents unequivocally declared democracy to be preferable to any other form of government, while only 20 percent said that sometimes a non-democratic regime might be preferable. Most described Tunisia's regime to be a full or nearly full democracy, rather than a flawed one.[7] All such surveys are likely to be at least somewhat affected by the course of particular recent events.

---

5. Youssef Meddeb, "Support for Democracy Dwindles in Tunisia amid Negative Perceptions of Economic Conditions," Afrobarometer Dispatch no. 232, September 3, 2018.

6. Daniel Brumberg and Maryam Ben Salem, "Tunisia's Endless Transition?" *Journal of Democracy*, Vol. 31, no. 2 (April 2020), pp. 110–24.

7. Center for Insights in Survey Research, "Public Opinion Survey: Residents of Tunisia, January 25–February 11, 2019," International Republican Institute, Washington, DC, pp. 64–65.

The surveys of politicians provide only suggestive evidence of democratic commitment on the part of politicians. What we might infer is that the emergence of a new dispensation from the Indonesian and Tunisian constitutional processes seems to have fostered the diffusion of democratic values.[8] Despite the negative trends reported, this also appears to extend downward to the population in Tunisia's case, more modestly in Indonesia's.

If we turn to democratic practice following the adoption of the three constitutions, we have a somewhat firmer basis for judgment. All three countries have maintained their democracies, but with varying degrees of difficulty. All are imperfect democracies, subject to periodic backsliding.

India's democracy was marred by a period of emergency rule from 1975 to 1977 during the regime of Prime Minister Indira Gandhi. This was a period of unlawful arrests, abductions for forced sterilization, and attempts to undermine the independent judiciary.[9] Importantly, however, the Indian electorate rejected the emergency and the Gandhi government in the 1977 elections, in which the prime minister herself and her son, who had been her designated successor, both lost their seats. There have been other challenges to democracy as well. Over many decades, India has also had bouts of very poorly controlled violence against a number of different minority groups in several different states, often with the connivance or tolerance of state governments,[10] and it experienced an upsurge of officially countenanced anti-Muslim discrimination, repression of dissenting voices, and questionable electoral practices during the

8. The cautious wording in this sentence is deliberate, as there is no evidence relating to those values before the constitutional process began or immediately after it concluded.

9. For a brief treatment, see Myron Weiner, *The Indian Paradox: Essays in Indian Politics* (New Delhi: Sage Publications, 1989), pp. 88–89.

10. See Steven I. Wilkinson, *Votes and Violence: Electoral Competition and Ethnic Riots in India* (Cambridge: Cambridge University Press, 2004).

regime of Narendra Modi.[11] Despite these challenges, Indians have habitually expressed high confidence in democracy and in their national government, even as they displayed divergences over time in party preferences.[12]

Indonesia left a certain amount of democratic business unattended during its constitutional renovation.[13] Thereafter, the country experienced backsliding in religious freedom. Blasphemy prosecutions, based on a decree dating back to the authoritarian 1960s, saw a dramatic upsurge. More than decade later, there were proposals to end elections of regional executives, a democratic innovation of the post-1998 period. Those proposals were defeated by a backlash from Indonesia's active civil society organizations. There was also a tendency, manifested around the time of the 2019 election and after, toward illiberal treatment of political opponents, including occasional prosecutions.

Undoubtedly, Tunisia had the greatest problems in producing a stable democracy. After its first post-constitution elections, it formed a coalition government of opposing parties and then a wider national-unity government. Both of these were prone to policy stagnation as a result of fundamental disagreements.[14] Important bodies, such as the constitutional court prescribed by the new constitution, were not established. Despite his limited powers, the first president intruded into matters entrusted to the prime minister. An overly broad anti-terrorism law was passed, and the courts were oc-

11. Sumit Ganguly, "An Illiberal India?" *Journal of Democracy*, Vol. 31, no. 1 (2020), pp. 193–202.

12. See, e.g., Grant Buckles, "Confidence in Key Institutions High as India Votes," Gallup Poll, April 11, 2019, displaying results going back to 2006.

13. On Indonesia's remaining democratic deficit after the conclusion of its constitutional process, see Horowitz, *Constitutional Change and Democracy in Indonesia*, pp. 207–60.

14. Sharan Grewal and Shadi Hamid, "The Dark Side of Consensus in Tunisia: Lessons from 2015–2019," Brookings Institution Governance Report, Washington, DC, January 2020.

casionally used against political opponents. The party system was poorly institutionalized, parliamentarians jumped from one party to another, and new parties arrived quickly as the old ones declined dramatically.[15]

Because Tunisia's list-system proportional electoral system provides no minimum threshold of votes for a party to secure legislative representation, parliamentary election results were badly fragmented. After the 2019 legislative elections, a disparate coalition of multiple parties, none with close to a majority of seats, was slowly patched together, but eight months later it still had been unable to form a government. In the 2019 presidential election, a non-politician, unaffiliated with any party, won the presidency in a landslide victory reflecting discontent with established politicians. While standing up functioning political institutions has proved difficult, public support for democracy has proved decidedly resilient. There were no real temptations toward authoritarian revival, whether civilian or military.

In fact, although all three countries are imperfect democracies, vulnerable to setbacks and occasional crises, there have been no serious proposals for a reversal of democracy. In each case, a constitutional process was created that made possible what might have seemed—and sometimes did seem—to be unlikely: democratic structures and a cadre of politicians who appeared, despite occasional slippage, to be committed to those structures as providing the only way to practice politics.

Bearing in mind that India, Indonesia, and Tunisia were all thought by some analysts to be infertile fields for democratic development, it is worth trying to uncover what may have been facilitating conditions that lay in the background or arose early the

15. On these difficulties, see Sarah Yerkes and Zaineb Ben Yahmed, "Tunisia's Political System: From Stagnation to Competition," Carnegie Endowment for International Peace, Washington, DC, March 28, 2019.

processes themselves. In India and Tunisia, some such conditions can be identified, but they were very far from determinative, as I shall show. Indonesia, by contrast, had more minimal facilitative conditions at the outset, and those that emerged were more proximate to the process itself. In all, it was clear that the intended destination was a democratic constitution, but in each case it took a long while to arrive there. Time to find agreement and determination to overcome any crises that appear along the way are both important facilitators.

In India, the long struggle for independence and the disastrous partition violence that came with independence, as the Constituent Assembly sat, intensified the desire on the part of political leaders to unite a fragmented society into a single polity.[16] The mass nationalism organized by the Indian National Congress in the decades preceding independence was linked to the emergence of democratic aspirations. These were important starting principles. As early as 1936, Congress made a constituent assembly elected by universal suffrage a central demand, and in 1946 it accepted indirect election of the constitution-drafting assembly only because universal suffrage would have entailed unacceptable delay in the face of the crisis that had come to the country. When Jawaharlal Nehru enjoined the constituent assembly to produce a dispensation in which "all power derived from the people,"[17] he was reflecting longstanding commitments of the Congress, but the assembly proceedings make clear that the meaning of the phrase in all its particulars would be subject to vigorous debate.

Congress was not a homogeneous entity by any stretch of the imagination. It was divided in multiple ways, along lines of left and

16. Khosla, *India's Founding Moment*.

17. Sumit Sarkar, "Indian Democracy: The Historical Inheritance," in *The Success of India's Democracy*, ed. Atul Kohli (Cambridge: Cambridge University Press, 2001), pp. 23–46, at p. 32. The discussion of the debates that follows draws heavily on Sarkar's essay and especially on Chaube, *Constituent Assembly of India*, 2d ed.

right, Hindu majority and multiple minorities, caste differences among high-caste Hindus, backward castes, and ex-untouchables. Muslims were the most politically significant minority. Before the partition of India and Pakistan, the Muslim League was demanding at least a great deal of autonomy for the provinces in which Muslims were in a majority. Other regional minorities also had similar claims: Sikhs in a Punjab that might be controlled by Muslims; Hindus similarly situated in Bengal; pro-India Muslims in the North-West Frontier Province,[18] aligned to the "Red Shirts," led by a secular socialist; and a number of others who aimed for degrees of separatism or protection from the larger communities around them. Princely states also had interests they were concerned to protect, and they were suspicious of Congress plans to absorb their territories without regard to their traditional identity and modes of governing. There were distinctive problems concerning tribal populations, many of them Christian, as well as ex-untouchables, known as Scheduled Castes, and others relatively low in the caste system, the so-called Backward Classes. Majority-minority differences across several dimensions could scarcely be avoided with the presence of certain conservative Hindus in the assembly and the refusal of the separatist Muslim League to participate in the body. The salience of the issue of untouchability was underscored by the appointment of Ambedkar, a highly respected lawyer and the most prominent leader of the ex-untouchables, as chairman of the drafting committee.

Left-right differences were also significant against the background of an active Communist Party of India, not to mention the socialist ideology conspicuous in some parts of the Congress, balanced by the presence in the assembly of notable conservatives concerned about protecting property interests. And, finally, there were differences of views among sophisticated lawyers and public figures

18. A province destined to go to Pakistan if there were to be partition, which the Red Shirts resisted.

concerning what should and should not be contained in the draft document and how it should be framed.

The concrete meaning of a democratic India had been fleshed out over just short of three years of wide-ranging debate, as we saw in chapter 5. Among the critical issues that divided the assembly were the reach of fundamental rights, the powers of a democratic polity to override cultural particularisms, the character of Indian federalism, and the emancipation of the least privileged members of the society.

The debates were complicated by the way these issues interrelated. On federalism, for example, the assembly began with a resolution guaranteeing autonomy and residual powers to its constituent units, a point especially important to governments of the princely states, which had sent delegates, some of whom were keen to preserve monarchy in their states. It was also critical to the Muslim League, which some delegates were trying, by moderating their positions, to entice into participating in the assembly. Like some Muslims, Christian minorities were fearful of a strong central government, with its accompanying homogenization and inevitably powerful Hindu majority. For his part, Ambedkar was keen on a strong national government, for he wanted the power to nationalize land and industry in order to benefit deprived sections of the population. The right wing of the assembly, however, resisted such provisions, as it also resisted the most extensive guarantees of civil liberties. Some feared that a strongly affirmed secularism—ironically because it would be accompanied by equally strong guarantees of religious freedom—might impair the power to act against untouchability, with its roots in Hindu religious doctrine. A different fear, of conversion attempts by Muslims and Christians, was met with proposals to limit the sphere of religious freedom by restricting conversion or providing for the removal of the children of converts. These proposals were opposed by Christians and by Ambedkar, whose conversion to Buddhism had inspired mass conversions of ex-untouchables. Eventually, these particular proposals were dropped. These various cross-currents affected debates over the strongest versions of secularism, of cultural practices of Hindus as well as Muslims, and of the powers of the states.

When the partition of India was announced in 1947, the debates in the assembly shifted. The need to entice the Muslim League to participate, which had produced great reluctance to advance any positions that might discourage League participation, dissolved. The previous consensus had favored a weak central government with residual powers in the states. Now the assembly tilted in the opposite direction. The remaining non-League Muslim delegates, who might have raised divisive demands, did not. The violence that killed hundreds of thousands and the migrations that moved millions of refugees promptly engulfed the country.[19] The assembly was persuaded to create a centralized federation, with residual powers in New Delhi, rather than the states, and rights guarantees were unambiguously stated, but without major concessions on cultural practices.

That did not end debate. Agreement was often hard won, especially on the scope of reserved places (quotas) for scheduled castes and tribes and religious minorities in various institutions. The exact form of government—the character of the executive, its relation to the legislature, and the role of the judiciary as constitutional arbiter—consumed a great deal of time. There were wide differences about parliamentary or presidential government and many related issues, and eventually the assembly settled on compromises regarding executive power vis-à-vis individual rights.[20]

Had the assembly not had a long period to deliberate, both in general and separately on each clause, a divided Congress might

19. There had already been Hindu-Muslim violence in Calcutta in 1946, but with partition a much stronger wave took place in Punjab and adjacent areas.

20. See Chaube, *Constituent Assembly of India*, 2d ed., pp. 193–213, 235.

have produced a very different constitution, possibly with strong dissensus remaining. The longstanding commitment of Congress to a democratic outcome was a start, but it certainly did not foreordain the agreed document that emerged. The commitment to a deliberative constituent assembly, with its formidable tolerance for argument and its ability to assess divergent views in the light of changing circumstances, was far more important.

Nehru had urged the assembly to try to reach unanimous decisions, and some debates were slowed down for this purpose.[21] On language issues, unanimity was not really possible, and a half-hearted compromise was produced after two close votes had been taken.[22] That votes had to be taken on particular contested issues does not impugn the ultimately consensual nature of the process. Real consensus can scarcely be produced without a full airing of differences and protracted efforts at persuasion. This the Indian Constituent Assembly had, with its 167 days of sittings. Of those days, 114 were devoted to debate.[23] Keeping the commitment to a deliberative constituent assembly was the decisive element.

Tunisia had some supporting conditions of a different sort, and it assuredly needed them. More than once, the constitutional project was in jeopardy, and it was saved by constructive interventions and determination to resume work after breakdowns.

As we observed in previous chapters, the exiled opposition, secular and religious, had met while abroad. During the constitutional proceedings, exiled leaders from the Islamic party Ennahda had proved to be more accommodating on issues of secularism than those party members who had been based in Tunisia. Yet those

---

21. Austin, *The Indian Constitution*, pp. 24-25.

22. Ibid., pp. 284, 300, 303.

23. Ibid., p. 110. During the same time frame, the assembly had many days of additional sittings to perform its functions as a provisional legislature. There were also many committee meetings during the three-year life of the assembly.

proceedings began with a great deal of suspicion of Ennahda's true motives on the part of many secularists and religious moderates, in and outside the assembly.[24] As Grewal has shown,[25] those who had lived abroad were critical to successful completion of the constitutional task.

Former exiles, however, were not alone in conciliation. Also important were relations among leaders of civil society organizations, secular and Islamic, who, years before the transition to democracy began in 2011, had formed a pro-democracy organization called the Collective. Over time, members of these bodies had achieved a degree of mutual understanding and an ability to accommodate each other's positions despite persistent conflicts among them. The Collective, however, dissolved in 2009. When the constitutional process reached a critical impasse in 2013, a National Dialogue, initiated by a "Quartet" of organizations representing labor unions, business groups, human rights activists, and lawyers, took an active role in persuading parties to resume negotiations. Former participants in the Collective participated in these efforts, which were then followed by the creation of the Consensus Committee that, as we saw previously, the president of the assembly had appointed.[26]

Previously established relationships, in Tunisia and overseas, helped overcome distrust and ideological differences, ultimately making a document reflecting consensus and compromise possible. At critical moments, the intrusion into the process from outside bodies reinforced the resolve of insiders to keep the process moving

24. Even before the process got underway, there was suspicion that Ennahda's professions of faith in democracy were uttered in coded and insincere language.

25. Grewal, "From Islamists to Muslim Democrats."

26. For the Collective and the Quartet, see M. Tahir Kilavuz, "Once Allies, Always Allies: Coalition Building Under Authoritarianism and Democratic Transitions in the MENA," unpublished paper, Harvard University, n.d., ca. 2020, pp. 17–22.

when it seemed that progress could not be made. Resources created before the transition were valuable years later, when success seemed most in doubt.

Like the work of the Constituent Assembly of India, that of the National Constituent Assembly in Tunisia was long and arduous. The assembly sat for two years. If it had had a deadline, it might not have overcome its differences and concluded its deliberations. The assembly was plagued by antipathy of some members toward Ennahda as well as by disagreements within that party. When Ennahda, with its large number of seats, was suspected of extralegal action or of untoward ambition, it managed to overcome the suspicion by abnegation, especially at junctures when it might have seized a disproportionate share of power. Its burden was to prove that it was not the fraternal twin of the Muslim Brotherhood in Egypt, and it managed finally to do so and to demonstrate its democratic credentials.

Indonesia's independence movement lacked the deep and wide democratic commitments of the Indian National Congress, and the extensive cross-ideological interchange of Tunisian elites, and the ability of civil society to break into the proceedings to resolve deadlocks.[27] The movement's main function had been to fight the Dutch, who, after World War II, had not given up on colonialism and had not been preparing their colonies for ultimate self-government. Among the Indonesians, there were also religious, ethnic, and inter-island differences as well as a fear shared in the Outer Islands of the ambitions of the strong Javanese plurality in the population. The powerful consciousness of being Indonesian had grown but was not uniformly spread on the periphery. A Christian group in eastern Indonesia was well represented in the Dutch forces that fought the

27. For a concise description of the Indonesian nationalist movement and its fissures, as well as of the independence struggle, see Ailsa Zainu'ddin, *A Short History of Indonesia* (New York: Praeger, 1968), pp. 169–238.

nationalists after World War II, and other groups on the periphery were fearful of Muslim hegemony.

During that war, Indonesia had been occupied by the Japanese, and some nationalist leaders had come under the influence of antidemocratic ideologies that then found their way into the 1945 constitution. That constitution had created an unchecked state with no real guarantees of individual liberty. It was the constitution in force in 1998, when Suharto was ousted as president. To make matters worse, as I mentioned earlier, Indonesia's only experience of democracy, from 1955 to 1959, had been unsatisfying, beset as it was with governmental instability. In 1998, some leaders of a divided military, heavily involved in government but temporarily discredited by the violence the armed forces had unleashed on civilian protesters, awaited a call to resume their previous civilian functions. That call did not come, but the initial odds were nevertheless against a successful transition.[28]

Indonesia's process was, like Tunisia's, accompanied by suspicion, but of a different and in the end less disruptive sort. The supralegislature that acted as a constituent assembly consisted of parties of Suharto's New Order and of extraparliamentary parties. Among the latter, some were established, while others were newly created in anticipation of elections announced by Suharto's successor, the former vice president B. J. Habibie. Soon after Habibie took power, he had committed himself to a democratic transition. Free elections were to be held within a year. Radical students were advocating violent revolution, and other political leaders were calling for creation of a revolutionary provisional government outside of constitutional structures. It was a time of great public disorder. The surviving parties of the old regime had no real choice: they declared their loyalty

28. As Edward Aspinall has written, there simply was no "credible democratic alternative at the point of the regime's collapse." *Opposing Suharto: Compromise, Resistance, and Regime Change* (Stanford: Stanford University Press, 2005), p. 240.

to the new democratic regime. The three most prominent extraparliamentary opposition leaders, from the three most prominent ideological streams, confident of their mass followings, did have a choice. They met and agreed to take their chances on the elections. Beyond that, their personal relations were often distant. Slowly, order was restored sufficiently to hold the elections.

After the elections were successfully concluded, there was considerable interparty cooperation, facilitated by the inability of any one party to govern alone. That cross-ideological cooperation was all the more remarkable because Indonesia had had almost no experience of democratic governance, and the little it had had, nearly a half-century earlier, had been marked by revolving-door governments and constitutional stalemates, recollection of which might have tainted the determination to renew the democratic experiment. Determined to avoid a constitutional stalemate that had defeated an earlier effort to frame a democratic constitution, the legislators avoided the imposition of constitutional deadlines that could, by their mere arrival, confirm a failure to agree.

When the 1999 electoral results came in, the vote and seat totals of the authoritarian-holdover parties were significantly clipped, so that they were in no position to dictate to the extraparliamentary parties, the largest of which had gained a third of the seats. The constitution-making body, controlled by no single party or cluster of parties, soon made clear it would proceed very quietly, making public its constitutional amendments only when agreed by all. In proceeding this way, the newly elected assembly was utilizing the preference of the former authoritarian regime for consensus decisions, but now in the service of producing a new regime. Official positions were parceled out among the parties, and during this period no idea of government versus opposition emerged. As they went about their business, legislators used the procedures specified by the constitution that most of them wished to displace in order to guide the process of displacement. When they had finished, the extensively amended and now-democratic 1945 constitution was, in form, somewhat similar to the original, but in content, hardly recognizable.

As the de facto new constitution was being crafted, the newly freed press and civil society organizations responded by recurrently expressing skepticism that the politicians would be doing anything other than making the deals that suited their own interests. The more the assembly operated in secret, releasing amendments only as and when they were agreed, the more conspiracy theories flourished outside. The greater the skepticism, the greater the assembly's determination to create a democracy that would not confirm it.

Skepticism among non-governmental elites did not abate, but the crowds had long left the streets, satisfied by the promise of elections, then by the actual exercise of a meaningful franchise for the first time in nearly a half century, and finally by the notable success of opponents of the previous regime in those elections. This enabled the constitution makers to proceed as they intended. By the time the job was done three years later, they had given up several of the most important powers the original constitution had accorded them, including the power to choose the president, who henceforth would be—and indeed has been—popularly elected.

Along the way, commitments to consensus decisions and to democracy were fortified by the action of the assembly itself. There was, for example, no desire to short-circuit the decision in favor of popular presidential election even when Megawati Sukarnoputri, leader of a secular-nationalist party for which many on the Islamic side of the fence had no affinity, hesitated long and hard to endorse such a decision. The proponents waited until she came around. Consensus decisions on every matter of constitutional change were the rule, and the rule was followed. A preference expressed by two Islamic parties, representing only 12 percent of the seats, for a provision stating that Muslims would be obliged to follow religious rules was opposed by all other parties and by the two largest Muslim organizations in the country. The proposal was abandoned in exchange for a clause committing the state to an education system encouraging "faith, devoutness, and character." This was a rare compromise in an otherwise consensual constitutional product. Democratic commitments were also on display in impeaching and removing Habibie's successor, Abdurrahman Wahid, who had shown a willingness to resort to authoritarian methods in order to stay in power. In short, successive bits and pieces of democratic praxis made the assembly's process and the initial democratic commitments more secure, until ultimately those in the press and civil society who stood outside the process had to recognize its accomplishments.

Still, there is no denying that, at the outset, Indonesia lacked the strong support of Indian nationalist history or even of Tunisian experience of cross-ideological cooperation. Had the process encountered internal difficulties, as Tunisia's did, there were no external resources available for a rescue. Elements of the most powerful external force, the army, would have been happy to help, but the outcome many of the generals would have preferred would have been very different.

All three of these processes began with apprehension at the outset about prospects for a democratic outcome, and leaders of all three exhibited determination not to be thwarted in its pursuit. For all three, a major democratic departure from the previous autocratic regime was essential, and that departure required unified support. All three bodies were explicit about the desire for consensus, and all three began and ended with inclusive assemblies created through elections (albeit indirect elections in India). All three deliberated extensively, both in committees and in plenary sessions. In spite of the need for compromises or divided votes on some matters along the way, all three concluded their work with universal or close to universal agreement on the overall constitution, two by nearly unanimous votes and one by consensus without the need for votes in favor of the final product. Although all three bodies involved representatives of groups with sharply divergent interests, none alienated those representatives by adopting provisions congenial only to bare majorities or to exclusive factions. None required a referendum to confirm the acceptability of its work.

Determination not to miss the chance; perseverance in pursuing it even when crises intruded; patience in proceeding without rigid deadlines; deference to rules for consensus across a broad range of participants, including those with disparate starting positions, some of which were not necessarily congenial to a thoroughly democratic outcome; reasoning together across party lines: these were the common elements across three disparate polities in producing results acceptable both to the politicians who crafted them and to their publics. It helped that most delegates in each case started with a democratic destination in mind, that in India the dominant movement had long sought democracy, and that in Tunisia the splintered opposition had been conferring during the authoritarian period and could be assisted in crises by interventions from coalitions outside the assembly. Indonesia's interparty consultations had been less intense, but the process was facilitated by agreement to use the serviceable parts of the authoritarian constitution as a ready-made procedural format for their efforts.

What this evidence shows is that actors who are committed to a democratic outcome at the start can design a process to produce that outcome. What it also suggests, although less conclusively, is that such a process is likely to enhance democratic commitment after the process concludes.

Against this welter of experience, it is easy to see where efforts elsewhere fell short. Sri Lanka and Nepal most closely approximated the best starting conditions. Their constitutional processes were, for a time, inclusive, deliberative, and consensual. In both cases, there were major differences in the starting positions of the polarized participants but also a good deal of deliberation—in Nepal's case, over many years—and a good probability of a consensus outcome. In both, however, efforts to reach a conclusion were undone. In Sri Lanka, the absence of the highest level of political leadership was visible early on, and the growing defection of participants reduced the chances for agreement as the de facto deadline created by the election calendar approached. Nepal, too, was vulnerable to an artificial, albeit unforeseen, deadline, the public demand for a resolution after a serious earthquake. At this point, inclusion was effectively reversed as dominant ethnic and caste factions in the Nepalese assembly took the opportunity to abandon the quest for consensus and embarked on a deal that excluded the concerns of the most significant minorities, provoking an extended period of violent protest and repression in the disadvantaged areas.

In Kenya, Fiji, and Iraq, there was little serious deliberation, and what little there had been was supplanted by deal making. In Kenya, it was a deal between leaders of two antagonistic political parties that left the interests of one ethnic group unattended. In Fiji, a deal negotiated in secret, in the quest to guarantee places in government, altered a carefully constructed constitutional arrangement. In Iraq, a major group was included only nominally in constitutional negotiations, which produced a deal between two other sets of participants, a deal that the excluded group found contrary to its interests and that produced a major upsurge in civil violence.

Interestingly enough, in all of these cases except Sri Lanka, where the constitutional project was aborted, a constitution was actually produced. Nevertheless, durable democracy in accordance with the four new constitutions was in doubt (or worse) in each one. In Kenya and Iraq, divisive referenda were held. The first national elections held after the adoption of the new constitution of Nepal were marred by more than a hundred explosions, many of them directed at political leaders. The parliament that was elected exhibited tendencies to centralize authority, to the advantage of traditional high-caste elites and to the disadvantage of some regions and groups to which power and resources were to be devolved. In Kenya, the new constitution was converted in practice into something closely resembling the previous strong-presidential system, thereby displaying the infidelity of the sitting regime to the constitutional design. The constitutional design in Fiji was given short shrift in the course of deal-making. The deal made it harder to achieve electoral results that were as robustly interethnic as the drafting commission had envisioned. Within two years, a paramilitary putsch had displaced the government elected under the new system. For more than a decade thereafter, Fiji was under military or military-influenced rule. As noted earlier, Iraq's constitution contained a number of important blank sections that were not filled in more than a decade and a half after its adoption. The country was subjected to internal warfare, terrorism, and abuses of authority that were slow to subside. Deal-making alone in constitutional processes did not produce unequivocally democratic outcomes.

Of course, it may be that Sri Lanka, Nepal, Kenya, Fiji, and Iraq were simply harder cases for both deliberative constitution making and democratic outcomes than were India, Indonesia, and Tunisia. Because the starting conditions of each were so different from those in others, it is hard to judge, but the immediate backgrounds in India, Indonesia, and Tunisia were decidedly more authoritarian than those in Sri Lanka, Nepal, Kenya, and Fiji.

Sri Lanka's parliamentary traditions went back to its first universal suffrage elections in 1931. They provided a stronger basis for democratic reform than anything in the history of Indonesia or Tunisia. Ethno-religious polarization was deeply embedded in Sri Lanka by 2015, but the need for fundamental constitutional change was widely acknowledged in parliament after the elections of that year.

Nepal had earlier undergone a popular decapitation of its authoritarian monarchy and an insurgency on behalf of disadvantaged sections of the population, followed by years of candid debate about constitutional remediation of its problems. This was far more debate than Indonesia or Tunisia had had. Yet Nepalese elites abandoned the task on the very edge of its success.

The deal forged in Kenya between former electoral enemies built on the foundations of the constitution rejected in a referendum a few years earlier could easily have given way to a more inclusive and deliberative process, but that was never contemplated. The most powerful Kenyan leaders, who, between them, commanded majority support, simply had other ideas all along.

Fijian politicians never thought they needed a wider process. They went from a commission report to a closed committee process led by two men, influential in the parliamentary select committee, and then to pro forma approval by parliament.

Undoubtedly, Iraq was a more difficult case than India, Indonesia, and Tunisia, but the Iraqis embarked on a process designed to be inclusive and then quickly abandoned it. The Iraqi process leaders saw advantages in two-sided negotiations that could lead each to control a region of the country.

In evaluating the impact of preexisting conditions, it is worth recalling that South Africa, whose preexisting conditions could scarcely be described as favorable, designed a deliberative process that led to an apparently durable democratic outcome. In Nepal, Kenya, Fiji, and Iraq, there was either the lack of genuine determination to contemplate the exigencies of a process that might bring them to a democratic destination or the willingness to give up on such a process when that proved convenient for an exclusive group of elites. In none of these cases were the environmental constraints so great as to obviate the ability to choose a different process. Those who make decisions at the outset or along the way often encounter a temptation to forego inclusive benefits for exclusive benefits that can impair the welfare of their opponents.

Differences in initial conditions seem much less important than what those in charge of the process actually decided, particularly with respect to whose interests counted. What stands out in all eight cases was motivated action rather than any sort of determinism. A deliberative process is a matter of choice governed more by the intentions and agency of actors than by forces beyond their control.

Well-chosen processes depend in part on determination to overcome obstacles and to avoid repetition of earlier adverse experiences. In acting on this determination, leadership, more than fortuity, is involved. Once India began its deliberations, there was no turning back. The same was true in Indonesia, driven as it was by the desire not to replicate an earlier failure. For its part, Tunisia created its democracy amidst enormous suspicion of Ennahda by some secular elements of its population. That suspicion was cured only by the frequently displayed modesty of Ennahda, Tunisia's largest party. The antecedent crisis conditions that seemed inhospitable in India, Indonesia, and Tunisia negate any possibility that their process choices or their success were foreordained. Rather, they were an achievement by those who managed the processes.

Superior leadership was a highly salient facilitating condition for building consensus. India, Indonesia, and Tunisia were fortunate in the careful, patient steps taken by their leaderships, coupled with a determination not to be thrown off course by crises that developed along the way. When leadership stumbled in Tunisia, organizations that had developed earlier moved in to help. Leadership was less conspicuous in Indonesia, and stumbles along the way were few, because agreement to proceed to consensus outcomes regardless of time constraints was widespread from the beginning. Civil society help, so useful in Tunisia, was unnecessary in India and largely shut out in Indonesia except with respect to advice regarding a presidential electoral system.[29] There were, in these cases, no preexisting conditions determining success and no single path to the same general

29. See chapter 2, n. 9.

destination. What they had in common were obstacles to overcome at the outset and along the way.

The determination to avoid hard and fast deadlines was particularly evident in India and Indonesia and notably lacking at the end in Nepal, where assembly leaders took advantage of the opportunity to short-circuit the proceedings, and in Sri Lanka, where the most prominent leaders failed to show any tenacity at all. The antecedent political conditions that seemed inhospitable in India, Indonesia, and Tunisia negate any real possibility that their process choices or their success were foreordained. Rather, they were an achievement by those who managed the processes.

Soon after adoption of the Indonesian and Tunisian constitutions, both countries were rated "Free" on Freedom House's democracy index. Despite slippage, India, Indonesia, and Tunisia have all had consistently higher scores on Freedom House's aggregate democracy index than have Nepal, Sri Lanka, Kenya, or Iraq.[30] In 2019, the scores of the first group averaged 68.7, while the scores of the four others averaged 47.3.[31] Similar results obtained for the Economist Intelligence Unit's Democracy Index for 2019, where the differentials were even sharper. The average scores for India, Indonesia, and Tunisia were rather tightly clustered, averaging 6.7, in each case amounting to what the unit calls a "flawed democracy." Scores for Nepal, Sri Lanka, Kenya, and Iraq averaged 5.1, and three of these were labeled either authoritarian (Iraq) or hybrid regimes (Kenya and Nepal), while only Sri Lanka counted as a merely flawed democracy—and this was the evaluation before Sri Lanka's widely expected authoritarian relapse in 2020.

---

30. I omit Fiji's scores in the late 2010s, because Fiji had two constitutional processes, in swift succession in 2012 and 2013, since the 1997 process I highlighted in previous chapters, and its later political development, democratic or otherwise, cannot be attributed to the 1997 process.

31. Even without Iraq, which pulled the average score down, the scores for Nepal, Kenya, and Sri Lanka averaged only 52.7, and this was before Sri Lanka's likely authoritarian relapse in 2020.

These scores, of course, can scarcely be traced entirely to constitutional processes, and they certainly cannot be traced directly to the democratic commitment of those who participate in them. Yet it is not farfetched to think that constitutional processes, as pivotal events, can begin a political trajectory in one direction or another. The finding of quantitative studies demonstrating the democratic effects of inclusive constitutional processes, cited in previous chapters, make it clear that some process characteristics can and do have consequences for the emergence and maintenance of democracy. The argument here suggests that more of these characteristics can be identified.

For a variety of reasons, the desire to avoid a relatively lengthy process associated with the criteria I have outlined can be great. It is not altogether surprising that many politicians, especially the vast majority without experience in constitution making, might simply prefer quicker alternatives or processes more congenial to their partisan, ethnic, or sectarian objectives.

On some matters, even a deliberative process may fail to find consensus or appropriate compromise, and even a process that succeeds in doing so may leave some participants unsatisfied. Commitment to the outcome is not likely to be uniform across all participants. Furthermore, it is not likely to be equally durable among all participants. Democratic polities produce a range of outcomes years after the event: they disappoint some as they satisfy others. Unconstitutional behavior and at least partial defection by some political actors are to be expected over time, even in quite durable constitutional regimes. Commitments can erode, but whether a constitution is utterly traduced or whether there is merely backsliding—nibbling confined to the edges of the document—matters, and so does the ability to redress violations through legal institutions. Protection against the worst outcomes can frequently be made more secure.

This point reminds us that the character and firmness of democratic commitments is affected by exogenous forces, such as the fear of an electoral backlash and the availability or absence of a functioning rule of law. The degree of commitment is also influenced by conditions internal to the process that has generated it. We have seen that inclusion can cause problems for the achievement of consensus and for the clarity and coherence of the product, and we have also observed that agreements reached through bargaining may be more vulnerable to defection than are those that result from genuine consensus, especially if the constitution must be promulgated by a divided vote that signals dissensus. Successful completion of a deliberative process usually indicates that a wide swath of participants are reconciled to the rules of the political game and are familiar with each other's objectives and constraints by the time the process concludes, even if they were not at the inception. Much also depends, of course, on something I have mentioned several times but not discussed in this volume: the aptness of the agreed institutional design for the polity in which it must operate.

Nevertheless, neither these process criteria nor the aptness of the design can constitute a surefire prescription for all times or all conditions. When theorists speak of "self-enforcing" constitutions, they are speaking in rough metaphor. That compound adjective cannot really mean that compliance depends entirely on the original insight of mutual advantage. If it did, there would be no need for good enforcement mechanisms to bind participants and those who follow them to adhere to constitutional commitments. Mutual advantage is recalculated over time, and it is affected by what the constitutional provisions actually produce once they are implemented as well as by the changing interests of later generations. Every new constitution in an existing state has, after all, supplanted a previous constitution, to which some people, perhaps most people, were committed at the outset. No constitution is really self-enforcing. There is still a job to be done after a constitutional process concludes, but a good process can make that work easier and more successful.

Index